"People at a crossroads in their life will be inspired by the story of how one woman created a life for herself—and helped so many in the process."
—ELLEN E. SCHULTZ, GRADUATE OF PURVIS' INTENSIVE WILDERNESS-MEDICINE COURSES, AVID BACKPACKER, AND FORMER INVESTIGATIVE REPORTER FOR THE *WALL STREET JOURNAL*

"A story of evolution and self-discovery…A good tale of an outlier doing well and the love of her dog and the impermanence we all face."
—JERRY ROBERTS, RETIRED AVALANCHE FORECASTER PRESENTLY WORKING FOR MOUNTAIN WEATHERMASTERS

"A spectacular love story about the beautiful bond between a woman and her dog…Prepare to be moved, enthralled, and inspired. *Go Find* is truly a rare and special find!"
—ANGIE ABDOU, PHD, AUTHOR OF THE *CANTERBURY TRAIL*

"Fascinating, moving, and well written…I cried and marveled and found myself in these pages as well. Bravo, Susan. I feel forever changed."
—KRISTEN ULMER, FORMER PRO EXTREME SKIER, THOUGHT LEADER, AND AUTHOR OF *THE ART OF FEAR*

"Challenges every professional service-dog handler to spend more time reading and responding to partners—both K9 and human…Dogs still have more to show us."
—SANDY BRYSON, CALIFORNIA COMMISSIONER, RET., LAW ENFORCEMENT K9 TEAM TRAINER

"Readers searching for meaning will find themselves somewhere on these pages…Susan Purvis takes us even deeper into the psychological landscape of lost and found."
—BRIAN SCHOTT, FOUNDING EDITOR, *WHITEFISH REVIEW*

Go
Find

Go
Find

MY JOURNEY
TO FIND THE LOST—
AND MYSELF

SUSAN PURVIS

**BLACK
STONE**
PUBLISHING

Printed in the United States of America

First edition: 2018
ISBN 978-1-5385-0760-5
Biography & Autobiography / Personal Memoirs

1 3 5 7 9 10 8 6 4 2

CIP data for this book is available
from the Library of Congress

Blackstone Publishing
31 Mistletoe Rd.
Ashland, OR 97520

www.BlackstonePublishing.com

To Pop. Since I left home at age seventeen, you visited me most Septembers, no matter where my feet were planted. You're a huge part of this adventure because you sat for endless hours in a rickety lawn chair amongst the turning aspen leaves, reading newspapers and drinking coffee, to play the victim for search-dog teams. You've lost your hearing, and now your memory. Pops, you now deserve to sit down in your chair and enjoy my story.

To Mom. Who really cares about all my dreams, achievements, and secrets, besides you? I walk through this world knowing your love lives on my sleeve. I wear it every day. You've offered me three gifts for a meaningful life: to love, laugh, and surround myself with supportive friends who care and listen. When I close my eyes, I feel your embrace and big smile. Since I left home, you've answered my telephone calls, even when I was worlds away.

To Tasha. For helping me find my way.

SEARCH: To look into or over carefully or thoroughly in an effort to find or discover something.

RESCUE: To free from confinement, danger, or evil.

Contents

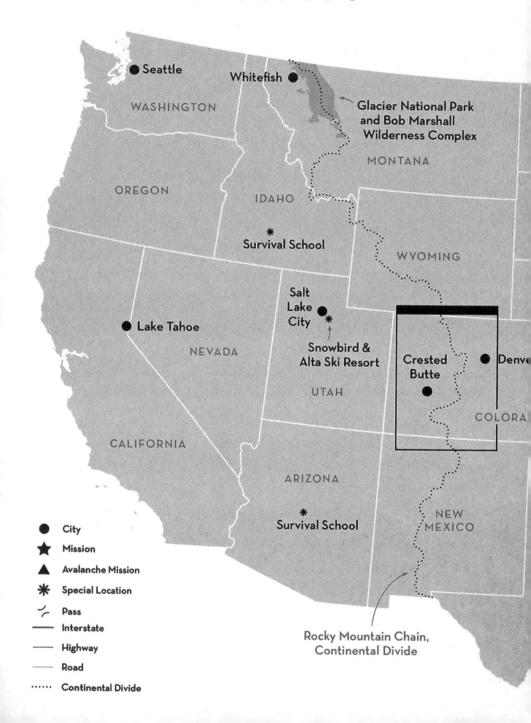

The Western United States

Seattle

Whitefish

WASHINGTON

Glacier National Park and Bob Marshall Wilderness Complex

MONTANA

OREGON

IDAHO

WYOMING

Survival School

Salt Lake City

Lake Tahoe

Snowbird & Alta Ski Resort

Crested Butte

Denve

NEVADA

UTAH

COLORA

CALIFORNIA

ARIZONA

NEW MEXICO

Survival School

Rocky Mountain Chain, Continental Divide

- ● City
- ★ Mission
- ▲ Avalanche Mission
- ✳ Special Location
- ⌒ Pass
- — Interstate
- — Highway
- — Road
- ······ Continental Divide

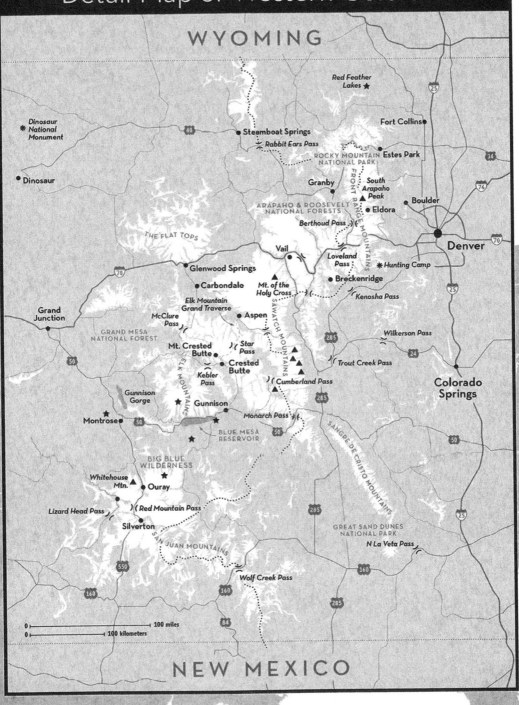

Detail Map of Western Colorado

WYOMING

Red Feather Lakes ★

* Dinosaur National Monument

Fort Collins ●

● Dinosaur

40 ● Steamboat Springs
Rabbit Ears Pass

● Estes Park

ROCKY MOUNTAIN NATIONAL PARK

34

25

Granby ●

South Arapaho Peak ▲

Boulder ●

ARAPAHO & ROOSEVELT NATIONAL FORESTS

● Eldora

76

Berthoud Pass

THE FLAT TOPS

Vail ●

Denver

70

70

● Glenwood Springs

Loveland Pass

* Hunting Camp

● Carbondale

Mt. of the Holy Cross ▲

● Breckenridge

Kenosha Pass

Grand Junction ●

Elk Mountain Grand Traverse

McClure Pass

● Aspen

SAWATCH MOUNTAINS

25

GRAND MESA NATIONAL FOREST

50

Mt. Crested Butte ●

Star Pass

285

Wilkerson Pass

ELK MOUNTAINS

● Crested Butte

▲
▲
▲

24

Trout Creek Pass

Kebler Pass

▲

Cumberland Pass

Colorado Springs

Gunnison Gorge ★

● Gunnison

▲

285

● Montrose

50

★

★

Monarch Pass

50

50

BLUE MESA RESERVOIR

★

BIG BLUE WILDERNESS

SANGRE DE CRISTO MOUNTAINS

Whitehouse Mtn. ▲

★

● Ouray

285

Lizard Head Pass

Red Mountain Pass

25

● Silverton

GREAT SAND DUNES NATIONAL PARK

SAN JUAN MOUNTAINS

N La Veta Pass

550

160

Wolf Creek Pass

160

160

285

84

0 ├──────────────┤ 100 miles
0 ├──────────────┤ 100 kilometers

NEW MEXICO

Introduction

Lost.

I was lost once.

Fresh out of college with a geology degree, I signed up as a survival instructor in the high desert of southern Idaho. No, I didn't have any previous experience, but I thought it would be more challenging—and fun—than working in a photography store.

After running several twenty-one-day courses without incident, I was promoted to lead guide. Then came a particular trip, leading six troubled teenagers on what we jokingly called a "hoods in the woods" trek through sagebrush country. Strapped to our back, each of us carried a wool blanket, wrapped in a second-hand military poncho for shelter, and a tin can for cooking. Ten days into the outing, I broke the most important rule about survival: I separated from my tribe.

And I got lost.

I wasn't supposed to get lost. After all, I was the so-called expert, the person who knew how to use a map and compass, find the North Star, set animal traps, and forage for edible plants.

I'd first learned to use a compass at age ten when my dad took me fishing for lake trout in his twenty-foot boat on Lake Superior. With his grown-up hand resting on mine, he helped me guide the wheel. "Honey, keep the needle pointing north and drive straight ahead." It was a big responsibility for a little girl who needed to stand on her tiptoes to see out the boat's windshield. I knew that if I screwed up and got off course, especially in the fog, we'd collide with the white rocks and drown. I kept my eye on that needle and told Pops, "I'll never lose my way."

When I was fifteen, I learned to read a United State Geologic Survey 7.5-minute quadrangle map during my first backpacking trip to the Bob Marshall and Mission Mountain Wildernesses in Montana. As a teenager from the flatlands of northern Michigan, the grandness of the Rocky Mountains overwhelmed me. I stood at the trailhead, wearing a too-heavy backpack and holding a flat sheet of paper the size of a small poster. "How the heck do you read a map?" I asked our bearded guide. "I have no idea where I am."

Back then, I was a follower. I took no responsibility for where I was or where I was going. But I wanted to learn.

My guide showed me how to orient both the map and compass north, and how to read topographical maps. He explained how lines could create a two-dimensional representation of both natural and human-made features on the earth's surface. These maps, often called contour maps or quads, depict in detail the ground relief—the shape and changing elevation of the terrain—the rivers, lakes, forest cover, roads, and other features, using symbols, colors, and contour lines. Each contour line on the 7.5-minute series represents forty feet of elevation difference. The closer together the lines, the steeper the terrain. The farther apart the lines, the flatter it is.

Maps intrigued me and expanded my world, far beyond my clan of friends and the concrete sidewalks in my hometown. I set out to discover everything I could about finding my way. By studying topo maps, I could eventually see how these lines formed mountains, cliffs, and river valleys.

By the end of that two-week trip, I had learned to navigate through the wilderness on foot, using only a map and compass. This offered me a newfound confidence that made the start my junior year of high school a little easier.

Years of practice—hundreds of hours navigating hiking, backcountry skiing, and backpacking trips—allowed me to gain fluency in map and compass reading. (It's probably one reason I would later become interested in geology and gold exploration.) I could plot my location on a map anywhere in the world.

And I believed, on that day in the desert of southern Idaho, that I would never get lost because I always knew where I was.

But I did.

The problem started when I made a hasty, unilateral decision to "take a shortcut." I'd decided to bypass some rough terrain to escort Phyllis, an overweight sixteen-year-old girl who was emotionally and physically exhausted, to our next campsite. My coinstructor and I divided up our navigation equipment. He took the compass. I kept the map.

A horrible idea. Shortcuts, I'd learn later, can be an important teacher of what not to do. One step forward and two steps back.

We should have just stayed together at our location and camped. Instead, I watched five students and my colleague hoist their bedrolls to their backs and disappear into the forest.

"See you in a couple hours," I yelled after them, plotting my route on the map. "We're going to take the road north, then traverse west to the campsite."

Boy, was I wrong. I never met up with the group again. They were right where they were supposed to be. But Phyllis and I were not.

Twenty-eight hours later my boss, Glenn, found us walking down a dirt road, dehydrated and exhausted. We had scrambled over boulders, climbed steep slopes, and descended into a tangled watercourse during our ten-mile journey. So much for bypassing rough terrain.

On the positive side, Phyllis would tell me later that her life had changed on that trip, because she was forced into survival mode. When she had to focus on the task at hand, marching one foot in front of the other, she forgot about the old ways etched into her brain.

However, Glenn confronted me in the pickup truck, "How'd *you* get lost?"

I responded in a calm, confident tone, "I wasn't lost. We just got turned around. Look, we're here, aren't we?"

Because tragedy was avoided, I never really thought about the question again ... until twenty years later, when I started to write this book.

The writing process made me question such a cavalier answer. I was wearing a plate of armor around my heart to protect my ego, my all-business, always-competent persona. I know I didn't have it in me back then to admit I was a scared twenty-three-year-old woman, feeling like that little girl driving the boat. At the moment when I answered him, I had suppressed my feelings, buried them deep to save face.

If only my boss had explained to me, on the bumpy ride home, about the stages of being lost, I might have found the clarity to understand the situation much sooner. But back then nobody in my world was talking about it.

If he had known about Swiss psychiatrist Elisabeth Kübler-Ross, who talked about the stages of loss in her book *On Death and Dying*, or Laurence Gonzales, who offered a dozen revelations in the stories in *Deep Survival: Who Lives, Who Dies, and Why*, then my boss might have said, "Oh, Susan. You are in such a state of *denial*. This is the first phase of being lost. You were disoriented and, like most people who are confused, you just pressed on as fast as you could go. You were trying to make your mental map fit what you saw."

If he'd said that, I would have admitted that I had pressed on that evening and the entire next day, that I had set a death-march pace, allowing no breaks, determined to continue until I recognized something, anything. When nothing I saw matched the topo map or my mental map, I just said, "Let's keep going." Deny, deny, deny—that was my coping mechanism.

Most people who are lost can't let themselves see that they're lost, don't want to hear about it or feel it. And when they deny reality, they keep themselves from learning from it, from solving the problem that's right in front of them.

Next, I slipped into *anger*—or what might be better called *panic*. As darkness settled that first night, urgency to find my way blossomed into a full-scale survival emergency. I panicked, thinking, "What if I kill Phyllis? What if I kill myself trying to take care of her?" And I cursed her for being slow, tripping and falling, keeping me from reaching my destination.

I pushed us onward, trying to find terrain that fit either the map in my hands or the map in my head. I didn't consider staying right where we were, because stopping would mean that I was admitting my lostness. Instead, I was so in denial that staying put, starting a fire, and questioning how I got myself into this mess never crossed my mind.

Laurence Gonzales writes that everyone who dies lost, dies of confusion. Lost is then not a location; it is a transformation. It is a failure of the mind. It can happen in the woods, or it can happen in life. I'd gotten off my path that day. I'd lost my way. I thought if I didn't get back on that path, I'd lose myself too. So, I pressed on through last light.

The third phase of lostness is *bargaining*. As fatigue and mild hypothermia crept in on that rainy evening, I formed a strategy for finding someplace that matched my misguided mental map, even though there was no such place. We roamed the desert aimlessly. I silently pleaded with the terrain, as if it could answer me, "I'll never let this happen again. Help me find our way out."

I stumbled upon a wickiup, a structure made of grass and mud, built by the survival school in case of emergencies. This shelter bought us needed comfort from the rain and allowed me to get my head on straight, breathe, and reassess where I had been and where I was going.

Had I not bumped into the wickiup, my untrained, deteriorating, irrational, and emotional mind might have fallen into *depression*, the fourth stage of being lost. When all your strategies fail, and you just give up—when you no longer know how to cope with the situation.

Later, I would learn that in the final stages of lostness, when you run out of options and energy and become *resigned* to your plight, you *must* make a new mental map of where you are. You *must* become Robinson Crusoe, or you will die. To survive, you *must* find yourself. Then it won't matter where you are.

I could have survived in the shelter for days if I had stopped to build a bow-drill fire and controlled my panicked mind. Eventually, a search-and-rescue team would have found us. That day in the wilderness, it was impossible for me to admit I was lost because I didn't have the experience, the mental map, or the maturity to know that my survival depended on accepting what was actually going on. Instead, the one thing I decided that day was that I'd never get lost again, even if it killed me.

It took me years to learn that lostness doesn't only apply to losing the trail and going off the map in the wilderness. I didn't know then that people can get lost in emotion, in a relationship, in a marriage, in a business, or in a life. I was convinced that just happened to *other* people.

But I was about to learn just how lost one person could be.

CHAPTER 1

Last Ditch Effort

Summer 2005
Ouray, Colorado

If the helicopter shifts, we're dead. Dead like the guy we're looking for.

So much can go wrong up here. Peering out the open door, I look down at the fast-moving, unforgiving terrain. Far above the tree line, where the air is thin, volcanic rock breaks into huge spires and fins. Freeze-thaw cycles have crumbled the cliffs into strange, gargoyle-like shapes, and every crevice is filled with snow.

Tasha, my black Labrador retriever and avalanche-dog partner, is wedged between the pilot and me. Her bum presses against the pilot's right hip while she digs her furry elbows into my thighs and settles her barrel chest onto my lap. Her webbed feet, splayed wide from years of digging in avalanche debris, dangle off my leg and out the helicopter's open doorway. In our haste to hot-load the helicopter moments ago, I had nixed Tasha's restraining device. As the helicopter blades shave the air closer to the towering 13,492-foot peak, I vise-grip her neck with my arm, pulling her closer, concerned she'll try to jump or scramble onto the pilot's lap. Wiggling my toes inside my ski boots helps to keep them from falling asleep. That's all I dare move. If Tasha or I make a sudden movement, the two-seat crop duster helicopter, used to spray pesticides on cornfields, might fall out of the sky. We're about to land by putting one skid onto a couloir, a steep narrow gully, hemmed in by sheer cliff walls on the upper flanks of Whitehouse Mountain in the San Juan Mountains of southwestern Colorado.

As we near our forbidding landing site, I try to avoid looking down at the four-thousand-foot drop, where dawn just turned to daylight over the towering evergreen trees, now shrunk to matchsticks. Warm air turns to cold, and my knuckles are blue as I squeeze the grab handle above the door frame.

Thirty-nine days earlier, a single-engine plane crashed on Whitehouse Mountain, killing all four passengers on board: Richard Mills—the man we are looking for—his four-year-old son, and his parents. Days of bad weather, coupled by avalanche hazard and extreme terrain, had thwarted any rescue effort. Eventually, members of the local search-and-rescue team, Ouray Mountain Rescue, were transported to the wreckage one by one. Over several weeks of searching they found, strewn over a half-mile-long path, pieces of twisted metal, clothing, children's books, and three partially buried bodies. The team located all but Richard. Then, deeming the recovery mission too dangerous, the local sheriff had suspended the search. Until now.

All hope is on my sixty-pound retriever and five-foot-three me.

We're the last-ditch effort, and we've got one hour to find him.

After a decade as my search-and-rescue partner, Tasha has a few gray hairs on her chin, but still looks and acts like a pup. In human years, she's seventy and I'm forty-three. Her career is almost over, and then mine will be, too.

Tasha and I are one of a few elite high-altitude volunteer search-and-rescue dog teams in the United States. We live in Crested Butte, Colorado. We don't get paid for our work, not even a bag of kibble, yet we're up here risking our lives.

Inside the helicopter, Tasha's silky ears flap against her blocky head as air blasts through my side of the helicopter. Her chest swells and retracts, panting breathlessly as the air thins. Her tongue is pasty white. Her breath stinks. I can't tell if her excessive panting is from nerves or the food she gobbled down last night when she nosed open my suitcase and devoured eight cups of dry kibble, plastic bag and all. Her bloated belly feels like a stuffed sausage.

I want to wring her neck.

How could she do that to me? Ten years of training, sacrifices, and proving our worth to a community of doubters, many hoping I would fail. This mission is the pinnacle of our career, and because of Tasha's gluttony we might fail ... if we don't die first.

The pilot reduces power, and the helicopter edges closer to the mountain. Boulders as big as cars litter our search area with fresh gray rubble, evidence of violent daily rock fall. Because of the danger, we only have *one* hour to get in, find Richard's body, and get out: the morning sun shining on the avalanche path will cause snow to melt, releasing rocks that could pierce our flesh and crush our bones.

"Sue, see that speck down there?" The pilot's voice crackles in my headphones. "That's Bill." He points to a narrow, snowy couloir in front of us. "He's chopping out a landing zone." The pilot stares straight ahead at the colossal mountain and concentrates on placing his skid onto the thin landing strip—no wider or taller than I am. I squint out the bubble-shaped window but can't see Bill.

A sharp wobble of the helicopter jolts me with adrenaline. My body jerks. I cling to Tasha. I don't dare let go. To calm my nerves, and her nerves too, I hum a soothing melody into her ear, one she's been hearing for a decade. "Good girl, Black Dog, *doo-tee-dooo* ... I love you." I shut my eyes, praying the blades don't hit the slope. I put my boot against the bubble window and press an imaginary brake pedal to stop our forward momentum and brace for impact. The chopper edges toward the sheer wall. Somewhere on this peak, a family's despair is buried beneath tons of avalanche debris. Will *my* family soon join in their despair?

Suddenly, I spot Bill running toward a rock wall, protecting himself from the rotors and shielding his face from the growing blizzard of blowing snow. He's engulfed in the white tornado whirling beneath the chopper blades. I lose sight of him. The helicopter's skid thunks onto the landing strip. Tasha jerks up and digs her nails into my legs. It's painful, but I don't move a muscle.

My eyes fixate on the pilot for direction. He focuses on the blade whapping an arm's length away from the snow. "Time to go," he yells.

Yanking off my helmet with one hand, I pin Tasha into my lap with the other. The deafening roar of the engine makes giving verbal commands to Tasha impossible. I rely on our years of communicating through eye contact and hand signals to show her when to exit. Bill crawls on hands and knees to meet us. He waits in a crouch, as directed by the pilot, until the bird steadies.

"You're going to have to jump!" the pilot shouts at me.

"Jump?" I worry about Tasha's distended abdomen. She could rupture her gut if she lands on her belly. Then I remember the raspy plea of Ed Jones, the uncle of the missing man. "I'm not leaving Colorado until all my family members are accounted for. I've been scouring these mountains for over thirty days." Ed's desperation had convinced me I had to come out here. We're his last hope. Ten years ago, when I blindly launched into this volunteer search-dog career, I promised I would never leave anyone behind. I've kept my word … so far.

The helicopter shudders. I clutch the handle and, for an instant, I question what I am doing here. My husband's pissed. He told me not to come, tried to order me not to get on the chopper. Yet here I am, in the path of an avalanche, risking Tasha's life and my own. Somehow, I find it easier to jump out of a helicopter than to talk to my husband about our relationship. Is my ego driving this? My promise to the family? Or is it that I have something to prove?

My eyes lock onto the pilot's. He nods, *now*. Before I ease Tasha into Bill's extended arms, I look to her to tell me something. Anything. I know I'll never bond with another being like I have with her. Everything we've struggled for hinges on this moment. Her kind brown eyes, full of confidence and foggy cataracts, stare into mine. Her calmness quells my shaking body.

"Tasha," I whisper into her ear, "Time to go."

After cuing her with a wrist flick, she lunges out and spread-eagles onto Bill's face and chest, knocking him backward. The two regain their feet and run together toward the rock for protection. Slipping off my seat, I sit on the floor. One at a time, my boots find a purchase on the icy skid. Slinging my pack over my shoulder, I let go of the safety handle and jump.

CHAPTER 2

Purple

Fall 1995—Ten Years Earlier
Denver, Colorado

It all began in Denver.

Knock, knock, knock.

Alone on the doorstep of a stranger's home in the Denver suburbs, I pound the wooden door with my knuckles.

The dry, Rocky Mountain air is a world away from the Dominican Republic, where I just spent the past month in heat, humidity, and congestion. This calm of the suburbs seems unfamiliar: there are none of the honking taxis, men carrying machine guns on their shoulders, or street dogs pillaging through garbage I've become accustomed to.

At my knocking, barking dogs raise a chorus from the back of the house. I take out a crumpled piece of paper and double-check the ad from the *Denver Post*:

> 5½-week-old purebred black Labrador retrievers.
> Hips and eyes certified.
> Parents AKC registered.
> 5 males, 4 females.
> Ready today. $500 each.
> Call Wyman if interested.

Earlier that morning my husband Doug had thought I was insane when I told him I needed a puppy, today. I had kissed him on his lips, snuggled under the warmth of our down comforter, and begged, "It's time."

"For god's sake, we're leaving for hunting camp in a few hours," he said while pressing his muscular body against mine. "And where are you going to find a puppy today, in this town?"

We divided our time between working in the sweltering jungle and respites at our condo in Gunnison, Colorado, one of the coldest places in America. The little cow-town condo was two thousand miles and three time zones away from the DR, and it wasn't so much our home as a storage box for our raft, skis, and outdoor gear, a place to land when we returned from our exhausting work stints. Gunnison had appeal because of the airport and its close proximity to the last great Colorado ski town.

On this particular Sunday, Wyman had the only litter in the state ready for adoption. I learned this when I jumped out of bed, threw on my green sweatpants and Doug's oversize hoodie, and biked to the nearest newsstand. The thermometer read sixteen degrees.

I live by instinct, and my instincts told me I had to have a pup today. Otherwise, life might suck me in another direction, back to the Dominican Republic for another two years, or to some field camp in Mexico. I had to act now. For years, I'd dreamed of having a soft, fuzzy puppy to call my own, but Doug and I found ourselves several years into a million-dollar gold exploration program. We had established an office in Santo Domingo, struggled to communicate in Spanish, secured an unlimited expense account, hired a few Dominican geologists and maids, and rented a field house in a very remote part of the country.

Until now, because of our constant travel to Latin America for work, we could never have a puppy. And since we agreed to not have kids, this seems like the next logical step. Today, I am ready to settle down—a little, at least. Today, I want a dog to fill an open hole in my heart.

I push my nose against the door's window and peer through the glass. Squinting, I hope to get a glimpse of the surprise waiting inside before I meet the dog breeder. Before I can size up the place, a large man with a big belly and a bad complexion stares back at me. Startled, I step away from the door.

"Hi, my name is Sue," I yell through the glass. "I'm the gal who called from Gunnison." I smile, hoping he might smile back.

The door opens, and he gestures with his index finger. "Come on in."

He coughs, takes a long drag of his cigarette, and closes the door behind me. Cautious, I look back as the door shuts.

"I hope it's not too late to see your puppies?" I say, reaching my hand out to greet him, trying to distract from my disheveled appearance with friendliness. In my haste this morning, I hadn't bothered to shower or put on a clean shirt.

"My name is Wyman." My palm disappears in his big, rough hand, and he offers a softer look as we shake hands. Bloodshot eyes scan my body. Looking into the street, he notices my rusty old pickup truck and scowls.

A few steps into the dim living room I smell the sweet, distinct aroma of new puppies. Across the frayed carpet, a blockheaded, stubby-nosed, short-legged black Labrador bitch darts toward me. In the Dominican Republic, dogs can rip fingers off. I jam my hands in my blue jeans pockets.

"Sammy's the mom. She won't hurt you. She loves everybody."

"Ah, she's beautiful. How old?"

"She's five. Had four great litters."

I can't imagine so many litters in so few years. Sammy is obviously a moneymaking breeding machine.

"Her puppies are calm, well-mannered." He exhales a puff of smoke through his nostrils. "Just the nicest dogs. Sammy's an English Lab—from the show-dog line. She's the perfect house dog."

"Great." I look around. I recall Doug's parting words as I loaded the truck for the six-hour drive to Denver. "No field-trial Labs that need to run twenty miles a day. And I don't want one that bounces off the walls like those border collies. I just want a nice normal family Lab. And no males. They pee all over everything."

Following Wyman through the house, I ask, "How many grown dogs do you have anyway?"

"Four more dogs penned up in the garage."

I hide my disapproval at the cruelty of caging dogs inside and get to the point. "Can I see the puppies now?"

"As the first buyer, you get first choice. They're forty days old, almost six weeks." He holds the door.

"Isn't that a little early to be taking a pup away from her mother? I thought pups didn't leave their mom until eight weeks?"

"Nah, if you like one, take it. If you don't like it, you can return it."

His used-car-salesman pitch grates on me. But from the corral, the nine black, romping puppies have nabbed my attention.

"Oh, my gosh, they're so adorable. How will I ever choose one?"

"Just pick one, ma'am. They're all the same."

I select the four females from the enclosure in the kitchen, and we bring them outside onto the grass. Lying on my back, I let the puppies—each the size of a well-fed hamster on steroids—climb on me. The alpha latches onto my nose with her razor-sharp teeth. I tug her from my face, losing a few drops of blood, and set her aside. Next, I rule out the runt. I stand up to see if the two remaining candidates will run after me. They do. I roll each one over and onto their backs. The first pup submits without a fight. The second one squirms, whines, and punches the air with all four legs, trying to escape. When I wave a small twig in her face, she chases it.

"Ah, a fighter *and* a retriever. I like you."

I pick her up and look into her baby-gorilla-like face. "Hi there. You're cute." My mouth nuzzles into her soft ear. Her warmth and baby smell oozes out, nearly dropping me to my knees.

I tie a purple ribbon around my pup's neck to mark her, then stand back to watch as they all attack their mother for feeding. The fatter male pups wallop the others with their feet to keep hold of the teats. But like a linebacker, the purple-ribbon pup shoves a sibling out of the way.

I nod at her, satisfied.

Within thirty minutes of handing the puppy breeder a check, I drive off with my black fur ball. I stop at PetSmart, where a veterinarian pronounces her healthy.

"How much should I feed her?" I'm thinking about careful measurements.

"Give her all the food she wants." He hands her back to me. "Don't worry about overfeeding. She'll know when to stop eating."

"Okay." Was this good advice? I don't know … I feel like a naive parent with a newborn. I have no Labrador operating manual, no freshly painted room, no toys stacked neatly in a cedar chest. Marching out of the store, I'm determined to do better than I had in college with the house plants I'd killed through neglect. Conscious of my new responsibility, I tote a five-pound bag of puppy chow in one arm and a delicate furry body in the other.

I place her in the copilot seat in my truck. Lifting her paws, as if the seat were hot, she looks up and locks her eyes on mine. Dropping her nose, she sniffs then circles a few times before plopping down into a ball and closing her eyes. I cushion her with two rolled jackets—one near her head and the other by her tail—and clip the seatbelt around her.

Through my rearview mirror, I watch Denver's concrete jungle and toxic, chocolate haze recede. My hand on her small body, I promise my new puppy that she will never live in the city—and she'll certainly not be held prisoner in a cage. "Purple," I stroke her head. "You're exactly what I need right now."

❁ ❁ ❁

Twelve hours later, in an unfamiliar bed in a hunting cabin, a thud wakes me from a deep sleep in the middle of the night. I spring up like a jack-in-the-box. Squinting in the darkness, I sort out my bearings. Doug and I are in a remote cabin at the base of Mount Evans with our best friends, Amy and Big, and their toddler, Junior, to bowhunt for elk. Normally, we'd camp in tents by Elk Creek, but between our crippling exhaustion after weeks in the Dominican heat and Amy's pregnancy, we'd decided to rent the one-hundred-year-old cabin.

Patting my palms beneath the bed covers, I feel for the puppy. But my hands encounter only sheets.

"Doug, wake up." I nudge him.

"What?" His voice sounds like tumbled gravel as he wakes from a deep sleep.

"I can't find Purple!" I throw off the feather comforter that stinks of mothballs, the cold autumn air sending goose bumps over my naked body. I pat my hands across the bed to feel the puppy and pray I haven't suffocated the poor little thing. "She's not here. I heard a thud—like she hit the floor."

"What?" He lifts to a sitting position. "That drop will kill her." His voice has a scolding tone.

"I know. I know," I mumble, as I do every time he treats me like a child. I want to call the pup's name, but she doesn't have one yet.

"Help me find her," I whine. "Check your side of the bed. But be careful. You might squish her." I lift an oversize feather pillow, hoping to touch a misplaced puppy, but feel the empty sheet.

Doug shoves the heavy blankets to his ankles. "What time do you think it is? Looks like it's almost shooting light."

My voice escalates in frustration. "I don't know." My missing dog took priority over killing elk. "Why isn't she whining or crying? Does that mean she's dead?"

"Wasn't she between us when we fell asleep?" On his hands and knees, he searches the bed. "I told you she needed to be in a crate. I warned you last night." He speaks with exasperation.

I snap back. "She was sleeping on my chest. And now she's gone." I slide my legs over the edge of the bed. The distance between the mattress and the floor exceeds the reach of my short legs. The four-foot drop would hurt—and could kill—a six-pound puppy. If only I'd listened to Doug.

Stretching for the wooden floor, I roll my weight onto my feet. The boards creak. Skimming the floor with my toe pointed like a ballerina, I feel for warm fur.

Nothing.

"Sue, we need some light. Where's the switch?" Doug whispers.

"I'll get it." Like a snake looking for a warm, fat mouse in the night,

I crawl on my hands and knees, reaching out blindly for a lump of fur. I bump into the bed, making the lamp on the bedside table teeter.

For a moment, I think about Amy in the next room, sleeping soundly with her husband and Junior. What if she woke in the night to find her boy missing? How do parents handle being responsible for such tiny, helpless beings? A month before, I had joked with Doug, sitting at the table in our Santo Domingo apartment and watching Nena—the local Dominican woman we hired to help clean and cook—"I'll only have kids if we hire her as our full-time nanny."

Doug had cackled back, "In your dreams! There's no way I'd live down here full time and have kids."

I climb my hands up the table, feeling for the switch on the lamp's base. My fingers click the light switch, and the room floods with an amber glow.

Doug flings the bed covers back to look under them. I kneel down to scan the floor under the bed. My breathing races toward hyperventilation. I'm ready to have a nervous breakdown because I can't seem to find my puppy.

But then, curled up into a tight ball, her chin resting on her thimble-sized paws, her eyes closed, I see her. My puppy looks like a one-day-old baby bear. With my white, naked butt in the air, I dive under the bed frame. I hold my breath to see if she is breathing.

My hand on her soft fur, I feel her chest rise and fall. "She's okay!"

When I pull her from under the bed, she licks my fingers with her warm wet tongue, curls up in my arms, and closes her eyes again. Jumping back under the covers, I cuddle Purple in my arms to warm us both up.

"She is one tough little dog," I turn and smile at Doug as he steps into his camouflage pants, jacket, and hat. "What are you doing?" I whisper, disappointed he's choosing to head out hunting instead of snuggling under the covers to bond with me and the newest member of our family. I wonder for a minute if he's angry that I won't be a good puppy owner or maybe pissed I'm giving my puppy more love than him. I hold her even closer.

"I'm going to go make coffee," he answers with a grumpy edge. "Big and I will be back midmorning. Hopefully, with an elk to eat for dinner." He leans over, kisses me on the forehead, and turns off the light. "You keep that puppy on a leash from now on," he lobs as he shuffles out of the room.

My skin crawls at Doug's inability to understand how I'm feeling. But I'm grateful he isn't making me return her. I roll over, hug my dog close to my chest, and feel a tear drip down my cheek.

Later that morning, I awake to the smell of sizzling bacon and Dominican coffee. The bed-jumping pup lies awake at my side, imprisoned by four pillows.

"Puppy, puppy. Where puppy?" Little blond Junior tries to scale the mountainous bed. His hand barely reaches mine on the edge of the mattress.

I lean over to look at him with one sleepy eye open. "Do you want to come up and see her?"

Jumping on his toes, he nods, "Yes!" I lug my twenty-pound godson onto the bed, his plastic diaper sagging.

Purple yawns, slaps her right paw on the pillow, and then fixes her gaze on the boy. She licks her lips, perks her ears forward, and flaps her three-inch tail against the pillow before squirming over to him on her belly. She worms her way into his soft, white baby hands, clawing her talon-like toenails into his skin, followed by a quick nip with sharp milk teeth.

"Waaaa!" The boy screams like he has just been attacked by a hungry grizzly bear.

"No biting." I grab the pup by the scruff of her neck and growl into her ear. She rears her neck back as if ready to fight. I toss her into the pillow corral. "You can chew on me, but no one else. Bad dog," I bark.

Amy, waddling under her watermelon-sized pregnant belly, lumbers into the room. "What happened?"

I roll my eyes like I do whenever Junior screams. I smile through clenched teeth. "Junior wanted to see the puppy. He has a few scratches. No blood. Sorry about that."

"Are you okay, honey?" she coos, lifting her son off the bed and onto her left hip. "You'll be okay. She's just a puppy, and she didn't mean to hurt

19

you." Kissing his red scratched arms and hands, she wipes the tears from his face. Junior's lips stop trembling and his tears ease.

The pup lets out a high-pitched whine. Junior turns his attention to the bed and points. "No, puppy. Bad!"

Amy counters with pragmatism. "I think we need to keep you two apart for a while. Otherwise, you'll look like a zebra with red stripes instead of black." She lowers her boy to the floor, scoots him along, and walks away, rubbing her round belly.

After bacon, runny eggs, and cowboy coffee, I let Purple loose to roam the cabin. She promptly sniffs a spot on the wood floor, squats on her hind legs, and pees.

"Oh, you! I can't have you peeing in here. Come on, pup, let's go outside."

She ignores me and walks the other way. Following her nose, she snorts like a baby pig, searching for a tidbit of food.

"You little stinker," I retort. "You can't ignore me like that. I am in charge." I crouch down on all fours, call a random name, "Black Dog!" and slap my palms on the wood floor.

She stares at me, cocks her head back and forth, and raises her ears.

"Come on, puppy, come here," I squeak like a teenage girl. Black Dog charges me. "Good girl."

Perhaps envious of the attention, Junior darts from his bedroom. Boy and dog collide midstride. Falling to his hands, Junior scrapes his knee. He screams. Black Dog slams into the side of Junior's diaper and flips over backward. She scrambles to right herself. Junior picks himself up, wailing and unstable on his fat, wobbly legs.

Digested food oozes out of his Pull-Ups leg holes. The brown mess runs down his legs as he sprints down the hall toward the safety of his mother, shrieking, "Aaaaaah! Puppy!"

Only a few strides behind, Black Dog darts on two-inch legs. Her razor-sharp teeth aim to tear open a fresh, warm breakfast diaper and possibly filet Junior's back with lifelong scars.

My eyes bulge. "Holy crap!" I envision a pending lawsuit and a five-year friendship permanently severed. "Grab your boy! He's coming around the corner." Catastrophe averted … barely.

At dusk our guys return, empty-handed. The four of us sit under the moonlight outside the cabin, quietly listening to the fire's embers pop and crack. The forest vibrates with the electricity of aspen leaves quaking and bull elk bellowing out screams of anguish and anger in their lust to find a mate. This gathering marks the fifth trip for us together in the woods, an annual ritual, just like the elk breeding season.

The elk rut is one of most phenomenal displays of nature I have ever personally witnessed, and I get to share this magic with Doug, our friends, and their growing family. To watch it, you have to get up close, within a few hundred feet of the animals. I love tiptoeing around the woods with Doug. We'd learned that, during the seventy-degree autumn days, the big bulls liked to hole up in the high, impenetrable timber, which provided protection and relief from the heat and bugs. As the day cooled, the bulls would blow their cover by charging into the open meadows, bugling, stomping, and snorting in hopes of luring a mate. From my tree stand, I could watch the competing males rip at each other with their antlers. After gigantic battles, wounded young males would stumble away into the woods. (And all for the sake of reproducing? I wonder if men's hormones ever rage in the same manner as an adolescent bull elk's.) During the weeks of the rut, these hormonal bull elk were vulnerable to Doug and Big's lethal broadhead arrows.

The cold mountain air settles around us, and I jump into Doug's lap and tease him. "Hope I was worth fighting for."

Nibbling my ear, he replies, "Yes," and wraps his strong arms around me while our puppy nestles into my lap. It is a perfect night. I stroke her head with my fingers, thinking I don't want Doug's affection to end.

Junior snores in a crib under the cloudless night sky while Amy serves up homemade chocolate cake, layered with hand-picked raspberries and covered in a thick, creamy fudge frosting. Big pops the cork off the champagne bottle and fills our glasses, then Doug hands out short, stubby Dominican cigars—*gordas*, they're called. The four of us have a lot to celebrate. We raise our glasses above the fire.

We toast to the fall equinox—a time of harvesting, friendship, change, and Amy's and my birthdays. I am turning thirty-three and Amy, thirty-six. We are soul sisters, and our husbands are college buddies and best friends. Four years ago, Amy and I worked together as environmental geologists on the twenty-fourth floor of the Arco building in downtown Denver. I carried a briefcase and wore black, midthigh skirts with nylons and heels, and so did she. I lasted nine months at the job, and Amy made it several years. She is short and athletic; so am I. She married a geologist named Doug, and so did I. She hunts and kills, and so do I. We both enjoy being in the middle of nowhere with our guys. The only difference between us—she had decided to leave the office behind to stay at home and raise babies. Me, I am about to leave the field for a while to stay home and raise a dog.

I lift my champagne glass, draw hard on my *gorda*, exhale the thick white smoke to the sky, and bless a healthy birth of baby number two.

Amy raises her water glass and announces, "May Doug, you, and that nameless dog have a fulfilling and adventurous life together. To a new beginning and a new career."

Amy vocalizes my exact thoughts. I smile, puff, and watch the embers glow at the end of my cigar.

My husband chimes in. "Here's to good friends and family. May we continue our tradition every year, no matter what life throws at us."

"Here, here," toasts Big with a smile. "Now, let's name that dog of yours."

"What about Equinox or Elk?" laughs Amy.

I don't want the puppy's name to end in a *y, i,* or *e*—like Mickey, Pattie, Molly, or Susie. I hate those names. I want a quick, sharp, and to-the-point kind of name. Around the fire, I poll the jury.

"How about a Russian name?" someone tosses out.

Perhaps the tobacco and champagne cloud my thought process. I don't want my puppy to have a sissy name, but a stoic-sounding, confident, intelligent, strong-willed name—perhaps all the characteristics I had noticed in her over the past two days.

22

"Like what? Natasha?" replies Doug.

"No, too many syllables," says Big.

"How about Tasha?" I shout.

"I like it," smiles Doug.

I lift the sleeping puppy from my lap, toward the moon. She cracks open her eyelids half-mast and hangs in my grip, "Black Dog," I announce, "you have a new name—you are Tasha."

A few days later, while the men are hunting, Amy and I guide Junior and Tasha on their first big adventure—a hike in the woods. Junior wears wilderness warfare armor for protection: laced-up brown leather boots— so cute and tiny one could hang them from a rearview mirror—blue bib overalls, a turtleneck shirt, a baseball hat, a fleece jacket, and a paperback-size backpack. The only protective covering he lacks are a motocross helmet, goggles, and kneepads.

Amy, in the lead, waddles down the game trail. Her seven-months-pregnant belly sticks out more than half her four-foot-eleven-inch height. Wearing flip-flops and baggy clothes, she clutches a food basket and a small tent.

Falling in behind her, I tote camp chairs, magazines, extra clothes, and baby toys. Tasha, unfamiliar with her surroundings, walks at my heels. Tasha's view of the world along the game trail looks completely different than mine. At five feet above the trail, my eyes scan far out into the forest and the meadow. Small birds fly away and leaves flutter in the wind. Tall grasses, wildflowers, sagebrush, and bushes blanket the forest floor like a first snowfall.

Tasha's nose and eyes hover only a few inches from the cool, moist earth. Her world revolves around the smells and sounds adjacent to the footpath. Fallen aspen leaves crackle under her feet. Every smell captures her attention. She scampers with her nose down, nostrils flaring, inhaling all the information on the trail—animal and human hair, scat, skin, food, and footprints left behind by field mice, ants, flies, robins, coyotes, and deer. Even the smallest of creatures, like a chirping grasshopper clutching a blade of grass, stops her in her tracks. Mesmerized, she cocks her head to one side and fixes her eyes on the nearly invisible insect. Wanting to examine it closer, Tasha leaps toward the grasshopper, both disappearing into the tall grass.

As Junior explores, Tasha gains the courage to leave my side and follow in his footsteps. I keep a close eye on Tasha. She darts back and forth across the game trail like a fat black rat gathering food for winter. I'm on alert, knowing that she'll look like lunch to any owl, fox, or mountain lion that may come along. Not long after this trip, I hear a horror story from my distraught neighbor, whose shoebox-sized pug was literally snatched by a great horned owl, ten feet in front of her. The bird and dog flew away, never to be seen again.

A few steps later, Tasha stops to sniff and paw at what looks like nothing on the trail, and Junior bends down next to her to investigate. Together, one head white as linen, the other dark as night, they poke at the dirt, two companions playing in a dried rain puddle.

Near the end of the trail, my two little amigos run out of steam. I carry Tasha in my shirt, rolled up like rice in a sushi roll. Junior soon demands a free ride too. He whines, asking for his mother, but she strolls ahead to set up a tent for nap time. Junior drags the left toe of his leather boot, leaving behind a long, single line in the dirt.

"Sorry, bud," I say, "my hands are full. You're going to have to walk."

Our adventure reminds me of my mom's routine as she schlepped three kids on day-trips to the fine-sand beaches of Lake Superior, just a few blocks from our house. Mom would park her firm, wide fanny in the sand and let us explore our world without the confines of walls and rules. The building of sand castles, testing the too-cold water, and tunneling into the warm sand ... all good examples of what I want for Tasha—freedom to explore her new surroundings in a place free of pesticides, concrete, cages, and constant nagging from me.

I won't tolerate an unruly, misbehaving, rebellious dog, so my only option is to try the same tactics my mom used on me at the beach. My unleashed, free-spirited, no-rules approach to puppy parenting would soon unfold during our inseparable days in the woods. Amy, the kindest soul I know, would also teach me love, compassion, and discipline as I watched her raise her boys.

We arrive at our destination, a picture-perfect meadow. Junior eagerly nests inside the tent, grabbing his binky and blankie and settling into a nap. I gently place Tasha next to Junior and zip the flap closed. She sniffs his hair. With her paws tapping the floor of the nylon tent, she makes three tight concentric circles and plops down near his head.

Amy and I cherish our reprieve. I lounge in the sun, replenishing a body tired from long work days. Even if it were only a single, solitary hour of relaxation, I'd take it. Amy, so big now, sits heaving for air, belly between her spread legs, catching up on the latest adventures in *Outside* magazine.

When I wake, Amy says, "Sue, it's so great to have you here. We really miss having you around." She squeezes my hand in that loving, sisterly way.

"I know, I know. Look at us," I laugh. "We just sit around and read, dream, and play with puppies and babies. We're the luckiest girls in the world. Our guys are keepers—smart and handsome, supergeek go-getters. But Amy ..." I pause to work up the nerve to say this. "Sometimes, I just curl up and cry 'cause I can't speak Doug's language. I have such a hard time telling him how I feel. It's hard for me to live in the shadows of Doug." I tiptoe toward the tent. "I feel a bit lost."

Staring at me through the mesh netting, Tasha sits like a little Buddha figurine. She doesn't whine, bark, jump, or try to scratch her way out of the temporary shelter. I unzip the tent, scoop her up with one hand, and carry her over to our blanket. I admit to Amy, "I'm a shitty geologist. I feel like I ride on Doug's coattails."

"I hear ya, Sue. I feel the same way. Big said I need to get a job after this baby's born."

"Really? You going back to geology?"

"I don't know what I'm going to do," Amy says.

"Me neither. The one thing I know I want to do is write. But I'm just too chicken. Besides, Doug wouldn't support it. He wants me to make money. I don't think I can go back to the DR. Man, I get so lonely down there. Doug refuses to compromise his career, but I could. I'd do anything for him."

Sitting in the woods with Amy that week I share all the feelings I've been experiencing over the last few months, all the things I will never say and that Doug will never ask about, no matter how quiet I get.

Tasha's nose nudges my hand. "Okay, okay, you're hungry." I free-pour a baggie of kibble onto the ground, and she devours the dry puppy nuggets within seconds. With her snout, she nudges my pocket for more. Little do I know that no amount of food, not even a ten-pound bag of dog food, will ever fill her bottomless pit of a stomach.

Just then, we hear Big's huffs, "We got one. I … shot … an elk," He rests his hands on bent knees to catch his breath. Doug trails behind him. Breathless, he continues, "We … we need to go back and track it."

"Wahoo!" I fly into Doug's arms, wrapping my legs firmly around his body.

Tasha jumps up, too, digging her claws into Doug's camo pants and joining in on the dance. I smile down at her. "She doesn't want to be left behind."

Doug, Big, and I tiptoe our way through dense timber looking for traces of blood from an open wound dripping like a slow-leaking faucet. I carry Tasha inside my jacket, supporting her with my arm. She pokes her head out, acting like my third eye. She observes the forest from a new level now. With her ears perked forward and her big brown eyes wide open, she scans the forest from a much higher vantage point than when she scampers on the ground. Her nose lifts to catch the scents blowing across the mountains.

We inspect the forest floor, searching for wet, red blood splattered on dried yellow leaves. We spot a drop and move from one drip to the next like an investigator looks for clues at a crime scene.

I sense death nearby, and the closer we get, the bigger the blood drops. "There it is." I point to the ground just in front of me. I nearly step on the beautiful animal as I climb over downed trees. My lower lip trembles. I want to cry and rejoice at the same time.

"This is the biggest bull I have ever seen," whispers Doug, as if afraid we might wake the beast from sleep. The bull elk, lying on its side, wedged between downed trees, is bigger than a horse. Its lifeless brown eyes, the size of silver dollars, are fixed and dilated. The ivory-tipped antlers jut four feet from the top of its head, displaying six points.

Doug runs his ungloved fingers over its thick hide. "It's still warm." He places his bow on the ground and high-fives Big. The bros pat one another on the back. "I can't believe you got that shot off."

Big wipes sweat from his forehead with his sleeve. "How much do you think he weighs? Eight hundred pounds?"

Lowering myself slightly downwind of the chestnut-colored carcass, I inhale. Trembling, I reflect, inwardly mourning the loss of such a magnificent creature. How is it that we have it in our hearts to kill another living creature? I ponder the question, justifying the death, knowing that it means food in the freezer.

Squirming, Tasha interrupts my thoughts. I look down at her. "You want out?"

She wriggles, catapulting her tiny body from my jacket. Landing on her face, she rights herself, and then her little pea-size nose catches wind of the giant. Cautiously walking toward the elk, she plants her feet firmly in the soil, body compact, unsure of what she'll find. She stretches her eight-inch-long body to get a closer look. Deep in concentration and only millimeters away from the elk's fur, her little, wet black nose tickles its golden face. She sucks in air, making little guttural noises like a baby pig.

I watch. *What is my dog thinking?*

Her little nostrils flair in and out.

What does she think of Stinky Bull? Is this too much, too fast?

I bite my lower lip as she interacts with the elk and—like a mother watching a toddler taking her first steps down a flight of stairs—I ready myself.

Tasha's skin stretches slightly across her skull as she leans toward the elk. The hairs along her back stay flat. Her tail sways in a slow cadence in neutral position, not curled under, nor pointing high toward the sky. Curious, Tasha lifts her paw and swipes at the elk's nose as if to say, "Hey, get up."

"She's trying to get a reaction out of the beast," I chuckle to Doug. "All right, girl, that's enough." I pick her up from the ground. "You've had a big day." She curls up against my chest and yawns.

"Doug, did you see that? She is so brave and curious. Stinky Bull didn't scare her."

"Let me get a photo of Tasha with the bull," Doug says. He's sharpening his hunting knife. "She's so little. He's so big. It will make a great photo, Sue. One you'll always remember—and Big too. It's the first elk he killed with his bow and arrow." Doug beams with pride, smiling ear to ear.

I place Tasha on top of the still-warm beast. She sniffs the fur between the elk's left shoulder blade and rib cage, finds a nice flat spot, circles three times, drops to her belly, places her chin on her paws, takes a deep breath, and falls asleep. A photo is taken for the family album.

We prepare ourselves for the slicing and butchering of Stinky Bull. This wasn't the first time we had packed elk on our backs. Doug had killed several elk in this area over the years.

The three of us say our blessings, slice into and quarter the animal, and carefully remove all the meat we can salvage. Doug hoists a thirty-five-pound pack of raw meat onto my back. My shoulders and back bend forward to compensate for the weight, and I walk out of the woods like a little old lady with a slipped disk. Stinky Bull's right front shoulder, with its hairy leg and black hoof, sticks out the top of the pack like a flag pole. As I hike the several miles toward camp, Tasha sleeps comfortably in my jacket. The guys follow with loads twice the size of mine. This would be the first of several trips we would make that evening.

As the sun drops I reflect upon my life, only a week earlier, without a dog. Now I have a pup adjusted to the outdoors, to our life, and to her own newfound confidence. How could I have predicted that an elk hunt with my six-week-old dog would play such an important role in her future?

On this day, she smelled death—the death of an animal, a very different smell from human death. How could I have known that her ability to differentiate between human and animal scents, between the living and the dead, would determine our successes and failures? That her reputation and mine would depend on it?

CHAPTER 3

Montana to the Dominican Republic

Before 1995

A few years earlier, I'd had no dog, no home, no community, and no real purpose. My fiancé, Doug, and I were working in the Dominican Republic, searching for gold. He was the boss, and I was his assistant. Doug, with a master's degree specializing in Caribbean geology, had signed on as exploration manager for an international mining company on the condition that they would hire me, too. I had a geology degree and years of experience working in Montana, Texas, and, most recently, Colorado. Our life together seemed perfect.

Doug had caught my attention in physics class in the early 1980s at the University of Montana in Missoula. He strolled into class wearing a pair of Levi's original 501 button-down jeans that showcased his long, strong thighs. His blue-gray wool sweater matched his sparkling eyes. He didn't notice me, probably because he had a girlfriend, but also perhaps because I still carried that "freshman fifteen" weight. I sat in the back of class, doodling, squirming in my chair, and passing notes back and forth with my equally restless friend, Munson. "PowDa Dayyyyy. Going skiing today?" I'd scribble on a three-by-five note card and slip it to him. Munson told me that I reminded him of his childhood dog, Skip, an adolescent black Labrador retriever that darted here and there, chasing this and that, and trying desperately to please everyone and everything.

Doug, on the other hand, seemed more like a German shepherd: methodical, precise, and contemplative. In physics class he was "that guy," the one who sat in the front row, asking the professor for definitive answers to complex problems with laser focus. He was intense and practical, serious, and a semi-introvert. Even though we had never met, I liked what I saw. He was everything I wasn't, yet wanted to be. Maybe I had something to learn from him. Doug told me later that he'd wanted to be a surgeon, but he didn't think he was smart enough or had hands steady enough, so he studied geology instead.

Five years after the first time I saw him in class, I finally met him on a chairlift at the local ski resort. Fresh out of grad school, he was broke, jobless, and uncertain what to do with his new degree.

"I could get you a job," I told him as we skied off the lift. Doug and his buds chased after me the rest of the day as we dropped a knee one turn at a time through deep powder on our Telemark skis.

Later that night, I met Doug at a mutual friend's party. We both showed up alone, hoping to get to know each other. While drinking cold beer on the outdoor deck, I created a mental map of what my future might look like with him. You know, the Cinderella story my childhood girlfriends and I would talk about when we played Barbie dolls behind the couch in the living room. Subconsciously, I was ticking off the requirements of what I considered to be a creative, passionate, life-affirming partner: smart, sexy, family man, dedicated, motivated— someone who'd take care of me, support me. I didn't think much about where we'd live or what we'd do because I was still adrift. That night, we shared stories of heartbreak and past relationships. He confessed he hadn't had a girlfriend in three years. "My college sweetie went to medical school."

"Funny," I smiled back. "My first love left for vet school."

Then, our conversation turned serious. "I just lost my dad," he frowned. "He was fifty-five. Just sitting in his chair. My mom found him the next morning. Cigarette still in his hand."

I didn't know what to say, so I hugged him.

"Man, I miss him."

He squeezed me so tight my ribs hurt. He didn't want to let go. I loved the way he smelled and held me. I felt something wet on my cheek. "Are you crying?" I asked.

"Yeah. It hurts, you know."

Wow, a man with tender emotions. I had never seen my dad, or even my mother, cry. I rarely saw affection between them. In our household we shoveled our emotions away like we scraped the dirt off our shoes into the red shag carpet, hoping that someday somebody else might clean it up. But I liked emotional Doug. Throughout college, my colleagues had told me, "Oh, Sue, you're so tough." I had begun to resent those words.

The next day, Doug asked me out. Soon after, we jumped into the sack, which might not have been a good idea since I still had residual feelings for my first love. I never shared that with Doug, though, because I didn't want to hurt him. It was winter, and Doug got hired by the gold-exploration company where I worked. We both sat in an office giggling, playing footsie under the table, and plotting gold anomalies—rock formations that contain gold—on topographic maps. The map of my world looked promising. He earned seven dollars an hour with a master's degree. I earned fifty cents per hour more because I had been working in the office a bit longer. Within a few months, the company promoted Doug to project field geologist. But not me.

We were inseparable after that—except for a nine-month breakup when I took a job in Antarctica. Doug begged me not to go. It was difficult to leave him, but I was twenty-six, restless, and not ready to settle down or commit to a serious relationship. I needed to see the world and figure out what I wanted to do, who I wanted to be. Unsure how to handle a separation, I promised to be faithful. I didn't know I was making a promise I couldn't keep. Halfway through my stay in Antarctica, I broke our vow when I met a writer working on assignment. *A writer?* I had never met a writer before. He was a friend of a friend and had just written a book about flying around the US in his Cessna. We had a lot in common, and I thought I wanted his life. When I returned home, I told Doug everything, and we broke up.

Months later, I begged Doug to take me back. "I love you. I made a terrible mistake."

He did.

But I had only asked Doug for half of what I needed. My mistake was not asking him for forgiveness. I should have rested my palm over his heart, stared him straight in the eyes and apologized, and asked him to forgive me. But I didn't.

Instead, we tried a geographical cure for what ailed our relationship; we packed our bags and moved to Chamonix, France, for the winter to ski and rekindle things. I went, thinking the past was behind us and that he had forgiven me. But our togetherness turned toxic. The smallest things I'd say or do would infuriate him. He would argue and pick fights. He was always right, controlling, and angry.

Doug would often remind me of my mother's imperfections, such as her incessant talking or her horrible eating habits. In the morning he'd say, "No half-and-half in your coffee. You don't want to look like your mother, do you?" Doug said I'd end up just like her if I wasn't careful. "Only one glass of wine tonight," he'd say and remove the bottle from my hands. His belittling comments were all too familiar to me after watching my father demean my mother or vice versa. All of this happened despite my telling him that I would never, could never be like my parents.

I'd watched my parents verbally abuse each other. No matter how horrific the arguments or how verbally cruel my parents behaved, leaving was never an option to them. That's all they knew. So, I learned to keep the peace by keeping my mouth shut and stuffing my emotions away to avoid conflict. I *hated* conflict. It was easier to smile than to argue. Back then, I didn't know how to navigate my way through conflict or stand up to it. Doug loved to win, and I put up with it because I believed that I *deserved* to be punished. It was *my* fault. I was guilty. I had sabotaged the relationship. So, I was going to take the hit.

Our sweet kisses and tender embraces became a memory.

I vowed, just like my mom, *to never leave*. And I wasn't about to break a promise, again. The angry phase will pass soon, I'd tell myself. He'll love me again, like when we first met.

To show my loyalty to Doug, I followed him from Montana to Texas, where he had been hired to manage a gold project in Jamaica. While Doug commuted to the Caribbean, I worked for an environmental consulting firm. Six months into my Texas gig, and fed up with our less-than-perfect relationship, I should have shouted, "I'm not putting up with your shit! I'm better than this!" But I didn't. Instead, I told Doug, "I don't want *you* to be miserable anymore. You can leave me. I'll stay with you, but I can't live here. I'm going to ask for a transfer to Amy's office in Denver." Conflict avoidance achieved.

Doug joined me in Colorado. His anger seemed to lift. We laughed more, and our intimacy sparked. I led him on a survival trip into the Utah desert, something where I was the expert, where I taught Doug how to make a bow-drill fire and scrounge food from the land. It seemed like Doug was learning to trust me again.

He'd forgiven me, and the past was behind us ... I thought. Right before Christmas, I asked him to marry me. At thirty-two, and six years into our relationship, I was finally ready to settle down, have a husband, get a dog, and be *normal*. "Loyal, I will be," I professed. He didn't say yes right away. I had to wait a few weeks for him and Big to go on a boys' trip to Denver. A few weeks later, he dropped to his knees and slid a big ol' diamond ring on my finger, in the mountains near Gunnison. I remember how proud that ring made me feel. I'd show it off and think that it proved he loved me.

Doug ended up in the emergency room that same evening. As he was sawing down a Christmas tree, a needle of a spiky spruce poked him in the eye and scratched it. He wore a patch, and his eye wept for days.

That should have been an omen. Three months later we said, "Till death do us part," and in my mind I was certain the words would heal his hurts, melt the ice around his softening heart, and rekindle our romance once and for all. We had suffered because of my betrayal, but now we were on our way.

❖ ❖ ❖

One afternoon, the year before, I was at our drilling site in the DR, swatting mosquitoes under a canopy of cacao and palm trees, watching three laborers use machetes to slice through dense vines in front of a bulldozer. Our two Dominican geologists, César and Tito, and a group of campesinos, the local subsistence farmers, followed behind, watching as the blade knocked over cacao trees and gouged a roadway through soil the color of sunset. Our Dominican geologists, with pesos crammed in their pockets, counted the toppled trees while landowners scrutinized with suspicious eyes from the sidelines. Doug was four hours away in Santo Domingo, finalizing other permits with the Miníera, the exploration and mining branch of the Dominican government. Permits granted us permission to drill for gold on anyone's land, as long as we compensated them for any crop damage while building drill sites and roads.

I fell behind when one of my rubber boots got sucked into the mud. I hurried to catch up to my team, slipping and sliding, clenching the road-building permit and map in my hand.

Over the rumble of the idling bulldozer, I heard voices rise. Spanish negotiations flew back and forth too fast for me to follow. Arms were raised, and feet stomped. I deciphered arguments about trees, but the rest sounded as muddy as the ground I stood on. The project meant quick cash and potential future commerce for campesino landowners who agreed to let us build the route up the steep mountainside. Every tree knocked over on their property had value. It was our job to count and pay compensation in cold hard cash.

"*La linea está aquí. Estos son mis* árboles."

Fingers pointed to imaginary property boundaries. One man drew a line in the mud with his bare heel.

As I strained to comprehend, two campesinos on horseback arrived with machetes hanging from their belts. A pistol was tucked into the waistband of one man, who also wore a cowboy hat. He dismounted in front of the bulldozer blade. Adjusting his hat, he postured with his hand on his machete. The other man, still on his horse, squared off on the geologists.

I retreated behind a thin coffee tree. Even the shade of the canopy couldn't stop the scorching sun from turning this place into an oven.

From my quagmire to the side, I picked out a few words in peasant Spanish: *Pare. Mas dinero. Oro.*

The clamor intensified, on top of the already-constant noise of the bulldozer.

My geologists argued that the landowners had signed agreements and the government had granted permission. But the two men advanced menacingly. The crowd of campesinos circled in on the conflict. One man grabbed his crotch, readjusting his overheated macho sacks as he threatened the geologists.

I recognized the man with the pistol. His mother was a landowner and he wanted *dinero* too. Right now.

I slinked away to my field truck. Sweat from my forehead dripped onto the receiver of my five-pound satellite phone. My shaking fingers punched the keys to call Doug back in Santo Domingo.

"I'm freaking out here, Doug. These guys think we're rich Americans, and that we've already found gold. They just showed up with guns." Caught up in the drama, I exaggerate a tiny bit. "Who knows? They might come and kill me tonight if we don't pay. They know where I live. I'm not paid enough to be here," I fumed.

"Calm down, calm down. Legally, we have the paper we need. We have permission from the Miníera to cross everyone's property. Just stand down while César negotiates with the landowners."

"Stand down? Doug, these guys have guns!"

"They're probably bluffing. Tell the bulldozer man to shut it down until we get it resolved."

"Doug, you need to get your ass out here!"

"I can't. You know our rule. No driving in the dark. Just let the geologists keep the peace. That's why they're there."

Hanging up, my anger toward Doug intensified as I recalled the time he introduced me to the president of the company as 'the other geologist' instead of his future wife. *I'm just another employee?* I ducked between the shouting campesinos. I plastered a smile on my mud-smeared face and tapped the shoulder of César.

The bulldozer shut down. The yelling subsided.

That evening, I returned to our gated field house on the two-lane, potholed La Carretera Oriental—a highway that also served as the human trafficking and drug trade route from neighboring Haiti to the town of Miches here in the DR, and was also a part of the escape route, via boat, to Puerto Rico. The electricity had been shut off all day, disabling the water pump. There was no water for a shower to rinse the mud from my skin. No fan to cool me.

Walking outside by the light of my headlamp, I looked for Augusto, the bony village elder who served as our night watchman. I usually found him perched on a wooden bench in the courtyard like a small garden gnome, cradling a machete. His blade also served to slap cockroaches, cut mangoes from the tree in our yard, and was used as an eating utensil. Even though he was nearly deaf and partly blind and never formally educated, we hired him because the locals told us no one messes with such a respected elder. Instead of circling the field house compound at night, he slept under the veranda overlooking the ocean, his machete tucked under the mattress.

But not even Augusto's machete or César, who woke every night at three, felt like enough protection that night. To make Doug and I feel safer, César had promised he'd hire a crew to build protective iron cages over the windows and door at our field house. But he hadn't done so yet.

Well after dark, I noticed César hadn't returned from the field. No doubt he was still dealing with the road politics or drinking cerveza at the local disco. Then, I saw Augusto sitting on the bench. "Hola, Augusto," I called. Between the convicts passing by our house on their journey toward America, today's confrontation in the field, and César's absence, I was feeling very nervous.

His big smile, lips curled inward to hide his toothless gums, creased wide across his face, was the first sign of friendliness I'd seen all day. He nodded. "*¿Suzanna, como 'sta 'sted?*" His stubby fingers reached out to shake my hand.

"*¿Tienes hambre?*" Hungry? I asked. I retreated to the kitchen for rice and beans with chicken, left on the stove by our cook, the neighbor. After mashing the food for the toothless man, I returned to the veranda and handed him the plate, which nearly toppled to the ground in his feeble hands. At the smell of food, the canine sidekick that served as his eyes and ears bolted up from cruising the garbage ditch for scraps.

"*Cyclone, ven acá.*" The dog, which looked like a mix between a small fox and Chihuahua, came closer, his ribs showing through his short-haired hide. I had dubbed the dog Cyclone after the last hurricane, which had nearly devastated Augusto's village.

I set another full plate on the ground for Cyclone. While Augusto muddled through eating, Cyclone wolfed his plate in seconds.

"Sit," I commanded, in an attempt to train Cyclone by the light of our lamps.

Cyclone didn't move.

I switched to Spanish. "*Sientate.*"

The dog cocked his head to the side and stared at me.

I looked at the mangy mutt and Augusto, fingering food into his mouth. With Doug in Santo Domingo much of the time, this pair were my only friends. Tears clouded my eyes. An adventure that had begun with the romance of finding gold and traveling the world with my husband had lost its luster, and now the loneliness of my situation hit me like a punch. I looked to the sky to prevent my tears from spilling.

I knew I cared deeply for these people, and the science girl in me was drawn to the land and the geology, but I felt I was stuck in mud, and that I needed to do something to move forward. I had sold my soul for dollars, and life was passing me by as I slaved away along a purposeless path of making money. Initially, Doug and I started working in the Dominican Republic with great enthusiasm and desire. But over the years, eleven-month stints shortened to two months, then mere weeks. I glanced at my watch, checking where I was in the fifteen-day countdown to jumping on an airplane and escaping. I screamed at the ocean: *I don't care about finding gold! I need to find a way out!*

CHAPTER 4

Crested Butte
Ski Patrol School

Winter 1995
Crested Butte, Colorado

My legs quiver from fatigue. The eleven-thousand-foot Colorado elevation steals oxygen from my lungs. I stand still and hunch over to catch my breath. Cold penetrates three layers of mountain clothing while a professional ski patroller shows several of us trainees how to execute an avalanche rescue probe line. Shoulder to shoulder, marching up the slope in sync, one step at a time, we slide twelve-foot-long aluminum poles down into the snow. Probe left, then right, then forward. A life-size dummy hides somewhere below our feet, buried four feet beneath the snow. Sinking to our knees, we aim to strike the dummy with the tip of the probe pole.

"When you strike a body, its feels like sticking a thermometer into a raw turkey. Your probe will pop and bounce back," shouts my teacher.

My breath escapes me as I wonder what it must be like finding people buried, alive or dead, in an avalanche and administering first aid—like my instructor has done dozens, maybe hundreds of times.

"Chance of survival in an avalanche drops to three percent after ninety minutes," he reminds us, adding more stress to the task at hand. "You've got a few minutes to get someone out of the snow or they're dead." Our pace picks up with the urgency in his voice. The session stretches long as the patroller has purposely buried the dummy one hundred feet away.

The cold stiffens my fingers, making it difficult to grip the probe pole.

Stumbling up the avalanche chute as I try to keep pace with my eight classmates, I'm embarrassed at my lack of physical fitness at this altitude. My excuse? My commitment to making money. I've always dreamed of ski patrolling but could never live off the minimum-wage salary the ski patrols get. Now I'm here by choice, at the frigidly high elevation, working my butt off in Crested Butte's fifty-hour ski patrol school. I can afford to give them my time for free now, take the time to learn about avalanche rescue and emergency medicine. With my frantic breathing hidden behind the snowy neck gaiter I have lapped around my nose, I press on.

The two-month ski patrol training—a long grind against bad weather, my own physical limitations, and the steepest avalanche terrain—pits me against burly twentysomething-year-old men. They force me, one of only two women in the course, to grow some competitive skin. At thirty-two years old, I stand only as high as their chests, and I am half their weight. In order to get hired by the ski company next year, I must pass the patrol test—to do this, I must be able to find two dummies in less than five minutes, each one strapped with an avalanche signaling device and buried under three to five feet of snow; manhandle a two hundred pound toboggan down an icy near-vertical mogul run; and ski every avalanche path on the mountain under nasty conditions.

I have my work cut out for me. These guys have had their feet in the snow for months, while I just pulled mine out of the steaming Caribbean mud. No one here knows that I commute to work in the tropics.

After we finish a morning of practicing probe lines—we failed miserably to strike the dummy within five minutes—we ski in whiteout conditions to the summit patrol shack. Snow falls at an inch an hour. Wind rattles the shack's windows. I shake snow from my shoulders and hat, hang my wet jacket to dry, and plop into a chair to remove the ski boots from my frozen feet.

"Hey, Purvis. Wanna come help me close some ski runs? This storm is skyrocketing the avalanche danger." Todd, a patroller for more than a decade, picks up his boots.

"Yeah. I'm on it. Just let me warm up my toes." I blow warm air into my hands and massage my toes to get blood flowing to them. Then I think, *Crap, Sue. You don't know shit about avalanches.* The one and only avalanche course I attended was in 1981, in college. So, I take the opportunity to learn. "Tell me what I need to know."

"It's all about stress, baby." He laughs and draws a triangle on a piece of paper, labeling the lines. Each side of the triangle represents a contributing factor for avalanches: *Snowpack, Terrain, Weather.* In the triangle's center sits the word, *Human Trigger.*

"Most avalanches occur on or around thirty-seven-degree slopes. A slope so steep that if you're standing on it, you can almost reach over and touch the face."

Colorado has the highest number of avalanches of all the states. Why? Because Colorado has urban centers near mountains, providing easy access to avalanche terrain. It also harbors a shallow snowpack, and cold, clear subzero nights create a temperature change between the snow laying on the ground (warmer) and the surface snow (colder). This strong temperature gradient drives a metamorphic process creating depth hoar, an avalanche term used to define snow as having the consistency of sugar. "Depth hoar literally falls apart in the palm of your hand," he tells me. It's considered an unstable or weak layer. This is a huge avalanche problem that lurks all season long once its buried by a stronger, more cohesive layer of snow, called a slab. "Out of sight, out of mind," he reminds me and draws, on the paper, this year's snowpack plunked on a steep angle. The entire mountainside is waiting to avalanche if someone skis across the slope.

"Stress versus strength." Todd stands up. "When an avalanche happens it resembles a lopsided teeter-totter: *stress* sits on the heavier, lower side and *strength* on the higher side." He uses the teeter-totter analogy to explain that repeated trips from skiers add stress to the snowpack. That's why patrollers use explosives to mitigate avalanche danger. The trigger—two pounds of pentolite—is a hand charge that will hopefully add enough stress to cause an avalanche.

I pause to let that sink in. "What do you think—am I going to get creamed by an avalanche on my drive home to Gunnison tonight?"

"Maybe. By the time this storm cycle is over, we'll have eight feet on the ground. Avalanche danger will be extreme."

Not knowing anyone in town except Amy's mom, who is staying at their vacation condo across the street from the ski hill, I ask his advice. "Should I stay at my friend's place on Marcellina Lane?"

Todd laughs. "Anyone who buys a condo on Marcellina Lane is an idiot. Tonight, I wouldn't be surprised if that slope avalanches."

"What?"

"You heard what happened?"

I shake my head.

"Six years ago, three kids were completely buried in an avalanche at Sunrise Condos." He gestures toward Marcellina Lane. "They were four and six years old, from Texas. They were playing outside a condo when the hillside ripped. All three buried. One was killed."

"A little kid died? In an avalanche? Here?"

"Yeah. Not in the ski resort, but across the street, out-of-bounds. We'd never seen that slope slide that big before. Smaller slides have hit the building, but never spilled over into the parking lot. Certainly never killing anyone."

Crap! A year earlier, when Doug and I had investigated buying a place in the valley, the real estate agent had taken us to that complex where the fatal avalanche happened. I remember him telling me, "There's some good deals here," as he escorted us into a ground-floor condo. When I threw open the bathroom shade to see a wall of snow packed against the uphill-facing window, I knew it wasn't a place I wanted to live. At the time I had no idea what had happened, nor that the hillside adjacent to the condo was in an avalanche path.

Todd tells me the whole story. Originally, the call came in that a roof slide buried three children playing in the snow. But when rescuers arrived they realized an entire mountain of snow had avalanched. One of the dads, loading luggage into the airport shuttle, heard a boom like a bomb going off. When he looked up he saw a white wall of snow rushing toward him. One minute the kids were playing in the snow. The next minute, they were gone. The dad, frantic, started digging through the snow with his hands to look for the kids.

By the time ski patrol arrived, a couple hundred people clogged the avalanche path, jamming whatever they had into the snow: broom handles, ski poles, mops, shovels. Police, fire, and ambulance crews were using PVC pipes, a swimming pool rescue hook, and conduit tubes to probe. One of the rescuers escorted the hysterical mothers off the debris. As Todd and other ski patrollers started forming systematic probe lines, they learned rescuers had just dug two of the kids from the snow. Blue. Not breathing. Rag-doll limp. But doing CPR, medics got them both breathing again. They'd been pulled out no more than six minutes after they were buried.

"You're kidding me. They survived?"

"Yeah. They did, but not the third boy—Stevie Reardon. We even brought in our avalanche dog to find him."

"Avalanche dog? What did the dog do?"

"Not much, really. He ran around the scene, sniffing here and there. It was so chaotic that I don't think he could smell the buried boy … because of all the bystanders and rescuers running around."

"Really? I thought they were trained to smell people buried in the snow."

"I guess. But the dog didn't do anything. Most dogs never make finds."

"How come?"

"Umm." He shrugs his shoulders then thinks about it. "Variety of reasons, I'd guess. Not trained, someone else handling the dog, lazy."

"But …"

"Someone with a probe eventually found Stevie, ten feet under the snow, an hour after he'd been buried. He was so deep that a backhoe had to excavate the snow away to dig him out. Medics tried to revive him all the way on the helicopter to the hospital. But later that night, the docs pronounced him dead."

Todd shrugs into his coat as he finishes the story. I fumble with my boots, jamming my half-warmed toes into the foam liners encased in stiff plastic. My thoughts run amok: avalanches, little boys, burials, screaming parents, rescuers, chaos, random probing, CPR, avalanche dog. I question my courage as we exit the shack.

Snapping into my ski bindings, I yell out. "So, where's the dog now?"

"After that, the owner and the dog left."

"Really? So, does the resort still have an avalanche dog?"

"Not sure." Todd clears his voice. "A few of the guys bring their dogs up to work, nothing formal."

My eyes light up. What if I got hired? I could bring a dog to work, train it, and save the next Stevie Reardon.

After school wraps up for the day, I walk through the storm, across the street toward Amy's condo on Marcellina Lane. My truck sits buried under a snowdrift.

Alone, on foot, in the dark, I'm the only fool out here. Locals fled the streets long ago. Snow pelts down hard as I scrunch my hood tight around my face. Wishing that I had worn my goggles, I squint as the snow stings my eyes. My legs push through knee-deep powder. Hurricane-force winds slice the snow sideways, knocking me off balance. Walls of snow line the roads. Berms tower above me.

Plodding uphill, I raise my eyes. Lights flickering in the windows of the Mountain Sunrise condos illuminate the adjacent slope. But at the site of the fatal avalanche, no signs are posted to warn of potential danger. There are no lights or sirens to warn residents that this entire slope could fail and bury anyone in its path. No one warns the tourists cooking dinner in their rented Mountain Sunrise condos that a tsunami of snow could blast through their windows and doors to suffocate them.

As I stare into the darkness, my anger swells at Stevie's senseless death. How, in 1989, could three young boys get buried in an urban avalanche at a world-class ski resort? How could the probe lines and even an avalanche dog fail to locate Stevie in time? Standing here today, on the tail of a weeklong snowstorm, I could be the next victim. For the first time, I ask myself the question: *What if I got a dog and trained it to save lives?*

CHAPTER 5

Tasha

Fall 1995
Gunnison, Colorado

Fresh off our two-week hunting trip, where I never left her side, seven-week-old Tasha has learned to trust by following me through aspen forests and stinky elk wallows.

Now back home, Tasha sits on the new Berber carpet in our condominium, looking out the sliding glass door, swamped by boredom. Her wet nose presses against the glass. Doug has gone back to the Dominican Republic and his gold-drilling program. Tasha stares into the postage stamp–sized lawn that's barricaded by a six-foot-tall wooden fence. Not one grasshopper, leaf, or pinecone clutters the chemically treated, cut-to-perfection golf course, condo-style grass that we share with seven other owners. Imprisoned, with asphalt out one door, a major highway out the other, and a "No Dogs Allowed" policy on the golf course, we have no place to romp. Scooping Tasha off the floor in one hand, I grab the truck keys with the other.

"Tasha, this Gunnison condo has to go. I know where you need to be. Back in the mountains and aspen groves, where we both felt alive."

Forty-five minutes later, we arrive in Crested Butte, an old mining town tagged as the last great Colorado ski town. Walled off in three directions by impassible mounds of snow in winter, it nestles in the Slate River Valley at the Highway 135 terminus, surrounded by white-capped peaks that rise to 13,500 feet. Hundred-year-old, dilapidated miner shacks and dirt roads have morphed into a yuppie haven, where most of the thousand year-round residents have college degrees. Competitive, young, athletic, and rich, the new Crested Butte residents pursue outdoor passions—skiing in the winter, mountain biking, boating, and hiking in the summer.

The town has planted mansions with quarter-mile-long heated driveways on the mountainsides overlooking the rugged Maroon Bells and West Elk Wilderness. It lures movie stars and "trustafarians," young ski bums who own homes but don't need to work. Those who work compete for jobs in thirty restaurants, three liquor stores, and seven T-shirt shops, all supported by tourists.

Tasha and I spend the afternoon trotting around the town with a real estate agent. Unable to afford the present-day luxury of the old mining town, we move outward to Mt. Crested Butte, the ski resort's bedroom community of three hundred residents. At 9,400 feet, it perches three miles above town.

When the real estate agent shows me his list of condos to see, I nix one pronto—the condo complex across the street from the resort, the site of the deadly avalanche. This time, with Doug's approval, I place a bid on a condo a half mile from the resort. The going rate to live in Paradise is as steep as the ski runs. One hundred, seventy-two thousand dollars buys a doghouse-size condo with a mortgage large enough to force us to return to the Caribbean to drill for more gold. But, in the town of Crested Butte below, the same 1,110 square feet goes for double the price.

Located a block from the ski resort, our soon-to-be-home is surrounded by hundreds of avalanche paths, slicing deep into the bellies of the rocky peaks. The avalanches have demolished dense stands of timber, leaving distinct scars. Our property line sidles up to vacant land where the city has posted a sign: KEEP OUT. AVALANCHE DANGER. Immediately after Stevie's tragedy, the town and the local police met with ski patrol personnel to solicit suggestions for future avalanche operations. That was six years ago. And now I suspect everyone hopes—including the private landowners and real estate agents—that avalanches just go away.

Later that evening, while rolling a tennis ball for Tasha on the carpet, I call Doug in the Dominican Republic.

"Hon, just think, you'll be able to walk right out your door and hike, bike, and ski. We'll have instant friends and a community. All the joint aches and pains you always complain of will disappear. Crested Butte is the best medicine." His objections of big mortgage and zero earning potential for me disappear into to my visions of a bubbling future. As I paint a rosy picture of our life in Crested Butte, Tasha intercepts the toy with her nose. I laugh as she sinks her sharp puppy teeth into the ball almost as big as her head.

"You need a job." I level my finger at Tasha, a few weeks later in Gunnison, as we wait for the Crested Butte condo to close. "You can't just sit around here and get fat." I say that after just watching her devour a day's worth of food in six seconds without chewing one bit of it. Now, I watch as her eyes grow heavy. She drops her head between her paws and sighs. I stroke her velvet fur.

A radio announcement about the local Western State College Search and Rescue Team piques my interest. I call the Gunnison Sheriff's Department to learn about this opportunity to use dogs with search and rescue.

"Yeah, we use dogs in searches," a deputy tells me. "We have four independent volunteer search-and-rescue teams in Gunnison County, but none have search dogs. We have to bring dogs in from elsewhere. We usually call SARDOC. That's Search and Rescue Dogs of Colorado."

"Really? What do they do?"

"They're a group of volunteer dog teams that find missing people."

"No fooling."

"Yeah. SARDOC teams do good work. In that manhunt last year for the two fugitives who murdered Sheriff Coursey and his partner, a li'l redhead and her border collie from SARDOC found the two bastards. After four weeks with no leads, we called SARDOC to check around the vehicle one last time for any clue of the fugitives' whereabouts, dead or alive. A handful of canine handlers drove from Fort Collins to help."

"I remember that," I say. "FBI. Sheriff's vehicles zooming down the highway. Sirens blasting. Road blocks."

The deputy goes on. "That dog found the two fugitives rolled up in a sleeping bag under a tree, a couple hundred yards from their abandoned car. Two hours after arriving on scene, that dog team solved a nationwide manhunt."

I crawl on my belly, grab the tennis ball from under the chair, and roll it to Tasha. She springs to her feet and bats the ball back and forth with her front paws. She nudges the ball in my direction with her nose.

"The autopsy report revealed they shot themselves soon after they shot the sheriff."

"That's pretty cool the dog could find them."

"SARDOC teams are good. But other dog teams, not necessarily."

"What do you mean?"

"Not all dog teams are created equal. A notorious police-dog handler told the FBI that his hound tracked the fugitives down a narrow creek to the main highway. That steered the search in the wrong direction, across miles of terrain, and eventually to the Midwest. That was a real waste. The guys were right here the whole time."

"So, what about Gunnison County? Why don't they have search dogs? Or an avalanche dog?"

As I listen intently, Tasha stops batting the ball, stands tall on all four legs, cocks her head and stares at me.

"Good question. We don't even have a police dog. But, we're thinking about it."

My eyes widen at the opportunity.

With further investigation, I learn that SARDOC dogs search for people missing in avalanches, wilderness, and water. Before canine teams can respond to missions they must build solid "Air-Scent" or "Trailing" foundations, pass rigorous tests, then move onto specialty disciplines like avalanche, cadaver, and water. Certification in wilderness search takes an average of three years, requiring a series of tests for both human and canine. In order to be a member, I must join a local search-and-rescue team to serve as my fielding organization. Crested Butte Search and Rescue, one of the four in Gunnison County, would be mine.

A tendril of a plan emerges from the kernel of Stevie's avalanche death and nourished by the fresh inspiration of SARDOC. Tasha plods over to me, wondering what's up. I lift her off the floor, bringing her face close to mine.

"What do you say, Black Dog? Ready to *go find*?"

I speak to SARDOC's representatives on the phone about dog training. The woman on the phone directs me to a possible mentor. "The nearest certified avalanche dog handler lives in Aspen and she trains a poodle."

"A poodle?"

Three days later, I load the truck with a week's worth of camping supplies for a road trip to learn firsthand about how dogs find people.

I could only imagine what I would say to Doug if he were on his way home after a three-week shift from the DR. I raise Tasha up above my head then practice my speech to Doug on her. "Oh, Honey, good to see you, but I've got to run. We'll be back in five days. The cereal is in the cupboard."

With Tasha in the copilot seat, we drive through the Roaring Fork Valley to Aspen. Brilliant yellow, orange, and red foliage lights up this isolated Rocky Mountain sanctuary. The manicured town clusters around the river, which snakes through million-dollar neighborhoods. Tourists parade down Main Street with Gucci bags and alligator-skin shoes, while I wear a stinky white V-neck tee that's covered in black dog hair (from earlier, when Tasha and I slept together in the back of my truck, on the side of the road).

Climbing the steep Red Mountain grade, past monstrous stone palaces, my rusted-out four-cylinder pickup loses steam. I downshift to chug up the road to reach an older remodeled house that's six times the size of my condo.

Peeking into the rearview mirror at my face and taking a quick whiff of my armpit, I swap my tee for a fresh one, twirl my shoulder-length hair into a ponytail, and brush my teeth with a squirt of toothpaste on my finger.

A woman named Carla bounces out of the house and greets me with a big-sister hug that picks me up off the ground. In her late thirties, the lean blond in running attire looks very Barbie-meets-new-age-mountain woman. Her three-year-old poodle, Cassidy, named after a Grateful Dead song, stands as tall as a miniature pony. Her untrimmed, eight-inch, kinky fluff looks like a mountain goat's fur in winter—long, frizzy, and thick. Strands of white hang over her dark-brown eyes.

"That's a poodle?" I ask.

"People judge us by our looks. If I want to get respect from the big egos in the search-and-rescue community, I can't have a classic-looking poodle."

I give Poodle Lady—her new name—a blank stare, unsure why the search-and-rescue community would be so judgmental. As we chat, she shares that she can run the eighteen-mile, four-mountain pass loop with her dog in twelve hours.

"Poodle Lady is badass," I mumble under my breath.

"Ready to teach Tasha how to find humans?" asks Poodle Lady.

A half hour later we arrive at Hunter Creek Trailhead. My ankle-high, roly-poly Tasha, Cassidy, and I hop out of Poodle Lady's 1960s Willys Jeep. As the dogs relieve themselves, we shoulder our packs, and I leash Tasha to keep her from disappearing in the hip-high grass. Aspen leaves rustle in the afternoon breeze. Tasha leads us, hiking single file down the trail toward the creek, dry leaves crunching under our feet. Cassidy is off the path, exploring.

Poodle Lady startles me by shouting at Cassidy. "No crittering! Bad dog." The poodle freezes, retreats from the bushes, and drops her head. Poodle Lady grabs the dog's scruff. "If you're going to have a search dog, you can't let it critter. Tasha can't chase animals or animal tracks. That is an automatic flunk for a search dog."

Without missing a beat, her dog walks a perfect heel. "That's only one of twenty-two SARDOC expectations for new handlers and dogs," she informs me. "SARDOC has some of the toughest standards in the country. Standards are important, otherwise any Tom, Dick, or Harry can claim they have a search dog."

I cringe, foreseeing potential failure in my future. I want to be the good puppy—a good handler, a good trainer. But I imagine getting scolded, "Bad Sue! Bad dog owner!"

As Tasha drags me down the trail, I have the urge to control her by yanking back on the leash. But she's only eight weeks old, and fear of cracking her tiny windpipe, the size of a sipping straw, prevents me. Instead of correcting her tugging, I skip to keep up with her. But Tasha speeds up, racing down the trail.

To impress Poodle Lady, I give Tasha's lead a slight wrench. She flips backward, landing her on her butt in the dust. I rush to pick her up and coo apologies to her.

"I never had to do that with my dog." Poodle Lady reprimands me. She's pulling small chunks of prime rib from a plastic baggy and offering them to her dog, as if spoon-feeding a baby.

"How did you train your dog to be so perfect?" Squirming Tasha lunges nose first out of my arms. She lands on her face in the dirt and starts scouring the ground, looking for bits of prime rib Cassidy dropped.

"My dog was easy to train. I didn't have to do anything." She pets her dog, offering me zero obedience tips. "Poodles aren't rambunctious like Labs. You have your hands full."

But, I can't wield an iron fist with my dog. I will raise Tasha to be a free spirit, just like my parents raised me.

Near Hunter Creek, a gurgling, fast-flowing stream, we set up a training exercise on a trail that cuts through an aspen grove. Tasha's chin lifts, and her ears pull back at the chirping of migrating songbirds. A minute later, she whips around at the buzzing drone of a grasshopper.

After tying up Cassidy, Poodle Lady crouches on her knees. One hand grasps Tasha's collar, the other hand rests gently on her furry chest. She explains how to do the introductory trailing exercise, which is a variation of hide-and-seek.

As instructed, I fling my arms up in the air and sprint down the trail, squawking nonsense. I hide in the bushes and drop to my belly, calling, "Tasha, come and find me."

Tasha rears up, punching the air with her front paws, eyes locked on my movement. Poodle Lady holds a firm grip, but Tasha slips through her fingers, scrambling away. Gaining momentum like a sprinting Olympian, Tasha gallops down the trail, spit flying from her mouth in excitement.

I tuck my nose into the dirt as Tasha hurls her body at my head. Her needle-sharp nails scratch my scalp. Teeth tear into my ponytail. I pry her off to come up for air. "You've got some fight," I tell her.

We repeat the exercise, this time with Poodle Lady and I swapping positions. Tasha finds her with the same gusto. As her reward, they play tug-of-war using a stick.

"Now we're going to up the ante by challenging Tasha to use her nose instead of her eyes," Poodle Lady announces. This begins a primer for me on why dogs can discriminate one person from another by scent. She explains that humans shed *rafts*, dead skin cells mixed with bacteria, that float with scent, just like the cloud of dirt swirling around Pig Pen from the *Peanuts* comic strip. Each person gives off a unique perfume.

"If you're lost and I give Cassidy your underwear to sniff, she'll know to look for only you."

"Really?"

"Dogs smell like we see."

I file away more facts: humans lose fifty million rafts per second, one-third of which fall to the ground, while the other two-thirds rise to float in the air.

"So, Cassidy tracks the scent in those fallen skin rafts?"

"Yep. She's a trailing dog, dropping her nose to the ground to retrace the invisible path left behind by rafts. Air-scent dogs on the other hand, lift their nose aloft to find scent lingering in the air."

I feel the information wash over me, almost too much to absorb.

Poodle Lady reaches in her search pack and withdraws green flags, the same wands used to mark electrical lines. "Let me show you." As she walks toward the creek, she flags her footprints. "These flags will let you see my exact scent path. If Tasha wanders off the trail of the flags, shove her nose into the footprints. That's how she'll learn to follow the scent." At the end of her flag trail, she cuts right out of sight.

Kneeling and supporting Tasha's chest, I whisper into her ear. "Ready, Tasha? *Go find!*"

Tasha rears on her hind legs, bucking like a racehorse, whining to get away. She ducks to escape my cupped hands. Little black paws scamper down the dusty trail, crushing leaves in her wake.

Charging full speed, Tasha ignores the flags. She ignores Poodle Lady's scent and misses the right-hand turn. I watch Tasha launch off the edge of the riverbank and drop out of sight.

"Oh no!" I bolt after her, imagining a sputtering black puppy swept away in rushing water.

Poodle Lady sprints from the bushes. We both peek over the embankment, holding our breath. Rustling out of a pile of leaves, Tasha looks up, tail wagging. She scrambles to climb the riverbank. Her two front legs, three-inch-long stubs, reach for a perch. She hops on her rear legs, trying to gain momentum to ascend, but falls backward onto her rump. Hopping down the embankment, I rescue the pup.

Back at the Jeep, I crack open two Budweisers. Our cans clink as we cheer the future. I prod my new mentor for an assessment of Tasha. "Do you think we have what it takes to save a life? To be a certified avalanche dog team?"

"Oh yeah." Reaching into the plastic bag, she offers Tasha her first taste of red meat. We watch as Tasha devours the treat. "Our ski patrol adopted SARDOC avalanche standards, and so did most major resorts in Colorado. We'll bury people three feet under the snow for Tasha to find. Come back this winter, and we'll train on Aspen Mountain."

"Really?"

"Whatever you do, get on and stay on ski patrol. Kiss their ass, do whatever it takes. Otherwise, it will take years to certify in avalanche. We still aren't wilderness certified, which means I can't deploy Cassidy in the summer. You need patrol, and they need you."

Kiss ass? I grin, certain we'll be welcomed with open arms. Everybody likes me. But without any other dog handlers in Crested Butte, much of our training will have to be on our own. Just Tasha and me.

Poodle Lady moves closer to me, nearly pressing her nose to mine.

"And your husband? Where does he stand in all of this? Our guys have to have our backs. My husband is my number one supporter. Doug must be yours."

"Oh, no problem. He's with me." I can feel that lie crawl up and blow off the back of my neck.

After returning home, I call Doug in the Dominican Republic. Stuttering, I give him a rapid-fire rundown of the road trip, like a movie in fast-forward. Doug sounds less than impressed. He's no doubt counting the days until I return for drill duty. I don't dare express the excitement I feel about Tasha's training and my connection with the Poodle Lady. I avoid mentioning that it's going to take two years of hard work—here in the States—for Tasha and me to get certified as a dog team. And my mind reels as I review the list of hoops I'm going to have to jump through and the organizations I'm going to have to join before we can actually go work. SARDOC, ski patrol, Crested Butte Search and Rescue. *Crap*, I think, *I haven't belonged to anything since Brownies and 4-H in grade school.*

"Tasha's our pet," says Doug. "I just want a dog we can take hiking. I don't want you running all over the state with our dog. You have to get your ass back down here and make *real* money. Don't think you can just goof off while I'm down here paying the mortgage."

Had I stopped at that moment and put myself in his shoes, I might have heard his vulnerable self saying, "I'm lonely. I hate it down here without you. Don't get so distracted that you forget me." That could have changed my course of action. But his hurt from our past seemed to come out sideways, always in the form of control of money, control of career, and control of my life. I resented that, and I felt like I was the dog in the cage. So, there was a piece of me that decided right then to prove to him I didn't need to lean on him for anything.

To appease him, I agree—sort of. "I hear ya. Let's just see what happens."

We settle on that. I don't dwell on specifics, figuring I'll have to renegotiate if the avalanche work pans out. Poodle Lady told me that once I get on ski patrol I'll have a trained and certified avalanche dog in no time. I believe her. Doug and I agree to balance one foot in the Colorado snow and the other in the Dominican mud. For parts of the year I can be the stay-at-home wife with a chance to saves lives with my dog—two duties I know very little about.

CHAPTER 6

Crested Butte
Search and Rescue

Fall 1995
Crested Butte, Colorado

"I've got to get on ski patrol this year, Black Dog, otherwise we'll be thou-sands of miles apart. You'll be in doggy daycare or doggy jail, and I'll be in our Dominican apartment behind an iron gate and window bars. Your cage is no different than mine." I whine to Tasha, who runs ahead of me, sniffing dry grass. "I want to take care of you, not some stranger in a strange place."

Days after we settle into our new Crested Butte condo, we walk a dirt trail that leads from my front door to the ski run meadows. Autumn foliage glows brilliant gold and red. Quaking aspens shimmer in the breeze. Unlimited expanses of public land unfold before us. The pyramid-shaped, rocky peak of Mt. Crested Butte towers above us, the upper third sheared bare by avalanches in the winter and landslides in the summer.

As Tasha tires, I scoop her in my arms to snuggle en route to the ski patrol office. I'm hoping to sign on there.

I'm thrilled to be far from the sweltering mass of humanity in the DR, where temperatures rise to 120 degrees. No wonder gold exploration offers a gigantic salary. Otherwise, who'd work there?

The downside is that the available jobs in my new community of Crested Butte hold no appeal for me. A neighbor offered me a real estate position, where I could make several hundred thousand a year selling condos in avalanche paths to unsuspecting people. No thanks. Shuttle bus driver? Already did that in Antarctica. Science teacher at a private school? I'd make more money serving tacos at the local Mexican joint.

I pull out the ski patrol application tucked in the back of my white jeans. Eyeing it one last time, I marshal the gumption to enter the new patrol director's office with Tasha cradled in my arms.

He takes my application, no doubt checking that I had met all the requirements.

Feeling confident, I smile. "Completed my Emergency Medical Technicians course this summer. Two grand and a month later …" I chuckle. "My husband nearly dropped dead when he saw the bill."

Seeming less than impressed, he gets down to business. "This job is physically demanding. Are you sure you're strong enough?" He looks at me askance.

"Of course. And …" I clear my throat, "Please, meet Tasha. I'm training her to be a certified search-and-rescue dog."

Ignoring Tasha, he shakes his head in disapproval. "Well, I'll just have to see who else applies. We should have an answer by mid-November."

Walking out of his office, I don't feel so strong.

Within a week, I inquire about joining the Crested Butte Search and Rescue Team just like Poodle Lady instructed me to do. She had reminded me that the two organizations were completely different. In Crested Butte, professional ski patrollers are paid employees who work for a private corporation and stay within the confines of the permitted ski area boundaries. Conversely, the search-and-rescue team consists of volunteers that are called upon by law enforcement agencies, specifically the county sheriff's department, to aid in all matters of search and rescue.

I try to calm my nerves as my truck bounces down a pothole-riddled dirt road in the old mining town. Tasha bobbles on the seat beside me. Following crude directions scratched on a piece of paper, we're headed to meet Sam Gast, president of the team, at one of their informal trainings. After being second on scene for Stevie Reardon's avalanche, Sam became a medic, joined the ambulance crew, and ramped up his participation in search and rescue.

Earlier, on the landline, Sam gave me the inside account. "We're probably the smallest US rescue organization, and the most laid-back. Maybe a little unorganized, too, since most of us who show up are on the volunteer fire and ambulance crews. We're lucky even to have a shack donated for our cache." No dog team, either. They rarely look for lost people. Most of what they do is snowmobile rescue—drive up the hill, put the injured party on a sled, and tow them down to an ambulance.

Driving through the small industrial center, I squint to find the official Crested Butte Search and Rescue headquarters. But the sewage plant captures my attention with its monstrous open green-brown pool.

"An open pit sewer sitting right there?" I say to Tasha. "No fence? No warning signs? It's 1995, in the USA, and this looks just like the Dominican Republic. People are living right next to this shithole."

Brown foam floats on the surface of the sewer pond. I lean across Tasha's seat to roll up the window before the foul stench can waft into my cab.

The cache is a twenty-by-twenty-foot shack tucked between the four-stall dog pound and the pristine trout waters of the Slate River. This provides a place for the team to meet, train, and respond to missions. Despite the stench of raw sewage, the cache sits on prime real estate with mountainous vistas.

Before entering the sorry one-room shack, I steel myself for the contrast to the Aspen Mountain Rescue cache Poodle Lady had shown me a few weeks earlier. Aspen's two-story house looks like high-tech command central: radio station, map drawers, multiple telephones, large meeting rooms, full kitchen with a beverage-filled refrigerator, running water, bathrooms, upstairs lecture room, personal lockers, team jackets, and a two-vehicle garage that houses official trucks and specialized rescue equipment.

Through the window before me I see a rescue litter in the rafters, a tattered couch, and a handful of men.

I take a breath to bolster myself for meeting strangers. *If I'm going to have an avalanche dog and work with SARDOC, then I have to barge right on in with a smile wider than Niagara Falls, listen, learn, smile some more, and make friends with all these guys.* With my teddy-bear-size pup swaddled in my arms and my résumé in my back pocket, I thrust open the door.

"Hi guys. I just moved to Crested Butte and I'm really interested in search and rescue." I toss out my hand and introduce myself.

Several men offer me blank faces. "This is my new puppy, Tasha," I add to break the awkwardness. "I've heard there's no avalanche dog in the valley. I'm here to train one."

"Great to have you here." Sam steps forward with a few casual introductions. He, and two others wearing radios, seem to be the leaders. Only Sam welcomes me with a smile. "Sue's hoping to get on ski patrol this year."

Setting Tasha down, I release her to investigate a floor festooned with mouse droppings.

A redheaded man in a baseball hat with a chipped front tooth scans my 110-pound frame and shakes his head in disapproval. "You? You want to get on patrol? Good luck with the God Squad."

God Squad?

He adjusts the radio hanging on his belt, puffs out his chest, and turns to his buddy, "You know … they think they walk on water. Better than the rest of us." He smirks.

I turn to pick up Tasha and hear him tell his buddy, "Someone's got to die or get injured before they'll hire her."

Another rolls his eyes. "Those guys are going to tear you apart. They've got some pretty big egos."

Not expecting this sort of animosity, Tasha and I retreat to the cold steel chair in the corner. I want to rewind the tape. I want to walk in again, sit quietly in the metal chair, and wait to be introduced.

What I do expect is an organized meeting, with discussion of rescue preparation for the upcoming hunting season. I expect to apply to the team for admission on probationary status, but at the end of the meeting Sam just tosses me a pager and a Crested Butte Search and Rescue ball cap.

I'm in the club.

As we drive home from the cache, I slap my new cap on sleeping Tasha. That was easier than I thought. Nothing like the trials of ski patrol or the organized, professional world I work in with Doug as the clear leader. And, that redhead. What an ass. I tap the hat to get Tasha's attention. "We'll just call him Stink Face from now on."

Weeks later the pager beeps, and I respond to a mountain-bike accident two miles from my house. Only one other team member, one who I had not met, meets me at the trailhead. I recognize the stranger only by his search-and-rescue hat.

"Where is everyone? I thought twenty people would respond."

"Nope. It's just you and me, probably because we both live so close. Let's just splint this biker's arm and get him in the ambulance."

After we assist the patient, I'm home within a half hour. No writing a report. No debriefing.

With the lack of mentorship on the team, I feel like I'm in the Wild West—I can just show up and be a hero. But in the back of my mind, I wonder if the redhead who acts large and in charge will reprimand me for laying hands on a patient.

During the ensuing weeks, Doug comes home, and I encourage him to join the team. And he does. With him traveling so often, I think this will be a great way for him to integrate with the community, maybe even find friends. He agrees, and I'm relieved, as I had read that couples who show genuine interest in their partner's joys were more likely to stay together.

We dig into learning all we can. Incorporated in 1988, the team helped organize the avalanche search for Stevie Reardon. Gossip in the valley used to tag the team as a loose group of pot-smoking, backcountry ski dudes. With several new members joining from the Emergency Medical Services, including ambulance and fire crew, the team began to find solid ground. Search and Rescue operates under the Gunnison County sheriff to handle backcountry emergencies—high and low angle rescues, avalanches, and wilderness-search operations—within a national forest the size of Connecticut. When a call comes in to 911, the sheriff's deputies decide which of the four SAR teams in Gunnison County should respond and for what duration.

Desperate for volunteers, the group performs the best they can, with no paid staff and minimal equipment, to serve the community without charge for rescues. On call twenty-four hours a day, seven days a week, most of us rely on communication via pagers and EMS radios.

It ain't Aspen, but it's all stuff I can live with.

As the first winter storm of the season brews over the Elk Mountains, and without a search-dog mentor, urgency sets in to train my rambunctious, now three-month-old puppy. Walking by Al's Coffee Cart, I plaster up a sign: WANTED: WELL-BEHAVED VOLUNTEERS TO HIDE FROM A TWELVE-WEEK-OLD SEARCH DOG IN TRAINING. CLEANLINESS IS OPTIONAL. SMELLIER IS BETTER.

Doug has been playing Tasha's training "victim," but he abandons the role when he leaves for a few weeks of work in the Caribbean. I need a replacement. My advertisement runs on signboards around town. I scout out the local coffee-drinking dirtbags, unemployed ski bums, and trusta-farians as potential volunteers. I flash my advertisement at them with a broad smile.

"Interested in helping me train an avalanche dog?"

No takers. They prefer to chat about big lines and endless powder. My ad should have read: FREE BEER FOR HIKING IN THE WOODS. NO WORK REQUIRED. JUST ACT DEAD.

Only one person answers my ad—Diazo, an exchange student attending Crested Butte Academy, a preparatory high school for local kids and foreigners.

"I help you. I have dog. I'm from Japan and miss my dog." Diazo's big, white, perfect teeth fill his wide smile. Long black bangs drape over his brown eyes.

"Very … nice … to meet you." Unsure of the cultural differences, I extend my hand, even though I'd rather hug him because of our immediate bond as outsiders in Crested Butte.

While Diazo holds Tasha on his lap, we jounce down the bumpy dirt road to the Slate River Valley. Large wet snowflakes drift sideways, and the temperature drops below freezing by three in the afternoon. Hopping out of the truck, we walk a footpath toward a clump of pine trees and leafless aspens, which provide us with a little shelter from the wind. Knee-high sagebrush tugs at our legs. Armed with only Poodle Lady's advice—no workshops, no books, no obedience trainer—I launch into a training regimen for Tasha.

"Act like a goofball to pique her interest. Run down the trail fifty steps and duck behind the pine tree," I tell him. "When she finds you, jump up and play with her as a reward. Diazo, do you understand?"

He nods. "Yes." But confusion clouds his face.

So, I demonstrate. I fling my hands into the air, shake my head, and scream like a squeaky toy as I run down the trail. "Get it? That's a goofball."

Diazo smiles and strolls down the path like a cool, silent Japanese kid on the bustling streets of Tokyo.

"Run! Move your skinny butt."

He skips a few steps, then resumes his normal pace. Good enough.

I unclip Tasha from her leash, set her little feet on the snow, and hold her by the chest, my fingers under her purple collar, thwarting her urge to chase. Tasha lunges forward against my hands, and I feel her tiny heart beat faster.

"Easy, girl. Look at that, Tasha. There's Diazo's footprint." Squatting next to her, I focus her on the impressions in the snow from Diazo's sneakers. His scent alive, the prints give Tasha a reason to place her nose to the ground and sniff.

Tasha bucks. Her desire to tear up the cuffs of Diazo's blue jeans makes me clench the scruff of her neck.

The snow sticking on the ground gives today's training a bonus: being able to see Diazo's tracks enables me to see the path of scent. For the first time, I can actually see what Tasha might smell—the tracks in the snow making a scent map or scent picture, a tangible outline of where skin cells land.

"Crap. I forgot to make notes." I fumble for my all-weather Rite in the Rain spiral notebook with one hand and restrain Tasha with the other. I attempt to fill in the required documentation for our training: Tasha's name, time, location, weather, wind, precipitation, cloud cover, ground moisture, and temperature. But as I write, the wind whips the notebook out of my hand. As I try to catch it, Tasha pulls loose, charging toward Diazo.

But Tasha sails past him. My hands shoot to my temples. "Call her name!"

"Ta … sha." He fluffs the word into the wind.

"Louder!" I snap.

"Tas—sha!"

Tasha slams on her brakes, quarter-size footprints streaking the snow, and spins backward. She darts toward Diazo, who is lying with his face buried underneath sagebrush. Sharp nails claw at his hide, and baby teeth sink into his skin. When I catch up to the pair, Diazo acts as if he is dead.

"Okay, get up." I yank him by his arm. "We gotta do it over again."

With my first training exercise a failure, I employ the standard operating procedures Poodle Lady dictated: I strap Tasha into her harness, clip her to a leash, and grip it with an iron fist. I instruct my helper clearly on the teaching goal of the exercise. I give him Chew Man, Tasha's favorite soft squeaky toy, to use as a reward. Taking notes in my log, I control Tasha until I'm ready.

"Diazo, run like a goofball."

This time, the Japanese teenager flaps his arms like a snow goose, squawking, as if he were taking off for flight. Diazo runs sixty feet and drops to the ground. I kneel, lean over, and whisper, "Go find!"

Tasha darts out like a shot. She homes in on Diazo's head, like a bullet to a target. He jumps up, yips, hollers, and dances around in the snow. I flash on Poodle Lady, eager to tell her how easy search-dog training is.

The next day, under an azure alpine sky, with snow sparkling like diamonds, we motor up toward Kebler Pass, one mile west of Crested Butte. Kneeling on the ground, I hand Tasha's leash to Diazo and tug my training book from my pack, intent on being as methodical as Poodle Lady recommended. I fill in the first line of my logbook: "Sky: clear. Temperature: twenty-eight." An eight-inch piece of dental floss trailing from the notebook picks up the wind direction. The fine strand barely moves. "Winds: two miles per hour out of the north," I scrawl. Next, I hand Chew Man to Diazo and give him explicit instructions on what to do and where to go.

I add an incremental change to the training by introducing Diazo's stinky sock to Tasha. His sock—a scent article belonging to the victim—is tucked in a Ziploc bag. Used as a training tool, the sock will teach Tasha how to discriminate one human scent from another.

Diazo walks the prescribed route. When he drops down behind a bush, I let Tasha sniff inside the bag, taking pains to keep my fingers off the scent article, so Tasha won't think I am the person to find. Taking a quick whiff, she bucks at my hold, and I let her go. Running in a straight line, she bounds down his path, finding the foreign exchange student within a minute.

We complete six more trailing exercises using the scent article. Tasha sometimes wanders off the trail, but she rights her route when she finds Diazo's footprints in the snow. I plan to call Poodle Lady to brag that Tasha glues her nose to the ground 90 percent of the time.

Two days later Diazo, Tasha, and I head to the cross-country ski trail northwest of Crested Butte, where the afternoon sun has shrunk the snow into small islands on the sagebrush hillside. No tracks from chipmunks, rabbits, or human runners contaminate the snow, giving Tasha the best chance for success in adding a new skill—searching for old scent.

Like Poodle Lady with her flags, Diazo tromps through patches of snow placing small, multicolored flags on his footprints. His crunching fades into the distance as he places flags every five steps. He lies down beside a bush, and we wait thirty minutes for the trail to age. His scent grows old, dissipates and brews with the shifting wind and sun.

A dog's ability to sniff out anything from nitrogen in bombs to a single cancer cell is due to both a large nasal cavity and a large portion of the brain being devoted to processing smell. Canine noses contain a high number of scent receptors, making their sense of smell one thousand to ten thousand times more sensitive than humans. Dogs can detect scent at one part per *trillion*.

Eager to chase Diazo, Tasha licks her chops. She stares down the trail, locking onto his tracks like an eagle to a mouse. She squirms backward, trying to slip out of her little purple harness.

"Tasha, are you ready?" I let her smell Diazo's new scent article—dirty underwear—now stuffed in the plastic bag. "Go find!"

I let her run but keep her on-leash. She pulls me along the trail like a horse dragging a cowboy with one foot caught in the stirrup. To teach her to slow down, I keep resistance on the leash. Working too fast can mean missing clues or failing to find a victim. In the past few training sessions, her gagging forced me to abandon the leash. But running free allows her to use her eyes rather than her nose. This time, I tighten my hand on the leash to force her to follow the scent.

Tugging on the leash, Tasha sprints like a racehorse, directly for Diazo, who sprawls flat on his belly with his face in the snow. In anticipation of the five-pound piglet pounce, he digs the toes of his boots into the snow. He peeks up, his big white teeth showing in a contagious smile. Snow flies in Tasha's wake. She tears into her prey with sharp puppy claws but draws no blood. Her hundred-foot dash using a scent article on an aged trail is completed in thirty seconds.

Like a proud mom, I beam at my human-seeking missile.

Our end goal for wilderness trailing certification is to pass a twenty-four-hour aged track over two miles in mountain terrain. SARDOC tells me the certification process takes two to three years. I'll shoot for the eighteen-month plan, the same amount of time it will take to pass avalanche certification.

If we fail, I'll be back deep in Dominican mud.

CHAPTER 7

The Student

Fall 1995 & Winter 1996
Crested Butte, Colorado

After extracting my feet from knee-high Sorels, I rip off my puffy down jacket and strip down to long underwear in the ski patrol room. I'm heated up from the six-minute uphill snow-slog for my first day at work, and I fling open my locker for the black Gore-Tex pants with suspenders and reinforced knee protection. Holding the pants by the waist, I shake the tangled legs free. The bottom seams of the pant legs touch the floor, and the waist reaches my nipples. It's sized for a man a foot taller than me.

Crap. This isn't going help with first-day impressions. Several weeks earlier, the human resources assistant had assigned me one of the last uniforms on the rack.

Sliding into the sack-of-potato pants, I pray that suspenders can soak up the excess and keep me from tripping. But my petite frame swims in the oversize things. To avoid being late, I yank a piece of webbing from my rescue pack to cinch the pants around my waist. The suspenders slide off my shoulders; I pull on the jacket to keep them in place.

My red patrol jacket, with its large white medical cross on the back, hangs nearly to my knees. I cinch the belt of my first-aid pack tight, trying to pull the jacket up around my waist. In this uniform, no one will know that I have a waist, or even that I am a woman—one of only seven women on the fifty-person crew.

With only minutes left to catch the 8:00 a.m. chairlift to the ski patrol morning meeting at the summit, I hustle to put on my boots. When I stand, my pants smother them. I try to bend over to roll up my pant legs, but my sleeves swallow my hands. Shoving up the sleeves, I roll each pant leg twice. Grabbing my hat, goggles, and gloves, I rush to hop onto the chairlift, my confidence melting into the wallow of my uniform. *How am I going to be able to ski dressed like the Pillsbury Doughgirl?*

The rest of the day I'm assigned to work some of the nonglamorous parts of the job, like cleaning the Clive—the pit toilet, that collects human waste near the top patrol shack—and spooling out the orange rope that defines the ski area boundary, two duties I'd hire campesinos to do for three dollars a day back in the Dominican Republic. I don't dare complain about my sagging uniform or rookie job assignments. Any whining could squash the chance for Tasha and me to save lives.

But after work, I order my own ski patrol vest and lay out my own black ski pants to wear.

One evening, after ski patrolling all day and training with my search-and-rescue team in the evening, I am sitting with my team, sipping on margaritas at the local Mexican restaurant. A tall, thin, smiling stranger in his midforties approaches our table.

"Excuse me. Are you Sue? From ski patrol?"

Me? I look around, thinking he's speaking to someone else. I nod.

"My name is Dr. Tom Quatman. How would you like to work at my new ski clinic this winter?"

I choke on the tortilla chips in my mouth, unable to respond.

"I'm the new orthopedic surgeon in town. Just opened an urgent-care orthopedic clinic. Slope-side. I'm looking for ski patrollers to work with me."

Summoning composure from my margarita buzz, I extend my hand and stutter through introductions. Dr. Tom's title packs a double whammy. With both a PhD and an MD, he'd previously served as a weightless physiology rocket scientist, in line to join the crew of the *Challenger*. But after the shuttle explosion, Tom had switched careers, training as a sports medicine orthopedic surgeon.

"I'm banking on patients literally falling through the door of my practice," he laughs with affable ease.

"How's that?"

"The entry to the clinic is a garage-size door, slope-side. Injuries can get delivered right inside without requiring ambulance transportation."

Dr. Tom's offer seems almost too good to be true. In addition to ski patrol, clinic work would help me build more skills to diagnose and manage trauma for search and rescue. A perfect supplement to training Tasha as an avalanche search dog.

He prattles on about the clinic, offering me the dream of every medical school graduate and seasoned practitioner: to gain experience working with injuries, high-altitude sickness, and general illness. But then I hear Doug's voice nagging in my head: "Seven dollars an hour? How are you going to make a decent living on that? You need to earn some real money." Two minimum-wage part-time jobs won't fly with him. Ignoring Doug's voice in my head, I leap forward.

"Why, of course. I'd love to." How could I pass up the opportunity to work with a team of experts? And from my condo it's only an eight-minute walk to work.

Just after Dr. Tom departs the restaurant, I realize I can't work for him without addressing one last glitch. Bursting into the twenty-degree November night without my coat, I chase after him. "I'm training my dog in search and rescue. I promised her I wouldn't leave her at home alone."

The doc stops to listen and folds his arms.

"She'll be good. I promise."

Gunning my gutless truck to our first official training with SARDOC, I push the gas pedal to the floor. After seven hours driving, and overnighting en route, Tasha and I pull into Lory State Park near Fort Collins under a bright Saturday-morning January sun. Jenny, a member of the organization's Standards Committee, starts by giving me some one-on-one time.

"Sue, think my dog can find someone inside of the trunk of one of these parked cars?"

I peer down a row of vehicles in the snowy parking lot with doubt. Tire tracks crisscross in eight inches of fresh snow, like a tic-tac-toe game gone crazy. The scents of SARDOC participants and their dogs mix with fresh gasoline fumes, combining with all the smells of yesterday's visitors: joggers' sweat, cigarette butts, and overflowing garbage cans.

Snow crunches under our feet as Jenny escorts me to meet her dog Tassie, named for the Tasmanian Devil. Her truck, as others at the training, advertises her affiliations with magnetic signs: LARIMER COUNTY SEARCH AND RESCUE and K-9 SEARCH AND RESCUE. Standing as tall as my knees, Tassie sports a colorful vest covered in patches. Matching emblems cover Jenny's jacket: SARDOC, WILDERNESS TRAILING CERTIFIED, DOG TEAM.

SARDOC personal vehicles flash exterior radio antennas and sirens mounted on rooftops. Members carry handheld radios strapped to their chest. They look professional and important. My team refused to hand me a patch or a radio. I want the badges, but I got tossed a hat instead.

Tasha's new vest, hand sewn with thick Cordura fabric and oversized for her small-yet-ever-growing body, looks more like a clown costume than an outfit for a search dog in training. One day though, she'll look as official as all the other dogs.

With SARDOC's strict rules only permitting us to observe the first few sessions, four-month-old Tasha is left behind in the truck. She stands on her hind legs, nose barely reaching the window, and claws the slippery glass. Her yelps become distant as I hurry along to meet up with my teachers. With Tassie on-lead, Jenny launches into a demonstration of how her dog can find Candace in a car trunk.

"Think of Candace's body in the truck acting like a smoke bomb, pumping out a ton of scent. Warm air rises. When her scent hits the top of the trunk, some of it stays trapped inside while some seeps out of the cracks. From there, the wind moves it. That's what Tassie will search for."

Jenny looks to see that I understand. I nod. She goes on to describe how scent behaves like smoke, floating in the direction the wind pushes it. The scent disperses into the shape of an open Japanese fan, called the scent cone. With the scent stronger at the source, it diminishes in strength with distance.

"Wow! I had no idea." My eyes arch wide at the concept.

"Just watch—Tassie will stretch her nose high above the ground and home in on the scent, like a fly landing on food. That's how air-scent dogs work."

Jenny orders Tassie to sit, stilling her with a one-hand command. She lifts up a plastic bag containing a scent article, a sock. Tassie sniffs it for a nanosecond.

"Search, Tass." Jenny flicks her arm outward. Off leash, Tassie moves out into the parking lot. Eyes intense, she holds her nose two feet off the ground. Jenny walks alongside, letting her dog lead. I follow, enthralled with the interaction between Jenny and her dog. Tassie noses the air; Jenny seems to approve.

"My dog works completely opposite of most." She breaks out in laughter. "Normal dogs work with nothing in their mouths. They just sniff the air looking for scent. Tassie doesn't do that. She'll pick up something like a stick first, and then she'll start searching." Spying a plastic cup next to a parked car, Tassie clamps her mouth on it.

Tassie weaves through parked vehicles. Intent upon her task, she walks past a row of cars and trucks, the plastic cup crunched in her mouth. Two minutes elapse.

Jenny continues, "Now, normal dogs when they find the victim return to their owners to show that they've found the person. This specific action is called a *refind*: jumping, barking, or carrying sticks known as *brinsels* back to their handler. The refind is the most important element of search work. Dogs must bring the handler back to the victim."

I remember a sixth-grade picture book where a Saint Bernard brings back a brinsel stick to the owner.

Jenny continues. "Once Tassie homes in on the scent cone, she'll drop whatever is in her mouth at my feet. She adapted this behavior because I ignored her alerts too many times."

Tassie drops the cup. Her ears perk up, her chin lifts, her muscles stiffen, and she whines. Jenny takes note of the behaviors—all signs that Tassie has found the scent cone. "Sue, this is what we call an *alert*. My dog must *show me* where the person is hidden. That's her job." The dog darts toward the rear of a parked car. With nostrils dilating, Tassie attacks the trunk with her paws, scuffing the paint. When the trunk pops open with the click of the remote, Candace, cold and stiff, climbs out. I shake my head at how much Tasha and I have to learn.

"No trail, no track, no victim hiding in the bush, or behind a tree. How did Tassie figure that out?"

"If you keep training, Tasha will be able to find someone in a trunk, under the snow, stuffed in a culvert, buried in dirt, or even underwater."

Jenny's prediction looms, next-to-impossible to imagine. *Will Tasha and I ever be that good?*

The training weekend is filled with dog handlers relaying stories of search missions. Near Breckenridge, Patti Burnett and her dog Hasty— both members from Summit County Rescue Group and Copper Mountain Ski Resort—were flown to the scene of an avalanche that trapped a thirty-three-year-old physician. Hasty had located the body. In another instance, Patti's dog had also found a live person buried in an inbounds avalanche at the ski resort, something rarely done and talked about.

I hang on to hope for Tasha and me as I hear seasoned handlers' search stories of lost hikers, kids, hunters, climbers, skiers, anglers, mushroom pickers, and horseback riders. One mission I learn about required technical rope maneuvers and boats to access drowning victims. Often, dog teams are transported into search areas by snowmobile, on chairlifts, or in helicopters. I imagine each story I hear as a possibility for Tasha and me. And, on hundreds of missions over years of work, dog teams also find cadavers.

With snowflakes sticking to and then melting against the windshield, I leave Fort Collins armed with SARDOC bylaws, a procedures manual, stacks of dog handler news articles, and a giant laundry list of requirements to pass. "Ooh," I croon to Tasha. "That will be you and me next year. We'll whip out these requirements in no time and save someone's life." I pull over three hours later to pee, and I scan the documents.

Crap. They're going to make me drive across the state just to demonstrate I can hike up a mountain wearing a heavy backpack. Really? I schlep a pack on ski patrol. Prove that I can navigate with a map and compass when that's a daily skill I used in the DR? Doug and I literally land in foreign country and navigate our way out. Show I can survive in the wilderness for seventy-two hours? For heaven sakes, I used to be a survival instructor, clocking two hundred field days in two years. At least, with my EMT license and working at the ski clinic, I already meet their medical requirements.

The search-dog list of exams runs the gamut from written tests to multiple field tests on air-scent, trailing, and night navigation. Dogs must prove they can work in unfamiliar terrain, finding victims, returning to handlers, and refinding victims. Dog handler teams can specialize in disciplines such as water search, avalanche, and human-remains detection, once wilderness certification is achieved.

I want them all.

Rounding the last highway bend toward Crested Butte, exhaustion flows down my arms, then through my hands and onto the steering wheel. After driving icy roads over three snowy mountain passes and navigating through city traffic, my trip odometer tops the 350-mile mark. In my fantasy world, I had believed a puppy would settle me into domesticity. Now, to save lives, I face hours of training and days, weeks, months on the road. Doug's not going to be too happy when I'm not home and logging thousands of miles on my truck, not to mention buying more gear. Cash registers clang in my head at the looming time commitment and expense to become certified.

Conflicted about abandoning Doug and our life in the DR, I shrug off the thought of what I expect Doug's reaction to my new passion will be. I grab Tasha to snuggle my face in her velvet ear and rub her tummy. I breathe deep with a sense of purpose.

Leaving behind my new set of mentors with no heels to hang on to, I must blaze my own trail. Where no college, books, or instruction manuals can teach me how to understand and develop a working relationship with my dog, I must rely on instinct and let patience guide me. I must create a language for the two of us. "I can do this. We can do this."

Tasha stares back at me then leans into my arm and nibbles on my shirt.

CHAPTER 8

Ski Patrol 101

Winter 1996
Crested Butte, Colorado

The smells of rank socks and stale beer soaked into the carpet permeate the small ski patrol locker room. In the corner, a group of seasoned patrolmen swill down Pabst Blue Ribbon, some of them spitting chew at a can on the floor. Most of the spit misses by a long shot, and they guffaw loudly with each errant shot. One of them points to a pinup poster of a half-naked woman, sprawled with legs spread across a sports car. Another man chortles loud enough to rise above all the other conversations in the room.

"You big lunkhead, did you finally get that piece of ass?"

I hide behind my locker door to remove myself from their postwork ritual of "blowing off steam." But I barely change into my puffy jacket and sweats before one of them shouts at me.

"Hey, Purvis-Rookie, the rule is that when you screw up, you have to go get beer. You rolled the snowmobile today, and we need another twelve-pack right away."

With a forced smile, I nod in agreement, swallowing the bile rising inside me. If I want to work with my avalanche dog on ski patrol, I have to suck up to their game. A few minutes later, I stumble back into the locker room, lugging two six-packs and donning a cheery smile.

"Enjoy, boys."

"Get used to it," one pipes as the others grin, popping open new cans. The patroller nearest me tries to spit into his empty beer can, but when he spews the brown wad of chew it skims my sweat pant leg. I recoil.

"Excuse me?" I manage to say.

"Oops. I missed."

I storm out the door, wondering how I'm going to survive the winter. As I stomp downhill to my condo, I berate myself. "Come on, Sue. You've got thick enough skin to deal with nasty men. You've done it before."

But in the Dominican Republic Doug had my back when it came to others respecting me. He didn't tolerate disrespect, and he extinguished unprofessional behavior, like field workers urinating on toilet seats. With ski patrol, I must face my battles alone.

Stuffing an avalanche bomb, a two-pound hand charge into my patrol pack, I get ready to tag along on the morning bomb route with Brad. The ten-year veteran patroller sports tree stumps for legs, and I feel like a kid walking next to him. Now I can empathize with twenty-pound Tasha heeling next to me.

I grab my radio. A dozen patrollers in the summit shack, all men but me, hum in multiple conversations about this winter's extra-big snowfall already producing four Colorado avalanche fatalities in the first two months of the year. Colorado's worst avalanche killed thirteen people at Woodstock in 1884. More recently, an out-of-bounds avalanche adjacent to Breckenridge Ski Resort buried seven and killed four.

Today's buzz computes the high dangers created by last night's storm, which deposited several feet of snow with intense winds. We have more than fifty avalanche paths inside Crested Butte Mountain Resort, classified by the Forest Service as a Class A avalanche area, that need checking before opening to the public for the day.

Worried that Brad might test my abilities on avalanche paths such as Body Bag and Dead Bob's Chutes, I hide nervousness beneath a neck gaiter and goggles. The deep, heavy snow, days working at the clinic with maimed skiers, and the thin air at eleven thousand feet compound my anxiety. And the fact that I'm literally carrying bombs in my backpack doesn't help my jitters.

With a steady wind whipping new snow sideways, Brad and I ski a groomed track to the resort's south side, where avalanche paths point toward town and my condo. Outside the resort, only six miles away in the rustic town of Gothic, researchers have documented ten thousand naturally occurring avalanches in the 175 slide paths surrounding the town. When it comes to avalanche deaths in the US, Colorado leads the pack, accounting for a full third of the total. Since 1950, Colorado avalanches have killed more people than rock slides, bears and snakes, and scary ski runs put together.

Relieved that Brad skis in the direction opposite from Body Bag Chutes, I follow in his tracks to the top of a snow-buried knob, where we inch toward the exposed, wind-loaded edge. The slope rolls over the ledge, occluding the run below. The thirty-eight-degree pitch, along with the convex rollover, makes the double black diamond run prime for an avalanche to occur. Add the massive snowfall of this winter, and the threat climbs even higher.

"Look, there's my condo." I point downslope. I see Doug and Tasha playing in the driveway. Warmth fills my heart knowing the two are bonding while I'm at work.

Brad removes his pack and pulls out a bomb the size of a soup can. The bright orange canister is stuffed with two pounds of chalky explosive, topped by an eighteen-inch-long fuse that looks like two strands of licorice twisted together.

I hunch into the wind and try to strike up conversation. "The first time I ever saw an inbound avalanche was five years ago, when we were skiing here. I was riding the lift and saw an avalanche bury the road. Patrollers swarmed the debris field looking for victims."

"Yeah, we were lucky. No one was buried in that one. The debris pile was over five feet deep." His words clip curt, tight-lipped.

"I heard one of your patrollers was killed in an avalanche here."

"Yeah, about three years ago. He was a friend of mine. He went out alone into a closed area, violating one of the safety rules about skiing with a buddy. We found him a few hours later."

"No way," I spout, choking on my words between wind gusts. "Didn't you have another avalanche that killed a skier here?"

"Yep. A couple of local skiers ducked a boundary rope." He points past me toward Banana Chute, several hundred yards away from where we stand. "One was caught in an avalanche and killed. The survivor skied to the base area."

I gaze to the top of the rocky, windswept peak, wondering why anyone would be bold enough to ski under a rope.

"Get this. Dispatch got the call forty minutes after the fact from an anonymous caller. The source said, 'I think someone is buried in an avalanche.' Basically, the dude left his buddy for dead."

I know what that means from my training: once a skier leaves the scene of an avalanche to get help, chances increase that the buried buddy will die. Every second matters.

"And then, to make things worse, our patrollers rushed into the scene, and they all got caught in hang fire, another avalanche."

Hang fire is the threat that lurks over every rescue and rescuer. When an avalanche releases tension from the slope, danger remains. The adjacent slopes can still slide.

"Yeah, we were lucky that none of the patrollers were hurt or killed when the adjacent slopes let go."

"Holy sh—" I chew on the fact that rescuers may become victims.

In a smooth, well-practiced move, Brad uses the igniter to light the fuse and curls his upper body over the bomb to look for smoke indicating that the fuse lit. Confirming smoke, he backswings, lobbing the bomb in an underhand softball pitch over the rollover.

"Fire in the hole!" he yells.

Crouching down, I cover my ears in anticipation. Seconds tick by. I glance at Brad to see what's wrong.

"Sue, uncover your ears. It takes ninety seconds for the bomb to explode. You've gotta watch."

I stand up to look, but only widen my hands a little off my ears. The kaboom reverberates through the air. My muscles tighten in response. A stream of black smoke trails east in the wind. I let out my breath.

"Your turn. Throw it twenty feet either side of my bomb."

Taking off my gloves, I pull a bomb from my pack. My hands tremble so much that I fumble with holding the bomb and plucking the igniter from my vest. My fingers stiffen in the frigid wind. I try to bolster myself. *Crap, Sue. Just do it.*

Igniting the fuse, I toss the bomb as far away as possible, crouch down, hold my ears, and squeak into the radio, "Fire in the hole."

Brad rolls his eyes, no doubt planning to trade me out for a different rookie. My bomb explodes, the boom reaching us a split second before the smoke curls off in the wind.

I shudder, muscles tightening at the violence of the explosion. Then, I sigh, having ticked off another rite of passage into ski patrol.

Brad motions me to follow him to see the results of the bombing. An eighteen-inch-deep fracture line, the length of a tennis court, shoots horizontally across the slope. Below the fracture line or crown, a shiny glazed surface outlines the dimensions of the avalanche. At the bottom of the run-out zone, three-foot-thick snow blocks jumble in a pile.

"I'd hate to get buried in that."

"Yeah, and that's a small one."

It seems time to ask a question about my future, and the question I feared most. Perhaps deep down, I might know the answer. "So, Brad, I'm confused. Does this mountain have an avalanche dog program or not?"

He shrugs his shoulders. "Two seasoned patrollers are bringing their dogs to work. So, I guess they are starting a program. We had an avalanche rescue dog about five years ago … back when those three kids got buried at the condos, but the patroller left, taking his dog with him. This year, the dogs seem more like pets than working dogs."

"I have a dog. I'm training her to SARDOC standards."

He looks at me like I'm from Mars and shrugs his shoulders again. "Patrol is in a bit of disarray. With a new patrol director this year, who knows what's going to happen."

Assuming Crested Butte would have a top-notch program like Aspen or Copper Mountain, I push for more answers. "But the avalanche dog failed to find those kids?"

"All I know is the secondary handler brought the dog to the scene. Sue, to be honest, there were hundreds of people, with so much chaos. I'm not surprised the dog couldn't find that boy." Brad shook his head. "He was buried eight to ten feet deep."

"It's been six years since that accident." I stab my ski pole into the snow. "Patrol has lost a member, and a local." Expecting patrol to welcome Tasha and me to the dog program by now, I fume. What's it going to take? Another death?

Later, I learn even four-foot-eleven Betty, who's been patrolling for several years isn't even allowed to *handle* her dog on the mountain until she can prove herself in basic ski patrol duties. In the meantime, a dude, a veteran patroller, is training her dog.

I snort under my breath. *Do they have something against women? A rookie gal is training her dog, too.*

"I need a patroller to respond to a ten-fifty at the bottom of Twister. Possible head injury," dispatch squawks on the radio.

After the third call today, and my third attempt to be the first responder to the scene of an accident, dispatch once again hands off the accident to a more experienced patroller. I want to butt in on the radio, "Come on, give me the easy ones, so I can practice and build some confidence. Give me a chance." But I resist.

Dispatch isn't aware that I've been working at Dr. Quatman's clinic for the past few months. When tourists come in with altitude sickness, I set them up on oxygen. When Tom aligns smashed bones, I take X-rays, vital signs, and medical histories. When people hobble in with ripped knees after landing on rocks, I run the other way.

Fifteen years ago, when I took my first EMT course, I fainted twice in the emergency room. A kid had walked in with a hole in his nose from a BB gun. I felt the blood leave my brain as I watched the doctor remove the blood-soaked shirt the kid held against his face. I fainted right there on the spot. While recovering, a white-haired lady scampered into the ER wearing her slippers and nightie and holding a bloody towel on her head. Apparently, she had ripped her scalp off when she fell onto the bathroom toilet. In anticipation for another collapse, I ran for the door. The next day, I dropped the course. Fifteen years later, I pray I don't hit the floor on Tom's watch.

Patrol had denied me all week. Dispatch wouldn't call me for early avalanche control, and one training supervisor refused to let me carry a critical piece of rescue apparatus. "You'll never be able to use this," he had pronounced.

I hadn't had the nerve to confront him, to ask, "Exactly what do you mean?" I'd shrugged it off, like the other insults directed at me, wondering if I'd stepped into a job I had no business being a part of.

As dispatch ignores me, I ski away in a huff to burn off steam, slicing the inside metal edge of my downhill ski into the firm snowpack, forming big, wide S-turns with the force of a racer.

Dispatch calls two more wrecks over the radio. On the chairlift, I don't bother replying. As I dismount the lift, the dispatcher cries out for help with one more accident.

"Any patrol that can respond to a ten-fifty in Powder 8 Glades?"

I look up at the T-bar lift, scooting skiers to the experts-only Headwall, where Powder 8 Glades plummets on a double-black diamond, narrow chute in thick timber. Falling in the chute turns a skier into a pinball—bashing into trees, rocks, and fallen timber. I pull my radio close to my ear.

No one answers the call.

Clearing my throat, I depress the mic key, "Dispatch, this is Sue. I'm on the T-bar in ten seconds."

"Copy." The dispatcher fills me in on the thirty-five-year-old unconscious female. A beginner skier from Texas took off her skis to climb down the chute, but slid most of the way headfirst, caroming off trees.

"On scene in two minutes." My heart races the entire ride up the T-bar. *My first medical mission on ski patrol.*

After dismounting, I pole to gain speed and herringbone skate up a small incline to the ridgeline. "Ski patrol coming through!" I shout to pass intermediate skiers who obviously don't belong in this terrain. The effort and adrenaline cause me to sweat.

The radio blasts with more chatter, but I tune it out, intent on my mission. I navigate through the thickly timbered chute, yelling, "Ski patrol!"

"Help! We're over here."

I stop three feet above the injured Texan and call dispatch, "On scene."

With one ski on and one ski off, the woman lies, head pointing uphill, with one foot and ski twisted beneath her back. A small tree has snagged her, stopping her from careening to the bottom of the chute. Above her, a trail of blood ricochets between trees and rocks, outlining her trajectory. She moans, shivering in the snow, her eyes closed. Another skier standing thigh deep in snow holds her in position to prevent her from slipping downhill.

When I unclip from my skis to step into the snow, my legs sink thigh deep. "Crap." I flounder in the deep snow, wallowing on my hands and knees to the woman. In my haste, I forget to prop my skis in the snow in a crossed position, warning people there is an accident. Sweat drips down my forehead. Tearing off my gloves, I stuff them in my jacket to wipe away the sting from my eye. Inching toward the woman, I avoid the bloody snow.

"Hey, can you hear me?"

She groans.

I look at the guy holding her. "Did you see it happen?"

"No, I just heard her scream, so me and my buddy came to help. I sent him down to call patrol." His body anchors her to the steep slope, his hand clenching her ski pants.

From my crawling position, I spin around to sit on my butt, sinking into the snow, and spread my legs around her head to prevent myself from slipping. I place my bare hands on the sides of her head because my EMT training taught me to protect the cervical spine first. But now, in that position, I can't move because I'll slide into her, and we'll both shoot down the slope.

Time seems to stand still. I know we'll need at least six strong men to get her out of here.

I scan her body: shivering, one leg broken in multiple places, the other leg looks okay. Blood comes from somewhere, but I can't release my hands to check where. Blood binds her long, brown hair to her scalp. Strands of bloody hair are glued on her face. Eyes half closed, she lies in a contorted position only Houdini could accomplish.

I assess the scene: steep forty-degree pitch on the slope. Narrow chute that will cramp trying to get a toboggan on scene. Deep snow that will require patrollers to work with their skis on to avoid postholing. Technical rescue needed with ropes, pulleys, and belays. On the shaded, cold, north side of the mountain. Late in day.

But, I don't know what to do next. The warmth of her hatless head percolates into my hands. The guy shifts position, and the semiconscious skier slips several inches downhill. She lets out a loud whimper as the movement wrenches her broken body. I grip her head tighter, my arms stretched full length. The three of us cling precariously to the slope. Any more shifting could send us all sailing downhill.

When a male patroller's voice sails through the trees, I call back to guide him to us. With urgency on his face, Nolan tallies up the situation, radios for more resources, and puts on medical gloves.

Paralyzed, I stay in my spot, gripping the woman's head. *Don't let go of the head. Don't screw this up.* I sit, unable to do anything else. I look to Nolan for guidance.

His face says it all: we can't do anything without more help.

Soon, four more patrollers descend. Nolan takes the lead. He sends one team to set up an anchoring system for the toboggan and the other to build a platform in the snow to help with moving her into the toboggan. Stepping from his skis, Nolan sinks to his thighs. As he introduces himself to the woman and narrates what he is doing and why, he scissors the woman's clothing open to reach in with his hands to feel for blood. I tense, knowing I'd forgotten to communicate with her and check for bleeding other than her head.

With my loose hand, I swipe away a strand of hair stuck on my eyelashes. As I return my hand toward her head, my upright palm is bathed in red, sticky blood up to my wrist. I grimace. Flipping my other hand over in panic, I let her head flop. I had violated the first rule of medical training: I forgot to put my gloves on. I recall hepatitis in blood can live outside for weeks. We're trained to assume blood has HIV, hepatitis C, and the plague. I probably smeared blood into my eye.

I sit frozen at my own trauma, drooping in disappointment at myself. As two more patrollers arrive to help, I flush red like the blood, knowing they will see my hands and my mistake.

Nolan nudges me. "Sue, we got this covered. Head down to the clinic to wash? We'll see you down there once we get her out of here," he whispers.

I slide out of position as another patroller moves in to take my place. I shuffle uphill through the snow to where I left my skis. But they are gone. A quick sweep of the slope reveals my skis stuck upright in a crossed position, the way I should have left them. My shoulders sink at another one of my screw-ups.

Anxious to get away from the scene, I hurry back into my gear. The biggest punishment is forcing my bloody hands into my brand-new, hundred-dollar ski gloves.

CHAPTER 9

Snow Burial

Winter, Spring & Summer 1996
Crested Butte, Colorado

En route to work at the clinic, growing Tasha, now as tall as my midcalf, sprints up the driveway in two feet of powder snow. The days of a ten-pound food bag lasting a week are gone. I'm now schlepping forty-pound bags of kibble over my shoulders to appease her insatiable appetite. We broach a blustering winter morning wind. Our twin neon uniforms—Tasha in her bright orange search vest and me in my yellow storm parka—glare in comparison to the layer of new snow. At the end of the parking lot, I order her to stop.

"Tasha," I shout. "Stop! We have to watch for cars." She ignores my command. While in motion, moving one paw in front of the other, she squats, splaying her back feet out, as to not step in her urine, and tinkles the length of a yardstick. When finished she lifts and wiggles her bum and continues, sniffing, at a fast clip to cross the street. Instead of correcting her for not listening to me, I laugh, justifying her action as cute and something that doesn't warrant correction. If Doug had witnessed her defiance, he would have tackled her then chewed me out. "Will you frickin' train her?!" Ever since I brought Tasha into my life, I hadn't really left her side. We were pinned at the hips. Does she ignore my command today because I suck at obedience training or because she's still mad at me when I leave her behind to patrol? In my denial, I brush it off to the latter.

Once we cross the road, Tasha falls in behind my stride, so she won't posthole through the worn track.

As we hit the ski resort's groomed runs, she follows her nose, cataloging scents of yesterday's skiers. She swipes the snow and shoves her nose into the hole. I presume she's looking for food scraps covered by the new snow. Approaching the base area, I clip Tasha into her leash. Her once baby tug is now a full on drag as we pass by the main lift. I wave to two ski patrollers loading their dogs on the chair. Tasha hauls me toward the lift line, again looking for morsels. I force gaiety into my voice to garner their attention.

"You guys doing some training today?"

The bearded one looks up, but twists his attention instead to his dog. The other acts as if he didn't hear me.

Their snub stabs me in the gut. I want to load Tasha on the chairlift, but I'm only part time. I want to have an avalanche dog. I want to be a part of the club. But ski patrol seems to maintain secretive rules about who can train avalanche dogs and what the training entails. *I'll show them. I'll train Tasha however I can.*

As we enter the clinic on the first floor of a leaky three-story building, shared with commercial businesses and topped by penthouse condominiums, I glance at the now-familiar waiting room walls covered with medical-degree certificates surrounded by photos: astronauts in moon suits floating inside orbiting space shuttles, athletes catching air on skis, motorcycles, snowmobiles, and snowboards. One signed photo reads, "Thanks, Doc, for piecing me back together." A few framed jerseys sport the signatures of famous cyclists and US Ski Team members. A three-quarter-length curtain separates the waiting room from the main trauma room, which is decorated with mounted antique skis, turn-of-the-century ski boots and poles, and some of the first wooden snowboards. Above the sink, a shelf displays an assortment of treasures, including an amputated thumb floating in formaldehyde.

In the tiny waiting room, our first patient slouches in a chair. Moaning, he holds his arm and bandaged hand. The pale-faced twenty-year-old dude smells of last night's booze and today's cigarettes. I hold my breath to prevent gagging, no doubt another ski bum without health insurance, like so many others Dr. Tom fixes. Tasha tugs me toward the patient, but instead of saying hello by sniffing him, she drops her nose onto the carpet like a vacuum scouring for tidbits dropped from yesterday's M&M's candy bowl. I yank her back, hustling her toward her crate. Filling her bowl with water and removing her vest, I coax her into her cage with more treats.

When Dr. Tom arrives to see the patient, he asks me to clean the festering hand wound. The young man explains that he sucker punched his opponent in the mouth during a drunken brawl, only to find his hand ballooning to twice its normal size a few hours after the incident.

I unwrap the gauze adhered to his puss-covered hand. "I can't clean that! It's so nasty ..." I swoon with nausea and cover my mouth. I feel a fainting sensation flood my body and grab the counter. *Crap, my career is over, and I just got started!*

Although Dr. Tom didn't hear my exclamation, he reads my body language. Grabbing my arm, he ushers me to the adjacent room, where we sit down, his hand resting on my shoulder.

"You okay?"

"Yeah."

"Sue, medicine isn't rocket science. Rocket science is rocket science. I should know. I was a rocket scientist. Look, you don't need to be a doctor to take care of patients." Dr. Tom smiles. "If you want to learn, I'll teach you what you need to know."

"Really? You'd take the time to train me?" I swallow back tears to avoid crying in front of my boss.

"Of course. Come on. I'll show you."

I take a few slow deep breaths. Oxygen refreshes my blood, returning clarity to my vision. Tom cleans the man's hand. I watch every move. He takes out a sterile surgical set, runs the man's hand under water, scrubs all the dirt from the flesh, soaks it in warm water with Betadine, and begins to explore and irrigate with a high-pressure syringe.

"I can do that."

But Tom sees from my expression that indeed, I can.

"Go ahead and finish this. When you're done, I'll stitch him up, and we'll send him home with some antibiotics."

The clinic provides a place for my personality to shine—to recover some part of me that got stuffed away during my life in the DR, a piece that was lost somewhere between struggling to speak Spanish, feeling less-than as a geologist, and playing subordinate in my marriage. Here at the clinic, each time I care for a patient more of my heart opens. I love helping people, talking with patients and making them laugh—this work makes me feel important. Tasha helps, too. I don't want to live like the fearful little kid I learned about in the *Incident Field Commander's Handbook* anymore, hidden away in a hollow and covered up with leaves and waiting to be rescued, like I sometimes do when I'm working in Latin America or when I'm with Doug.

With ski patrol shifts few and far between, Tasha and I settle into the clinic as if it's our second home. I thrive on tending to an assortment of ski injuries and sick people with aliments such as high-altitude pulmonary edema, urinary tract infections, or gastrointestinal upset. I'm learning it's more than a ski clinic; we're treating just about everything.

Hating to tie Tasha up or kennel her before the ski resort opens, I allow her some freedom to greet the shop owners in the building. She establishes her early morning ritual like a doctor visiting patients on the surgical floor. Wearing her uniform orange vest, which I wrestle onto her each morning, she crashes through the clinic door, sometimes knocking down Tom's sentimental photographs, and dashes to the waiting area to scrounge M&M's off the floor. While I make coffee, I try to keep track of her, but the carpeted floors mute the tap of her nails. I shun putting a bell on her, to avoid the annoying incessant jingling. Plus, Poodle Lady told me to use the bell only when Tasha is working.

Sipping coffee, I take down the phone messages at the front desk as

Tasha sashays out the clinic doors. Like a snooping parent, I stop the message machine to follow her into the neighboring hip snowboard shop. Punk music blares while she greets her eyebrow-ringed bros and the gaggle of dudes who hang out wearing baggy pants topped with oversize T-shirts. We know them well since they visit the clinic regularly with injuries, chalking up medical visits as if they'll get frequent-flier points. Dr. Tom takes care of them gratis in exchange for free snowboard tune-ups and word-of-mouth referrals. Tasha waddles behind the counter to the tuning area to bond with the snowboard mechanic. He soothes her with soft baby tones while she rubs against his leg. He scratches her bum and underneath her vest. Satiated, she plods off through the coat section looking for crumbs of today's breakfast burritos.

"Tash, here!" I command. But the clinic phone rings, sending me running back to my desk in case Dr. Tom calls. As a pilot, he flies himself to Aspen a few days each week to operate, while a family practice doctor subs in at the clinic. But instead, the call is from one of Tom's patients, who laboriously details the slow, wrenching twist that torqued his knee, tearing his ligaments while skiing yesterday.

After finally hanging up, I return to the shop to retrieve Tasha. I peer for her under the racks, checking the usual spots.

Nothing.

"Hey guys. Have you seen Black Dog?"

"She was just here, but I don't know where she went." Replies echo each other.

I retrace my steps back to the clinic to search for her before rushing back to the snowboard shop. "Have you seen her yet?"

They shake their heads. "No."

Worry inches into me. Exiting the building, I case the not-yet-busy ski area for a black puppy. Sliding in the snow on my clogs, I scramble, using my hands to climb the small slope toward the clinic's garage door. Throwing it open, I peek inside, hoping to find a sleeping dog on the couch. I call into the clinic.

Nothing.

Desperation winds me into a knot. With fists balled up and anxiousness furrowing my face, I look like the hysterical mom who's lost her kid at the mall. I force a calm facade long enough to ask a stranger walking by, hauling skis on his shoulders.

"Excuse me, have you seen a little black Lab anywhere?"

"Yeah, I just saw her." He points toward the bus stop.

Dashing toward the stop sandwiched between commercial buildings, I accost the first person waiting for the bus.

"Hey, have you seen a black dog?"

"Yeah, she just walked toward the back of that building." He points to three giant commercial dumpsters alongside a loading platform behind a restaurant.

My thanks trail off as I hurtle down the small alley. A giant grease dumpster, stained black from years of drippings missing the mark, oozes a rank smell. I gag on the reek.

Movement catches my eye. Tasha, belly crawling, with her butt wiggling in the air, squirms to shimmy beneath the metal grease dumpster.

Crap. "Bad dog!" Grabbing her by the hips, I tug her from beneath the bin. She whips her head around to stare at me. Her fur shines with blotches of goo. One tendril of grease slimes her snout. Oily brown streaks smear her orange vest.

Clutching her collar, I drag her back to the clinic—me trying to blow the pique out of my system while Tasha prances as if she did nothing wrong.

Cleaning her up as much as possible, I shove her in the kennel with a firm snap of the latch. She stinks so much that I fear patients may complain.

I just need to keep a tighter rein on her. I mollify myself, refusing to use undue restraint. The freedom to explore is key to helping dogs learn: her skill at finding food interlinks with her expertise at finding humans. To squelch one may mean inhibiting the other.

The rest of the day, Tasha stays locked in the crate. Frequently, I glance at the caged dog. Her imprisonment eats a deep pit in my stomach.

I think of Doug in the DR without me, about the years we'd spent living in the cockroach-infested, barred, concrete, two-story apartment building we called our home and office. How each morning I'd get up from our king-size bed in the air-conditioned room in the heart of Santo Domingo and walk sleepy-eyed downstairs to Elma's apartment. With her door wide open, the smell of brewing coffee would lure Doug down later. Beautiful wrinkle-free, brown-skinned Elma, with her white hair pulled back into a bun, became my confidant and surrogate mama. Each morning when I came down to see her she'd greet me with a big smile and open arms. "Oh Suzanna. *Mi muñequita,* my little baby doll," and we'd kiss cheek to cheek. Before I could sit at her two-chair table and sip her strong, black coffee, poured into a cup not much bigger than a thimble, she'd ask, "How was sex last night?" She'd hang on the word *sex* in her Dominican accent until I blushed and stumbled for words.

How was it?

Her brown-eyed stare would penetrate deep into my soul, leaving me so exposed, as if she was mining truth from me. *How was it? I didn't know? Regular? Routine? Meaningful? Marital? Wild and crazy? Probably not. At least we're having it.*

That was usually about the time Doug would stride through her door. Greeted in the same fashion, Elma would confront him, "How was lovemaking this morning?" I'd watch his face turn a slightly different shade of red than mine. But that was about it. No emotion, no expression. Elma's question did force the two of us to contemplate how frequently we made love. We weren't like Elma and her Cuban boyfriend, Pedro, nine years her junior, who had nothing to do all day but watch porn films and make love. We had a business to run. She'd remind me, "You need to make time for love, Suzanna. You aren't doing it enough." I always wondered what Elma saw that I couldn't. I never had the courage to ask.

At the time, I would have disagreed, but in hindsight she saw something I couldn't. Her question to us wasn't about how often we made love but how it made us feel. At her table, we'd add a teaspoon of white sugar to our coffee and listen to her stories about growing up in *el campo* without shoes in the thirties and forties. By the time she was eighteen, she'd fled to New York City for a better life, where she raised two children as a single parent on a beautician's wages and eventually retired to Santo Domingo where she was living with Pedro.

After two cups, Doug and I would leave. We would sometimes hold hands together, like the perfect married couple, and head straight to the bedroom before our hired help clocked in. Other times we'd just march back into our separate offices and spend the rest of the day being colleagues and geologists.

Flapping a leather glove in the air, I stuff it four inches under the snow. Tasha dive-bombs headfirst, paws digging, and latches her teenage fangs onto the buried glove. Tasha and I play endless games of "Now-You-See-It, Now-You-Don't" to teach her to dig in the snow after scents. We repeat the drill daily, and she nails it each time.

With my warm breath rising into the subzero morning, we meet the Crested Butte Search and Rescue crew for Tasha's first avalanche burial training day. Since patrol forbids me to train at the ski resort, I train with my search-and-rescue team. We settle for a parking lot instead of deep snow in avalanche terrain. Eagerness rips through me to *finally* get Tasha locating people buried alive.

A young man, who stands a few inches taller than me with the carriage of an American Marine, volunteers to help. Contrary to the typical dread-locked, wool pant–clad Crestibutian with punk piercings, the fresh-faced young Mark Fisher with his half-inch, buzz-cut hair jars me. He sports flashy new Gore-Tex gear.

"Call me Fish."

Six-month-old Tasha jumps up on his black pants. She's strong enough to take my knees out but not big enough to prod the Marine. He encourages her behavior and drops to his knees talking like a kid, "Hello,

Babycakes. You're so cute." As he scratches her ears, Tasha lets out a moan and half smile.

"What brings you out to train on an early Saturday morning?" I ask. "Most guys your age are hungover."

"I don't have a life," he chuckles. "Just the outdoors and Western State College. I figured if I could get in with my horrible grades, I might be able to get a degree, too. I came to Colorado because I wanted to join the college search-and-rescue team."

"Nice." I smile wide at my new training victim, even though he doesn't know that's what he is yet.

Fish stands to his feet and continues his rant. "But the college team wanted nothing to do with me. They treated me like I had no experience and was a kid just out of high school. I had *four years* in field combat."

"I know the feeling."

"So, I joined Crested Butte Search and Rescue instead. They recognized my skill set and respect me. No rules here."

Wasting no time, I dive into standard operating procedures for training dogs in the snow. "For starters, you always need to have your beacon, probe, and shovel."

Fish opens his coat and shows me his toast-size avalanche beacon, a radio signal device, hooked to his chest harness. "I'm on it. I've climbed Rainer."

"Transmitting or search mode?"

"Transmit. Check me."

Unzipping my coat, I turn my beacon to search mode. The audio beeps. My display shows that Fish's signal is 0.6 meters away. I spend a few minutes showing Fish several snow caves I've dug inside a giant snow bank. "This is how we get started." Tasha follows, sniffing the surface of the snow.

Twenty feet away from the cave, I hold Tasha by her purple harness. Fish waddles like a duck, flapping his arms and squeezing down on Tasha's favorite squeaky toy, Chew Man. "Quack, quack. Come and find me, Black Dog."

We watch him crawl into a three-foot-deep hole.

Tasha rears up. Her stumpy front legs paddle the air in a dance. The bell on her harness jingles. The bell lets me know when she stops to smell something, in case I can't see her. She licks her lips, mesmerized by her new friend called Fish.

Fish drops out of sight into the cave.

"Go find," I whisper, releasing Tasha.

She soars through the air, kicking up snow in her wake. Tasha drops her nose to track him to the hole. Climbing the snow bank, she disappears headfirst into the depression. A few seconds later, a little black nose emerges along with a snowy Marine.

He rolls in the snow, wrestling with her as a reward. Tasha sinks her teeth into her Chew Man toy, strong enough to yank Fish across the snow on his belly in a tug-of-war. His baby-talk tone and praise for Tasha piques her play drive.

"Fish, you're a rock star. Perfect timing."

Then I tell the playful Marine why. Dogs are like kids. When a child comes home with a straight-A report card, the child wants the parents to go wild with praise. If parents fail to applaud the good behavior, then the child is not motivated to repeat the effort. Dogs respond the same way. In general, women tend to be fearless in their rewards because they can behave like young silly girls with an innate attraction to dogs, while men struggle with delivering enthusiastic rewards. When dogs fail to receive that reward, they lack the drive for searching. "Fish, you're the best squeaky toy on the market."

Next, we abort the cave mission and dig a small coffin-size depression. With the help of another volunteer, we bury Fish under a few inches of snow, leaving an air space and a radio with him in case he wants out. With Fish on his belly and his hood over his head, he is completely covered. He doesn't move although I watch the rise and fall of his rib cage as he breathes. Without using a scent article, Tasha will learn to look for any concentrated scent emitted from the snow.

"Go find," I command. Tasha runs to the pile of snow directly on top of Fish. But the loose snow separates her from the Marine and Chew Man.

With her nose held in the air, she sniffs. She freezes. She draws her ears back, and her mouth drops into a yawn. Her eyes plead for direction.

Making sure to avoid stepping on the snow smothering Fish, I squat down nearby to coach Tasha. "What ya got?" With my hands, I dig in the snow piled on Fish. Tasha tilts her head down toward my hands, her eyes following her nose. She sniffs the snow. Her whiskers flare forward. "That's it. That's avalanche man."

I burrow into the snow with both hands. She shadows me, using only her right paw.

"Dig, dig, dig."

Tasha swipes the snow like a fox batting an injured vole.

"No, Tasha. Dig. Like this."

Rearing up, she lifts both front paws in a fluid motion, attacking the snow with the weight of her chest and front shoulders, double-digging with both paws. Together, we dig until the buried victim emerges with her Chew Man reward.

As the rest of my search-and-rescue team bury avalanche beacons in backpacks, Fish and I pile snow over other volunteers for Tasha to find. Without an avalanche dog mentor, I muddle through progression steps, figuring out our own training regimen. We bury victims in different locations, and this time Tasha pounces on the snow using both paws, a double-dig, without prompting.

A few days later and excited about our success, Fish, a helper, and I travel to Washington Gulch trailhead, where the snow is five feet deep. We prep our site. Tasha chases each shovel of snow as Fish scoops out a snow cave big enough for me and my puffy coat. A two-foot ceiling of supportive, wind-swept snow holds up the structure, even under the weight of forty-five-pound Tasha. While I bundle up in gloves, hat, and goggles in preparation for my turn at being the victim, I haggle with Fish about my burial. I'm nervous. "I can't do it ... You go."

In disapproval, he shakes his head, "Sue, I learned in a Marine leadership course to *never* put someone in a situation that you wouldn't put yourself in."

"But I can't," I whine.

He points to the hole. "Go."

"What if it collapses? I'll frickin' suffocate."

"Nah, it won't. The slab above your head is superstrong." He pounds on it with his fist. "And, if it does," he laughs, "Tasha and I will dig you out."

I hesitate, then cross my arms over my chest and bat my eyelashes at him, hoping he'll renege.

He holds his stance, staring into my eyes.

I surrender. "All right then. But only for one minute." I slide into the hole feetfirst. Fish knows the longer the scent pumps from my body, the farther it wafts. Snow will filter it, terrain deflect it, sun burn it, wind swirl it, water move it, trees funnel it, and vegetation hold it. It's Tasha's job to find it. "Sue, at least twenty minutes."

"Ten."

I wedge into the cave, curling into a fetal position, with six inches of air space over my head. Tasha dive-bombs into the hole to check on me. As she licks my face, I push her away, my face now covered in snow. "Grab her, Fish, and tell her to stay."

He drops the first carry-on luggage size snow block over the entrance. "Ready?"

"Fish, if you hear me screaming you better get me the frick out."

Our helper restrains Tasha. Her brown, hooded eyes stare down at me. She lunges for me, but the helper holds her back. With my hand clamped on the radio, I watch Fish place more chunks over the opening, bits of light shooting through the cracks. Tasha whines as I disappear. I breathe faster. My heart thumps.

Fish shovels snow to close the gaps, obliterating the blue sky and cutting off Tasha's whine. It's just me in a tomb. Shivering, I try to move my legs, but the weight of the snow pins them like cement.

Even though enough light seeps through the porous snow to allow for reading a book, I close my eyes. Tasha's bark grows muffled as Fish dollops on more snow. My breathing speeds up, forcing me to grapple for air. An ice droplet of snow melts on my neck. My arms have no space to reach it.

"You okay in there?" Fish's voice comes over the radio. Tasha's bark continues.

"I'm good." *A flat-out lie.* I want to scream, *Get me out! Now!* But knowing I need to give Tasha a chance to find me, I steel myself into a Zen state, battling down the terror. As the minutes pass, I breathe the air trapped around my head, but envision snow compressing against real avalanche victims, filling their mouths and noses. The weight on the chest prevents expansion of the lungs. The thought of being pinned into place like most victims, upside down or contorted, flares panic in me. I try to move my legs again, but the snowy tomb still glues them in place. I have no place to go. I wait for Tasha in silence.

My mind races and my effort to breathe increases. How on earth am I going to train an avalanche dog when I hate the hole? At least I'm not denying it. Poodle Lady told me that by the time Tasha is eighteen months old, I'll have to bury over fifty people. How the heck am I going to get Doug and Fish to play victim in a snow cave all season? Fish had also admitted he felt awkward when he first met Doug, as if Doug was saying, "Who are you and what are you doing with my wife?"

Soon, crunching footsteps cross overhead. Disappear. Then return. I hear Tasha's bell jingle, her paws scratching the snow, and the light increases. With a blast of bright sun and a spray of snow in my face, a black wet nose drives into my neck. When the collapsing snow and Lab fur threaten to smother me, I push outwards with my arms to brush snow from my face. Fish pulls me free.

While soaking in the bathtub later that evening, I slip my head down under the bubbles and hold my breath. I can't see or hear anything. What if I got buried? I'd only have a few minutes before I'd suffocate. Who'd rescue me? *Doug?* He's in the other room watching television. I pop to the surface gasping. Tasha nudges open the door. Her thick tail whacks the porcelain tub. I pat her head to calm myself.

Form a strategy, Sue.

"I need a favor," I say to Doug the next day while he sits at his desk.

Over time, I would hand out Dominican coffee and rum to anyone who'd be a victim. And to my favorites, like Fish, I'd offer a hand-rolled Cohiba cigar brought back from the DR.

Still, the feeling of being buried alive haunted me.

CHAPTER 10

Derailment

Spring 1996
Crested Butte, Colorado

The snowmobile engine rumbles. At my direction, seven-month-old Tasha leaps onto the seat, squeezing herself between the driver and a passenger, both strangers. She looks and acts as if she's been riding snowmobiles for years, but she only practiced once in a parking lot. I wait on skis. When the passenger tosses a towrope to me, I grab it. The snowmobile jerks me into motion like a water-skier behind a boat.

Over snow that dazzles like diamonds in the early morning sun, the parade of skiers, snowshoers, snowmobilers, and dog heads west toward Kebler Pass for mock avalanche training. With a dozen fellow Crested Butte Search and Rescue team members, we intend to practice all the techniques for an avalanche search.

"Good girlie! Good snowmobile rider!" I holler to reassure Tasha.

She spins around in the tight space to keep an eye on me as the snowmobile pulls me ten feet behind her. Fifteen minutes later, with my arms straining to hang on, we arrive at a steep-sided hill, the site of our mock avalanche training.

A seasoned search-and-rescue member standing in the snow wearing a neon-orange Incident Commander vest organizes us into a group. "We're going slow and methodical. The newbies need to know how our team responds to a backcountry avalanche."

I hang onto his every word. I've been waiting for this day all winter. I smile. Finally ... a team to train with.

"Okay!" shouts the commander. "Here's the scenario: an avalanche has buried an unknown number of backcountry skiers. You're the hasty team, first team on scene. What do you do?"

"Turn on your avalanche beacon to transmit," Fish hollers. "That way, if any of us gets buried, our teammates will be able to find us."

I smile at him like a proud mother.

"We need our probes, shovels, food, water, and clothing, because we may be out here until dark," I toss out, well-honed from last year's ski patrol school.

"All right. You're ready. You have your personal gear. Now what are the big-picture problems?"

Several of us shout out responses. "Hang fire."

"Visibility."

"Radio and communication problems."

"Good. I'm the incident commander for this mission. I'll be on our TAC channel, and all communications come through me. For more resources, medical equipment, or assistance of any type. Now, everyone do a radio check."

We all dial to channel five while his voice bounces from one radio to the next. When the incident commander asks who will check beacons before going into the field, Fish volunteers for the task.

"I need a hasty team to check for victims wearing avalanche beacons."

Three members volunteer.

"I need three folks to follow the hasty team carrying probes and shovels. Look for clues, like gloves, skis, or backpacks sticking out of the snow!" he shouts. "Remember, this is the search component of the mission. Once we find the victims, then the rescue part begins."

I stand there, biting my lip, waiting for him to say, "Sue, you and Tasha search the debris for victims not wearing beacons."

But he doesn't.

What? You've got to be kidding me. My jaw muscles clench. I want to scream out, *We can find everyone faster than a team of thirty searchers!*

There is a glove attached to the strap of a ski pole lying in the snow, and our leader picks it up. "If you find a pole sticking out of the snow, just don't walk by it. Check it. An arm could be attached." Clapping his hands together to dismiss us, he adds, "Once you find someone in the snow, do a quick medical assessment and depending on what you find, we'll organize a rescue."

Feeling rejected, my head hangs low.

"Purvis," he commands. "You and Tasha head out with the hasty team."

I light up with a huge grin. I ignore the fact Tasha is a toddler in human years. She's never worked like this before, in a mock scenario, with today's distractions, full human burials, people standing on the sidelines, radios blasting. Feeling confident—fresh off a three-day avalanche course (without Tasha), where I learned how to recognize avalanche red flags, and travel through mountainous terrain with new awareness—I ignore the potential for failure and charge ahead.

Crusty snow crunches under our feet as we trudge the trail to the boundary of the mock avalanche path. The borders are outlined by small flags and churned-up snow. Tasha wears her own beacon, attached to her harness. I leash her, and we pass Fish for the beacon check.

Suspecting the scene may be too chaotic for Tasha's abilities, I hesitate, unsure how to proceed. With avalanche searches, scent articles are not used. Trained dogs are looking for scent wafting upward from under the snow. But, not knowing if someone is actually buried, I pull out the scent article for her. Tasha dips her nose into the bag for a second.

"Go find!" I whisper and unclip her.

Tasha looks around with momentary hesitation. She darts toward the chopped-up snow, sniffing and following every footprint on the surface. I stand back, watching her search for scent. Ten yards upslope, she stops, makes eye contact with me, tongue hanging from her mouth. She cocks her head. Her stare is fierce. I shrug my shoulders and stare back asking, "What?" Tasha's eyes fix on mine. I look to Fish or Doug, but they're no help. *What's she trying to tell me?* If I had a seasoned avalanche handler at my side, they'd tell me what she's trying to communicate. Frustrated, I break eye contact and stomp toward her.

For four months, she's been trailing human scent on dirt and snow with few distractions. Today, a snowmobile ride, radio babble, and chattering people add a miasma of interference.

A few mounds of snow hide partially buried volunteer victims in snow caves. But Tasha bounds through chest-deep snow to reach one of two members standing on the sidelines and watching. With her tail wagging, she circles the man as if communicating, "I found him."

"Crap!" I hurry to catch up to her. "Good girl. Let's keep working. That's not the person we are looking for."

With the probe line team trudging through the snow on our tail, the pressure forces me into action. To help Tasha, I stomp uphill toward one of the mounds hiding a victim. He's curled up in an open snow cave.

"Okay, Black Dog. Go find!" I point to the man in the hole.

She stands on top of the mound of snow, refusing to alert or double-dig. Tasha eyes the landscape looking for someone hidden in the woods. Her ears perk up as she watches a rescuer home in on a beacon signal buried under the snow. She snaps her head toward three team members marching up the slope.

"Tasha. Look. He's right here." I drop to my knees and dig on top of the snow. She stares at me with her head cocked. I dig. She watches but fails to copy.

Worried my weight could collapse the snow cave onto the man, I slide down into the cave's doorway. Tasha follows me. I point to the man hidden in the cave. She slithers in on her elbows with her belly scraping the snow. Her bum lifts, her tail wags. Tasha licks the man's face as if he's a lollipop.

I wag my hips back and forth, hands in the air, hooting out for everyone to hear, "Good job. You found him." Actually, I had to lead her to him, but I don't want to discourage her. I kneel into the snow cave after her.

Tongue and nose in fast action, she nips the victim's jacket.

I give a gentle tug on her collar. "Okay, Black Dog, enough."

But she continues licking and clawing at the victim's hat.

I yank her collar again, "Stop!" dragging her away from the man. I shove her out the doorway. "Stay. Sit."

While other hasty team members probe the snow for more buried victims, incident command assigns me to assess this patient for injuries as part of the exercise. The victim squeezes himself from the cavity. As I conduct a trauma assessment, Tasha dives headfirst to jump on both of us. Her nose nudges my pocket for her toy, but instead of rewarding the alert, I shove her up on the snow cave's rim with a brusque, "Sit."

Assuming she'll be obedient, I turn away and conduct a head-to-toe exam on the patient. A minute later I look back to Tasha in time to see her run to a rescuer bent over, searching with his beacon. She dives beneath the beacon to double-dig. Snow flies until she uncovers a buried backpack.

Self-rewarding, no doubt.

"Get your dog under control. She's in my way," the rescuer snaps.

Feeling like a scolded dog myself, I retrieve Tasha and tie her to my backpack as embarrassment flushes my face. Then I pass on the scolding to her with a sharp, "Stay!"

I depart our first mock avalanche mission, wallowing in my rookiness.

At six degrees, the window edges have frosted, occluding the ski runs but framing the distant Elk Mountains from the ski patrol shack, where I sit at the dispatch radio. Clearing my throat, I respond to my first call on my own.

"Copy, ten-fifty. Do you need backup?"

"Yes. Send a toboggan and oxygen."

"Copy, sending backup to Dead Bob's Chute." I finish my relay and shift to broadcast the accident to all patrollers. "I need a patroller to respond to Body Bag Chutes for an unstable knee injury."

No one responds.

Twirling my ponytail in nervousness, I repeat my command in case no one heard. "Can anybody respond to Body Bag Chutes for an injured skier?"

Behind me, the door bursts open with a cold flush of air. Ski boots stomp toward me, and a bony face pinches into a wide-mouthed grimace. The patroller radiates anger that matches the color of her red jacket. Her lips purse. She jabs me.

"Don't you know how to use a radio? You don't know the names of the runs, and you're sending patrollers to the wrong part of the mountain. Gimme that thing! I'll do it." She yanks the radio mic from my hand, ordering me out of the chair.

As heat rises to my face, I choke back words. I slither out of the chair as she shoves her bottom down to take over my dispatching job. As I slink into the adjacent room with my tail between my legs, I hear her fume into the mic.

"I need a patroller to respond to Dead Bob's, NOT Body Bag!"

In the adjacent room, patrollers on break glare at me. No one says anything. Donning my jacket and ski boots as fast as I can, I make a beeline for the door to escape my humiliation. Tears cloud my eyes and freeze on my eyelashes in the cold.

Before I can wipe my eyes, the patrol director skis up to the shack. Clicking out of his bindings, he pulls a booklet from his coat.

"I hear you've been inquiring about working your dog on the mountain?"

Pages rattle in the wind. Without making eye contact with me, he shoves the booklet into my hands.

"Management doesn't allow rookies to work avalanche dogs on the mountain."

You've got to be kidding. That makes no sense. I'd been dreading this confrontation all season. Wouldn't they make an exception for me? "Tasha and I are aiming to be certified." I want to scream, *You have no standards, no program! You need me, us!*

"Well, that's just the way it is. First, you need to be a competent line patroller."

"But the two patrollers with dogs up here are working dogs on the mountain that are pets more than working dogs. One even admits he isn't training his dog. They just do their own thing and claim their dogs are avalanche-trained without going after any real certification."

He glares at me. "Three years. Those are the rules." Spinning, he disappears into the building, where he'll no doubt hear about my radio screwup.

Taken aback, I stare at the booklet. Tears blur my ability to read. I suck in a deep breath, exhaling with defeat. My shoulders sink, and I want to melt into the snow, never to be found. If *denial* had teeth, it would have come out and bit me right then.

Forcing cold air into my lungs in another deep breath, I home in on the booklet to see the words. There they are: "All patrollers must work three years full time before handling a dog."

Three years? Are you kidding me? We don't have three years. Innocent people could die. Labs have a short lifespan. One injury would sideline us. The words seem to be written with vengeance. There's no way I can work full time ski patrolling. This job will tear my joints apart.

I scowl at the booklet. It stands as a symbol of a system wanting to crush my dreams of saving a life with Tasha. Rolling the booklet like a magazine, I jam it into my coat pocket. If *anger* had fangs, it would have sliced me in two.

I want to quit. But, I need ski patrol to keep my avalanche skills sharp … to expedite SARDOC avalanche certification. I need to live it, breathe it, do it.

I pray my knees, hips, back, psyche, and marriage will survive the duration.

Back at home, Doug greets me at the door. "I'm sorry, honey. I know you worked so hard for this."

He catches me, and I melt into his arms and cry. Tasha wedges her head between us, slapping her tail on our knees, doing her best to console me. For the first time, even with all my failures, I feel Doug's love and support. "Fuck Patrol," he tells me. "I thought they treated you like shit, anyway. We'll work something out."

I hold onto the moment as long as I can and accept my fate.

❧ ❧ ❧

Spring–Summer 1996
Dinosaur National Park, Colorado

Leaning out from the cliff top above me, a dog handler named Darren holds an armload of his whining chocolate Lab, Ranger. Clipped to Darren with a special canine harness, the dog quivers in fear. The pair, secured by a rope, are to follow the rappel that Tasha and I just did over a fifteen-foot sandstone cliff. Darren glares down at Tasha.

"Sue, are you sure you don't want to tie her up? I don't want Tasha to get us in trouble again—like at the first station."

In denial about what I am hearing, I reply, "Trust me. Tasha won't take off again. She got a butt slap after the last time." I glance sideways at Tasha with a command to stay.

On this cool, cloudy May day, all the big guns of SARDOC descend on Dinosaur National Monument, a juniper desert broken by rocky outcrops in Colorado's northwest corner. The training weekend, called Confidence Weekend, gives me a chance to learn from the state's top search-dog handlers. We meet Patti Burnett from Copper Mountain Ski Patrol and her dog Sandy. Patti, with nearly a decade of missions under her belt, has dug up more avalanche victims than almost anyone else I've met. I yearn to copy her. Hannah and her cattle dog are the pair who located the two dead high-profile fugitives. I heard about how Wendy Wampler, a stern, no-nonsense dog handler, and her Australian shepherd found a lost twelve-year-old girl alive in the wilderness. I hang on their words.

Earlier in the day, Tasha and I joined three handlers and their dogs to compete in the obstacle course, a doggy Olympics. A freelance journalist tagged along, looking for dog teams to feature in a story. One at a time, our dogs were required to jump into a canoe and sit-stay for ten seconds, then jump out, and crawl under a truck. Tasha refused to stay in the canoe and aborted the truck crawl several times. Our team earned last place.

At the rappel exercise at the base of the cliff, Tasha shakes her butt sideways and prances. She smells the dirt rather than paying attention to my orders. At nine months old, she tests her boundaries and my will. The experts today told me she seems a little short and stocky and a bit overweight for a Lab. For a moment I thought, *what is this, a beauty pageant?* Then, *focus at the task at hand.*

"Tasha. Stay!" With emphasis, I add that Darren will kick her butt if she moves. "I have to help Darren get down the cliff. I'm counting on you not to move. Copy?"

She avoids eye contact with me.

Ahead of us, four other teams of humans and dogs march through the desert. Behind us, three other dogs and their human partners wait their turn to rappel off the cliff. As I focus upward to help Darren and his dog lower off the cliff, Tasha sits.

Using a high-pitched baby voice, I coach Ranger off the ledge. But the dog's pads stick like glue to the cliff's rim. I try coaxing him, stretching up my hand with a big piece of white cheese. "Come on, Ranger, you can do it. Here, boy."

Darren whispers to Ranger. Finally, the big dog lets go of the cliff, settling into Darren's lap. Darren grabs his rappel rope with one hand and his dog with the other. With Ranger clawing the toenails of one paw into the last bit of sandstone, they lower off the ledge together. After they hang together, suspended in the air, the safety crew above lowers them to the ground at my level.

"Good boy," I squeal in praise, then reward Ranger with cheese. As I turn to reward sitting Tasha, I sense something wrong. Tasha, always the competitor for attention, had not begged for praise. Nor had she barged in when I pulled out the cheese. She's always the first to shove her black snout in a hand for treats.

"Tasha's gone," someone on the cliff yells.

Abandoning my rappelling station obligation, I dash along the human and dog tracks to search for Tasha. My calls for her echo off the low sandstone walls.

I pause to listen for her. Only wind whistles across rocky outcrops.

I repeat the routine three more times: run, yell, listen. But the voices of Darren and the crew call me back.

"She's here?" I huff for air, after galloping back to them.

Darren hands me a radio.

"Whose dog is this?" The radio voice of Wendy Wampler is harsh with unsympathetic disapproval. "Someone's dog is running around loose. The owner of this dog needs to get it under control."

My shoulders collapse in defeat. I turn to my teammates and swallow hard. Their well-behaved dogs, on lead, stand next to them. Sweat leaks from my armpits as I scan the surrounding terrain for Tasha.

"Wendy, this is Sue. Is that dog running around a little stocky black Lab with short legs?"

"Yes."

"That's Tasha. Could you grab her and hang on to her until I get there, please?"

"You need to get your dog under control. She's running around, agitating all the other dogs that are tied up." Then, with the finality of a court sentence, she enunciates, "This is not acceptable." That's exactly what Doug said to me three weeks ago when I allowed Tasha complete freedom to roam in the front yard. She journeyed back home an hour or so later. I shrugged it off to different parenting styles. Doug was pissed and told me, "You're an irresponsible dog owner."

After a mile hike, my crew and I approach Tasha. She's tied with a short rope to a stunted evergreen tree. She lunges at me, her front paws swimming in the air. The rope nearly pinches her airway shut, causing her to cough. Panting fast, her dry pink tongue hangs from the side of her mouth.

I untie her and firmly secure her on a short lead while Wendy approaches from behind. Her eyes bore into me. "What's next?" I ask, knowing it's too late to punish Tasha. The damage is done. I'm in total *denial* about what happened.

"Follow me. We are going to the next station, but this time you're going to keep Tasha on lead."

"Wendy, sorry about that." Tasha pulls against my control trying to pursue the next several teams in front of us. "Heel, Tasha!"

She ignores me. Her determined body pulls and drags me. I stumble, trying to keep up with her.

"Heel!" With all my might, I yank her backward, so hard that my hand bones nearly crack, and her neck likewise. She lands on her back, somersaults, lands on her feet, and stares at me. Instantly forgetting the correction, she darts ahead again, dragging me along with her.

"Sue, what is going on?" Wendy blurts at our tug-of-war. She stomps her foot into the sand. "Why do you let that dog do that to you?"

"Do what?"

"Yank you around like that. You're not in control of your dog. She's in control of you."

My face flushes. "I don't know how to get her under control," I confess.

"Do you mind?" She grabs the leash from my sore, bruised hand.

Wendy sends magic down Tasha's lead—enough that she corrects Tasha's tugging. Wendy crafts a makeshift noose with part of the lead and secures it around Tasha's nose. Every time Tasha lunges forward, the noose pulls down on her snout. Tasha squirms, desperately trying to remove the noose. Wendy holds tightly. Within five minutes, she hands the reins back to me.

"How old is this dog?"

"Nine months."

"You need to get her into obedience class."

Most of the time she behaves. I defend us in my thoughts. Wendy marches off. I should have told her, *I work alone. I thought I could do it on my own. I don't want my dog to be a robot, unable to free-think.*

My hands cramp from yanking the leash. The day is a disaster.

I should have been listening to Doug. He and Wendy must be from the same mold. From now on, I'll keep her on lead like everyone else. Then I take back that thought. There is plenty of space between freethinking and militant-style training.

I love watching Tasha travel through challenging terrain and diverse

109

environments. That's how she'll grow and learn. In order for Tasha to learn how to solve problems, she needs the freedom to roam in large, wild spaces, and to not always be looking to me for direction. I should know. My parents allowed me to run amok with my girlfriends in our tiny mining town. The streets were as safe then as they are now. I received moderate correction, when necessary, from my parents and friends. I learned from my mistakes ... and I turned out okay. I want a partner, not a subordinate. Isn't that what a creative, life-affirming partnership should be? Doug makes me feel like a whipped puppy sometimes, giving me correction and direction at times when all I want is understanding and love. Good thing Tasha can't talk, or she'd tell Doug how disobedient I am when it comes to his commands.

"Like daughter, like momma," my friend would share with me years later. "Apples don't fall far from the tree."

Without speaking, my team walks back to headquarters. Tasha heels the entire way at my left side. Only occasionally do I have to correct her. I fume in silent worry about the impression we've seared into Wendy, my group, and the entire SARDOC community.

CHAPTER 11

Licking My Wounds

Summer 1996
Crested Butte, Colorado

Instead of dealing with Tasha's obedience problem immediately (*denial*), I travel to Alaska. In typical Sue fashion and on the spur of the moment, with one week of planning, I explore Prince William Sound by sea kayak. Doug had insisted I go. "I'll stay here and hang with Tash," he said, supportively.

My fourteen-day adventure, paddling a boat three times my size and weight through twenty-foot tides and white-capped waves, gives me plenty of time to reflect. I think about how the separation might impact my bond with Tasha. I miss her terribly. *Have I done the right thing by leaving?*

Maybe my absence is the best way for Doug and Tasha to form a tight union. Sometimes I think she forgets everything I teach her. Doug teaches her to heel and stay during their time together, deepening their relationship. This brings joy to me.

While at sea, I miss Doug, too, but don't think about how our frequent times apart might impact our relationship. I assume my marriage is solid because we already went through a "divorce" before we even got married. Our vow to never split again is the one that will hold.

Upon my return I vow, "I must learn Dog, and Tasha must learn English." Fresh off my trip from Alaska and from the disappointments at Dinosaur National Monument, Tasha and I launch into language lessons in our Crested Butte driveway. With determination to turn around our poor performance, I dive into obedience training. Alone.

I hope learning each other's language will go better than the immersion Spanish lessons Doug and I took, five years earlier, before going to the Dominican Republic. I had expected the class to be a cinch. With a few years of high school Spanish, Doug was able to carry on halting conversations with the instructor. I heard only gibberish. After the first hour of Berlitz Language class, I bolted for the bathroom.

That evening in our Denver apartment, after flipping on a Latin television soap opera with Spanish punching too fast, I collapsed into tears.

"Doug, I can't do this. I'm so stupid!" I sniveled between inhalations. "I'll never figure this stuff out. My brain is just too slow … just go to the DR without me."

I'd been hoping for sympathy, but he'd fired back, "I know. You're pretty bad. How'd you get through high school without taking a language class?"

For six more days, I'd suffered through conversational Spanish. Most of the time, I cupped my ears with my hands and pulled back to listen to Doug and the instructor blabber incomprehensible syllables. Occasionally, they forced me to speak. The instructor had given me one long Spanish word to get my lips moving: *estacionamiento*. Parking garage. A really useful word. She also slowed down her speech to aid me with pronunciation. By the final day, I could bumble through basic travel phrases.

With Tasha, I hope for faster results, like … by the end of the day.

"Sit," I command her from three feet away.

She stands, eyes fastened on mine. A match of wills ensues.

I point at her and move in one step. "No." I sink into a deep, sharp voice.

She drops to her bum.

"Good girl." One English command down. Oodles to go.

Moving on to a second command, I tell Tasha, "Down! Stay!"

She ignores me while my words float in air. I try again. I am not in denial. I really think I can do it all myself. I should be reading the classic dog-training bibles—*Don't Shoot the Dog, Scent and the Scenting Dog,* or *Search Dog Training*—by Sandy Bryson, my hero, but I figure if Tasha loved me, she'll do what I say, sort of like how Doug and I communicate. Before I can enforce Tasha's obedience with threats and bribes, Doug joins the training session.

"She won't down-stay," I whine. "She just sits and stares at me like she doesn't understand.

"Down," Doug commands.

Tasha drops, slamming her body to the ground. The first time.

Interesting. She pays attention to him, but not me. The little stinker.

Together, we reinforce the two commands. Tasha obeys. We up the difficulty of the *stay* command. Doug stands over her while I walk away. Eventually, I move out of sight. Tasha holds her position in a sit. When she whines, I walk back to her and reward her with a big game of tug-of-war.

The next morning, I feel more in love with Doug than I have in a while. We had connected, communicated. I like that. With Tasha in her crate in the other room, we immerse ourselves in a long-overdue lovemaking session.

The next day, I explain to Doug what Wendy Wampler had impressed upon me. Search dogs are no good if they can't communicate that they've found a person. In addition to mastering obedience with a few English words and hand signals, Doug and I will have to teach Tasha the refind. Refinds are used in wilderness-search missions when the dog finds the missing person, returns to the handler, and then leads the handler back to the missing person. For a refind, a trained dog returns to the handler and jumps up with paws on the handler's chest or barks. This action needs to be so distinct that it can't be mistaken for anything else. Once the dog performs the task, the handler says, "Show me," commanding the dog to lead the handler back to the missing person.

Tasha's refind in an avalanche is digging in the snow with both paws. Her refind behavior for wilderness missions must be different. With no class on how to teach a refind, Doug and I launch into our own method, similar to a ping-pong game.

Starting twenty feet apart, Doug and I each hold one of Tasha's favorite toys. Doug waves an eleven-inch orange, soft, rubbery dummy from a rope, a dummy often used for field trial dog training. It's bright, so it's impossible to lose. It floats in water and resembles a giant dildo. I call it "the Schlong." I wiggle fuzzy Chew Man. While Doug holds Tasha, I run away from the pair, flapping Chew Man in the air, and take a sharp left, out of sight behind the condo. Doug releases her. When Tasha finds me, I yell, "Good girl! Where's Doug?"

Doug returns the call, "Tasha." She spins around and runs back to him. He encourages a big jump by teasing her with Schlong. I lean out from behind the condo, so she can see me. "Tasha!" I flap Chew Man above my head. Bolting toward me, Tasha springs off her rear legs and her front paws hit my chest. Doug commands her back, and the process continues two more times. We reward her with cheers and the choice of her favorite toy. Today, she parades with Chew Man clenched between her teeth. Doug drapes his arm around my shoulders, and we head inside for our own reward.

Tasha jerks on the leash, pulling me down the sagebrush-lined trail to find Doug, who hid thirty minutes ago.

August thunderheads build, roiling over the mountains; winds swirl upslope, gusting the clouds into different shapes every few minutes. Cloud shadows dance across the steep, rocky hills broken with intermittent dry creek beds, while I run behind Tasha as we test her refind in the field. Halfway down the trail, I release her leash. I must trust that she will find Doug and come back to tell me by jumping on me.

She weaves in and out of the trail, snorting as she goes, enjoying the freedom from the leash. Her bell tinkles. Crisscrossing the trail, she looks back at me. I can't tell what her eyes are telling me. I stop, and she spins away from me and moves in Doug's direction.

"Good girl. Stay close."

Five minutes later, after tracking Doug's scent, she returns to find me. Her behavior tells me she still hasn't found him as her gait is fast, her tail stands erect and her nose is to the ground.

I reinforce her job. "Go find!"

Tasha's ears perk up. She spins away from me and runs away.

Far in the distance, small green flags flap in the wind, a sign of Doug's route. "Good girl, Tasha."

She disappears into the quaking aspen forest. Wind drowns out the sound of her bell. I whistle for her. Minutes elapse before Doug's voice whispers over the radio.

"I'm hiding in a tree. She just circled it three times. Then, she looked up and found me. Tasha is using her hearing and eyes to find me. But she's so tired and hot that I think she forgot to return to you."

"Tell her to find Sue," I call back on the radio. Throwing my voice into the air, I call Tasha's name to assist her, followed by three blasts on the whistle, meaning *come.*

Her bell jingles. She appears with foam oozing out her mouth. When she spots me, she stops, her eye contact unwavering. Even though she stands twenty yards away and doesn't jump on me, I wonder if this is her refind.

"Show me. Did you find Doug?" I run to her, offering her water.

She whips her head around for me to follow. I mentally file away her refind action: stopping and staring, rather than jumping on me. That's her way, not mine.

During the quiet mile-long walk back to the truck, no words are exchanged. It hits me: Tasha's training me. I'm the trainee. She's the trainer. I can only wonder whether Dog and English really jibe.

❖ ❖ ❖

During the summer, Poodle Lady and Patti Burnett insist I train Tasha to ride chairlifts. While Crested Butte Ski Resort forbids non-ski-patrol dogs on chairlifts, my colleagues guarantee Tasha and me access to Aspen and Copper Mountain ski lifts. "Take advantage of jumping on and off snowmobiles, ATVs, horses, shopping carts, escalators, anything you can find," Patti told me at Confidence Weekend. "The more you put Tasha in ridiculous situations, the more she'll learn from you."

I hang on my mentors' words. Chairlift training starts in the living room. I use a dinner chair. We work on putting paws on the seat first. Next, I say, "Load up," I lift her bum onto the seat. She faces the back rest, unable to move. Her tail drops between her legs. Her legs shake. "Really, Tasha?" I ask her. "You're afraid of this?"

I help her. She scoots in a half circle to face forward.

"Sit."

She sits.

"Down."

She resists, so I yank her front paws out from under her. Her butt and wide feet dangle over the edges of the chair.

"Good girl."

Eventually, I leave her on the chair and walk away, coupling my action with a verbal "Stay" and a hand command for reinforcement.

To unload, I say, "Help," as the command and assist her in falling into my arms. Patti Burnett advised me to avoid letting Tasha jump down from the back of pickup trucks or high places due to the impact on shoulder joints.

"We have to take care of our special creatures," she told me. "We want them to have a long career. Don't let Tasha get hurt."

Within a week, Tasha jumps onto the chair on command, spins around to look at me, sits, and drops to her belly to wait. To simulate the moving chairlift, I rock the dining room chair back and forth, cooing, "Good girl."

Solid in our skills, we hike uphill to the ski area. Nervous of the slippery seat, I help Tasha load onto the idle two-seat chairlift. Together, side by side on the chairlift, we swing in the breeze.

While Tasha and I develop our communication, we see some successes. But she and I are still in a battle of wills. No matter where we train, she self-rewards with fodder of any type or the biggest stick she can find. One day she drags an eight-foot-long dead aspen tree down the trail and to our condo.

"Drop."

Her eyes intersect mine, teeth clenched on the wood.

I posture, stamping my feet and waving my fists. "Drop!" I up the volume.

No response.

With an angry look plastered across my face, I stomp toward her in a threat. She chomps the stick tighter in her jaw, ignoring my menacing comportment.

Not to be the one to lose the battle of wills, I grab her jaw to pry the stick out. I grunt and swear, my fingers straining against her iron jaw. With her lips curled, Tasha locks her teeth tighter around the stick in a death grip. With no other option but to up the ante, I wrestle her to the ground in a half nelson to wrench the stick from her mouth.

I win. Barely.

❁ ❁ ❁

Fall 1996
Elk Mountain Wilderness, Colorado

"Beep-beep-beep-beep-beep-beep." The pager vibrates across the dresser at 1:20 a.m. I jump from beneath the down comforter and fumble in the dark to silence the noise. "A mission. I told you so. Get up," I roust Doug.

A muffled Gunnison County dispatch voice requests the Crested Butte team leader call in.

Earlier in the evening, a fast-moving, mid-October cold front had barreled into Colorado, unloading several feet of heavy, wet snow into the mountains. Looking out my window, the blizzard prevents me from seeing the porch rail just five feet away.

When my so-called team leaders, including Stink Face, fail to respond, I call dispatch. The mission is twofold and three hours away in the West Elk Wilderness. I learn that a forty-nine-year-old hunter from Louisiana wearing light clothing and tennis shoes went missing hours before the blizzard. The sheriff's office dispatched the young, inexperienced B team from Western State College to search for the missing hunter, since the A team had been deployed to a high-angle rescue in the Black Canyon of the Gunnison National Park, a two-thousand-foot canyon that often entraps climbers. Now, the ten-member search-and-rescue B team, mostly freshmen and sophomores, were missing somewhere in the middle of the wilderness, in the snowstorm. *A fiasco on top of a mess.*

"Stink Face is going to rip you a new one for calling dispatch. Didn't he forbid you to talk to dispatch on the last mission?" Doug asks as we drive the dark, icy roads to the trailhead, three hours away.

"I had to call. We'll look like fools if no one answers. Someone might die."

After stopping several times to scrape icy glop from the windshield, we arrive in the West Elk Wilderness at seven in the morning. Frigid winds shoot wet snow sideways, and three feet of snow buries the ground. I bring fourteen-month-old Tasha along for companionship, knowing quite well she's too inexperienced to search. She'll stay in the car.

By the time we arrive, the ten missing college kids have been located. The kids, some dressed in sneakers and cotton clothing, had taken full backpacks with tents, food, and water. But in the race to find the missing hunter, chasing what they believed were a man's footprints, they failed to care for themselves, plopping down in the snow, exposed to the elements. Their two team leaders slipped into severe hypothermia. Too cold to function, the remainder sat on the ground, unable to help. Even the searcher who had located the two leaders lying unresponsive in the snow was now shivering.

When the core body temperature drops, the normal body shivers, the most efficient way to generate heat. But if the body temperature drops below ninety-five degrees, hypothermic victims can get sluggish and confused, start stumbling around and slurring words. As the body protects vital organs, blood flows to the core. Lips, ears, fingers, and toes turn blue. If the body temperature continues to drop, victims stop shivering because they have no more calories to burn. Heart rate, blood pressure, and respiration slow down. The brain slides slowly into unconsciousness and death if somebody doesn't get them warmed up—and that somebody *should* be at a hospital.

Even though I've only been with my search-and-rescue team for one year, I step into a deputy command role as my team charges into the field. With my leadership experience in the Dominican Republic kicking in, I lecture Doug and our team with some members of the college A team, who just showed up.

"When you reach the kids, feed them quick sugar, and when they start to get their strength and mental awareness back, hike them all out together." I explain the plan as the frigid wind pelts us with wet flakes. "Most of all, watch your own safety out there." With the team marching away from the command post, I shout, "Careful of the buried snags, the downed timber! A classic spot to wrench knees or break an ankle!" My words bounce off distant ears. Another reason not to deploy Tasha. The same thing could happen to her.

As my team heads out, including Doug, I collaborate with the Western State College A team and the sheriff deputy. He asks me about Tasha's training in-between traffic on the radio. I log communication, request more resources, and devise a plan for locating the missing hunter. A Black Hawk military helicopter from Fort Carson in Colorado Springs is summoned to evacuate the hypothermic team leaders.

Hours later, the helicopter skims the mountains in the few feet between the trees and the cloud ceiling. Without landing, it hovers above the victims, lowering a military medic on a jungle penetrator, to pack up one unresponsive leader for hospital transport. The blast from the blades spews stoves, packs, and clothing off into the trees, some not to be found again, including ours, which Doug volunteered to use to warm the lost students. After the helicopter returns for the second leader, our team hikes the remaining eight kids through thigh-deep snow out of the woods.

The deputy learns that the missing hunter had stumbled into a camp in the night, miles into the wilderness, where other hunters warmed and fed him. As he slept on a cot inside a sleeping bag, the college team nearly froze to death.

The chain reaction of a fast-moving storm, an unprepared hunter getting lost, followed by an inexperienced team trying to be heroes put lives at risk. We drive home with a lesson learned: everyone wants to be the hero, but if rescuers don't take care of themselves, they'll turn into victims.

My team says nothing about my call to dispatch. Feeling confused, I let it go hoping they're all beginning to trust me. Or is our call-out procedure so unorganized no one even noticed?

CHAPTER 12

Ready and Awake

Fall 1996
Crested Butte, Colorado

A big white SUV, souped-up with spotlights, sirens, several radio antennas, and an Eagle County Search and Rescue emblem, pulls up in front of our Crested Butte cache. In the predawn November light, Tim Cochrane, a former Marine, steps out of the SUV. With a commanding presence he, a lead evaluator for the Mountain Rescue Association accreditation test, surveys the scene.

Within minutes, many more rigs and evaluators arrive from other Colorado counties, boasting MOUNTAIN RESCUE ASSOCIATION stickers on windows and doors. Occupants wearing uniforms with embroidered titles and association logos disgorge from the vehicles.

My thirty team members mill about the cache, pacing enough to keep our bodies warm in the freezing air. Most of us stare at the ground to avoid looking at the intimidating evaluators, who are here to test us and determine if our SAR team is worthy. Our team, a mix of several alpine climbers and guides, paramedics and firemen, extreme skiers, an Alaskan fisherman, a lawyer, a metalsmith, a professional skydiver, and a wilderness-medicine instructor, includes only five women. Despite our matching team jackets, we look like a ragtag operation with only a used ambulance rig and unmarked personal vehicles for transportation. No emergency lights, no sirens.

Two weeks earlier, our search-and-rescue team pulled off the rescue of ten college kids in a blizzard, but now we must prove to Mountain Rescue Association evaluators that we deserve accreditation. MRA certification sets the operational standards for serious teams around the country, similar to SARDOC in Colorado. But some teams never affiliate with either. Over the weekend, we'll complete four tests: performing a high-angle rescue on a vertical rock wall, scree evacuation over a jumble of boulders, avalanche rescue on a mountain pass, and managing a hypothetical search. My armpits sweat. The potential consequences of any mistake—injury or death—require our focus.

Our team leader attempts to quell our nerves by launching into a pep talk.

"Once you save a life in the wilderness, you will never question why you are out there."

We suck up his words, but our anxieties still jangle. As evaluators move out to position themselves in the field, my team leader nudges me.

"No dogs allowed during this test."

"What? Tasha's part of the team. Why wouldn't we use her in search and avalanche?"

Rather than letting the "no dogs" rule drop, I approach Cochrane. Fourteen-month-old Tasha stands by my side, wearing her vest decorated with a Crested Butte Search and Rescue patch. I yearn desperately for SARDOC and sheriff's patches.

"I've got a SARDOC-trained wilderness and avalanche dog. We're not certified yet, but …"

Cochrane smiles and leans over to pet Tasha. "Sorry. This is a test for humans. No dogs allowed."

Curling out my lower lip, I rebut with several arguments, hoping to change the testing rule. My pleas collide with Cochrane, who wields the strength of a titanium carabiner.

"No dogs. I love dogs and call them right away for our searches. The good ones find people a lot faster than humans. But the point of this weekend is to challenge the humans."

I stomp away in defeat, wanting to call Poodle Lady and bitch. The rules prevent me from showcasing Tasha's search abilities, but I'm mollified knowing that a search-and-rescue state coordinator and examiner believes in SARDOC-trained dogs.

More waiting tweaks our nerves raw until the call comes in to rescue an injured climber hanging two hundred feet up a rock face. After driving thirty minutes to the site, I shift into my assigned job—to help with logistics on the ground and act as assistant incident commander at the base of the cliff. Since I don't feel comfortable hanging in a harness on rock, this assignment suits me. That leaves me available to help oversee the search-management scenario that will start midway through the high-angle rescue, in order to prove our team has both skills and smarts.

Every search-and-rescue team lives for a high-angle rescue with steep risks and technical solutions. Doug and a dozen teammates deploy to set ropes above the victim, with a main line, a backup line, anchors, and rigging systems. Evaluators observe the top crew while others dangle on ropes down the rock wall to assess every aspect of our procedure—teamwork, anchor choices, lowering and raising methods, safety, medical, and litter management.

The first rescuer descends the rock face on a rope to assess the condition of the victim and determine whether to haul up or lower the victim. Aiding the base incident commander, I ensure team members are doing their jobs. In the middle of lowering the victim on the rock face, a page summons our team to begin the search component of our reaccreditation. That's my cue to step away to comanage the next scenario, searching for a lost eight-year-old girl, a call that tests the depth of our team. I know full well that if Stink Face and his cronies were not involved in their adrenaline-fueled rock-wall scenario, he'd be large and in charge managing this search. Thank goodness, because I've been given the opportunity to showcase my ability to read maps and lead, a task I know will come easy to me.

My partner and I drive several miles away to a parking lot just off the two-lane highway, where the hysterical father waits for us. Tasha waits inside the truck, nose pushed against the window as she watches my every move. I ignore her whines and the equivalent of a two-year-old's temper tantrum, jumping, scratching, spittle flying, to do my job.

Evaluators with clipboards hover around, documenting my movements. Grabbing my own clipboard, and *Managing the Lost Person Incident Field Commanders Handbook*, I introduce myself to the parent, played by an MRA evaluator, who rushes to me with alarm about the fictitious scenario about to happen.

"We all were hiking along the trail. My stepdaughter started to fuss and said she was tired, so I told her to stay put. Two hours later, when I came back, she was gone."

"How old is she?"

"Eight. I know I shouldn't have left her."

"Tell me what she looks like. What is she wearing?" With my game face on, I walk through the necessary questions, following up with requests for her shoe size and medications. Jotting down his answers, I refer to my handbook for further questions regarding the behaviors of a lost child. Children between the ages of six and twelve get lost in strange environments. When upset, they intentionally run away and tend to avoid calling out for help for fear of being scolded. They have a greater sense of fear, loneliness, and helplessness than adults. I probe the father for more information.

"We got into a fight, and I wanted to teach her a lesson," he confesses, his shoulders slumping in shame.

Putting judgment aside, we retain the father nearby in case we need further information. We now refer to him as the *RP*, for reporting party. My partner and I discuss the tasks for the incoming deputy: to check the mother's home, calling the neighbors' homes, and other possibilities for the kiddo's whereabouts. We follow the search protocol for ROW, checking the "rest of the world" for the missing person. I question other possibilities—being dragged off by a cougar or kidnapped by mountain men. Back then, no one had cell phones, and it would be another half decade before the tiny device would dominate our lives. Our team relies solely on radios for communication, and in the mountains in central Colorado they rarely worked.

We set up a staging area in a parking lot off to the side of the road in a safe location. To set up a search strategy, I unroll the maps onto the hood of a vehicle. "We're right here." I point on the map to the exact location where the Taylor River, Highway 742, a parking lot, and steep cliff bands—illustrated by close-together contour lines—merge on the map. Validated by a nod of the head from the lead evaluator, I move on. Ninety-three percent of lost children are found within two miles of the point last seen. Designing a search method based on the weather, topography, direction of travel, and kid behavior, we designate five areas of probability and outline them with a marker on the map. My teammates trickle in from the previous test, I form five hasty teams of two and assign an area to each, instructing my searchers to yell out the name of the victim, stop to listen, walk fifty feet, and repeat. I also instruct them to look for clues and report those to me.

I list off requirements for searchers and warn them of a few anticipated hazards, such as cliffs, strange men, and rough terrain. "If you do find the child, and she is deceased, call on the radio that we have a *Code Frank* and mark the location with your GPS. Treat it like a crime scene. If the child is alive, administer first aid and protect any evidence there."

Handing each team a map, I ask them to search for an hour and return to base if they haven't found the kid. "Don't forget to test your radios before you leave." I send an additional team to walk the road for signs of the girl.

While the hasty teams search, I plan the next operational period of the search mission: calling in other resources such as more search teams, ATVs, man trackers, dogs, searchers on horseback, and Civil Air Patrol. Bringing in all of these entities, often all working independent of search teams, is a typical response for missions lasting more than one day. Search dogs are just one piece of the puzzle.

Our mock mission runs like clockwork. Within two hours, the evaluators deem the search test finished. I high-five my partner, knowing we aced the second of the four testing scenarios. We move on to scree evacuation, followed by an avalanche burial the next day.

After the weekend of testing, the evaluators give us our results late

Sunday evening. We pass all four disciplines. Where some teams take several tries to pass the MRA test, we ace the test in one weekend. Pride swells for our volunteer team, with our used ambulance, loose-knit operation, and dinky cache near the sewer treatment plant.

❖ ❖ ❖

Winter 1997
Aspen, Colorado

"An avalanche just buried two people. You and Tasha have got thirty minutes to find them or they're dead."

Wendy Wampler holds a clipboard in one hand and a stopwatch in the other. She stands atop six feet of snow and directs two canine avalanche testers, one from Aspen and the other from Vail, to assume their positions on the slope. Just like the MRA test, this trio of judges will test Tasha and me for our SARDOC avalanche certification.

I had planned and prepped for this moment since that first day I met Poodle Lady a year and a half ago. Dogs must be a minimum of eighteen months old to test, and I wasn't going to let the winter pass by without certifying Tasha. I made sure I had my ducks in a row and met the requirements. All the tick marks had been checked: ski patrol professional, SAR member, appropriate canine age, and most importantly, I had received validation only a month prior from SARDOC handlers that Tasha and I were ready.

Tasha, the rebellious toddler had matured into a complex teen, still a little unpredictable, but reliable and laser-focused when it came to "Go find." Since the MRA reaccreditation test five months earlier, I'd buried half my neighborhood, including the town manager, Chuck and the Harley Davidson–riding, one-eyed Texan who lost his eye to cancer, under the snow. I'd happily handed out Dominican schwag and asked Doug to replenish the supply each time he flew back home. Sometimes he would—other times not. Doug, Tasha, and I had traveled to Copper Mountain to watch Patti Burnett set up and test several SARDOC teams, since my local patrol wouldn't let us train on the ski hill. My training hours clock over two hundred, plus several thousand miles on my truck, and nearly one hundred avalanches and tracking problems. Two weeks ago, in preparation for this test, Poodle Lady and I buried our spouses under eight feet of snow on Rabbit Ears Pass near Steamboat. Even after lengthy preparations for safety, I panicked in the hour digging them out with the dogs. After that, I vowed to practice with only shallow burials, but felt proud and confident that Tasha could find someone under that much snow. If we pass our avalanche test, I'll add the SARDOC patch to my Marmot-brand team jacket, a patch only thirteen certified dog teams have earned in Colorado.

Just out-of-bounds at Aspen's resort, my ski boots are planted in the soft new snow on the upper boundary of our test site. I'm on my own for this one. Doug is back in Santo Domingo, and Poodle Lady stayed home to deal with some personal issues and to not be a distraction.

I look down onto the slope of simulated avalanche debris. Churned up with chunks and blocks, the white snow looks like a real slide. Tasha is hyperaware and stands at my side. Backcountry skiers zip past our test site on their way to cut virgin snow on unpatrolled terrain, a place where numerous skiers have been killed over the years.

From Aspen's sundeck, the aroma of hamburgers barbecuing drifts our way. Tasha's teenage mind might wander toward the scent of fat dripping from juicy burgers. A crowd of onlookers lining the testing zone adds more diversions.

Keep her focused. I bolster myself, fighting my own fatigue at yesterday's six-hour drive across ice-packed highways and a restless night's sleep. *Find the bodies. Thirty minutes.*

Adding to the complexity of the scene, another handler, Steve, and two-year-old Odie took their avalanche test before us, on the same site. Now Tasha's nose must work the site where Odie peed, Steve and his testers walked, and two live bodies were buried under snow. The residual scent may confuse her. I gulp at the difficulty and wrap her leash an extra time around my hand to take up slack.

There's no way I am going to let go of you until they say "Start". Do you understand me? I need this validation desperately. If I don't pass, I'll have to wait one entire year to save a life. By then, Tasha could be crippled, or I could be hunting gold again.

Tasha sucks in two quick snorts of high-altitude air, with her head lifted to catch the breeze of human scent lofting in her direction. Sporting her handmade orange search-and-rescue vest, she looks half clown, half sharpshooter. The vest hangs catawampus to the right side, ill-fitted to her stout, full-figured body. Panting hard, she presses her ears against her blocky face, her head and tongue tilting to one side in anticipation.

Wendy Wampler approaches us. She nods her head. "Ready?"

"Ready."

"You have one support person to help you shovel once your dog alerts." Wendy points to the test site and the two lone pine trees that mark the side perimeters. "Are you clear on your boundaries?"

I nod, "Yes."

"Anything else you want to know?"

"Are the victims wearing rescue beacons?" Tasha bucks.

"No beacons."

"Are there any more hazards like hang fire or avalanches that could kill Tasha and me?"

"No."

"I want to call in more dog teams."

"Good. I will call more teams in."

The formalities over, I grip Tasha's collar to kneel on the snow. "Tasha, are you ready to go to work?"

Tasha shakes; her bell jingles. Her eyes widen, ears perk up, and tail wags. Pulling hard, she bunny hops on her two front paws as I unclip her lead.

"Go find!"

Tasha tears from my grip to sprint downhill across the broken, ripped-up debris. Her nose hovers six inches above the snow. She darts across the simulated avalanche debris before zigzagging back and forth as she collects the scent data. I step forward onto the testing site and stop. My eyes focus on her.

The minutes ticking by seem like days. Sweat drips into my eyes. I pray enough time has passed for the victim's scent to rise upward through the snow. I step further into the debris, glancing at Wendy's facial expression for a clue that Tasha is on task.

Nothing.

"Okay Tasha, where are the buried people?" I follow her around. She seems to lead me around senselessly.

Tasha's nose rises into the air. Confused by her behavior, I clench my fist. "Are you still working?" I ask her, unable to tell if she has finished working. Could the wind have shifted? Is she confused about her task at hand after the long road trip, sleeping in the truck?

Tasha's nose leading, she sprints uphill, darting past Wendy Wampler and all the bystanders. She runs down the track, on the tail of skiers headed out of bounds.

Oh, shit. I blame the testers for making her wait on the top of Aspen Mountain all morning while Steve and Odie tested first. Stomping up the slope to the path where Tasha disappeared into a grove of trees, I pound my fists on my thighs as I call her. "Tasha, come here."

With no sign of her, I posthole, sinking to my knees to wait above the debris field for what seems like a million minutes. Defeat courses through me. My shoulders slump. I dare not look at Wendy Wampler, who no doubt recalls Tasha's previous lapse in obedience.

More minutes tick by, I face the inevitable and turn to Wendy. She gives me that look—the same disapproving look she gave me nine months earlier when I collected Tasha from her in the desert. I want to collapse to my knees in shame.

Finally, I hear the tinkle of Tasha's bell. Black dog reappears from the trees. Out of breath from diving through chest deep snow, Tasha returns to me with her tongue hanging from her mouth as if to say, "I'm done. Now what?" Calm, cool, collected Tasha with her tail relaxed is telling me she has already found the buried victims and left to see what else she is missing. *She wants to find it all.*

"What? You haven't showed me anything." I want to shake Tasha, but instead, bite my lip to regain a matter-of-fact composure.

"Wendy, Tasha is such a good tracking dog. She just had to go over there to make sure no one is hiding in the woods. She will get back to work. How many minutes do I have left?"

"Twenty."

Turning my attention toward Tasha, I grab her collar to start over. I give Tasha a big drink from my water bottle. She slurps up as much as she can without coughing. I hold her to force her to focus.

"Okay, girl, let's get back to work. Go find!" I release her again onto the test site.

Tasha runs toward an abandoned hole used in the previous test.

"Leave it."

She disappears into the hole. With anger rearing up at interference with her performance, I yank her out of the hole and off her feet by her vest.

"Go!"

Tasha moves out again, cutting in and out of the scent cone honing toward a featureless part of the debris. She stops one hundred feet in front of me and snaps her head toward me.

Aha! I pat myself on the back. There's that eye contact. She's found victim one.

Her head whips back, eyes and nose focusing on the buried prey in the snow. Her back legs power her two front paws into the air. With her big barrel chest, she drives both front paws into the snow in a double-dig. *Yes, the alert.*

"Dig, dig. That's it. Dig 'em up." Running to her, I mark the location with an orange wand pulled from my pack.

"Tasha's got an alert here. I need a probe pole and shovelers."

Tasha digs. I dig alongside her. Shovelers dig. Tasha's furious digging blows snow in my face.

"Sue, move her off that hole. Keep searching. You just have a few more minutes." Wendy lets a note of support enter her voice.

I drag Tasha off the new hole. But she runs back, diving in again, her tail wiggling in the air. She wants Chew Man.

"Let's go!"

Clawing her way from the hole, she obeys. Together, as the clock ticks, we dash to the other side of the debris to locate the other buried person. The silence on the sidelines and the deadpan stares from the SARDOC judges add pressure. I look up for a split second at Wendy, hoping she'll crack a smile or mouth, "Atta-girl." But nothing. She curls over her clipboard, writing notes. I fear we've done something wrong.

"Where is she?" I coach Tasha to smell the buried person.

She drops her nose to the snow and moves out, covering every inch of the remaining area before returning to me. At my feet, she swipes the snow with one paw.

I freeze to avoid giving her any cues, any encouragement, nothing that will alter her behavior, or force a false alert. I wait for the pounce and double-dig.

Tasha stares back at me, then drops her nose to sniff the snow under my feet.

"One minute left," pipes Wendy.

"Don't fail me, Tash. I have so much riding on this. I can't go home a failure."

She again swipes her right paw at the snow under my foot.

What? You're kidding me. At my feet? With all those burials under her belt, she's been 98 percent on her game.

My dog holds her ground, with all four pads planted on the snow. Her direct stare sears into mine. I scrunch my forehead to read her. *Where's the pounce? The double-dig?*

Tail swaying half-mast, her eyes still lock on mine.

"Time," announces Wendy as she waddles across the snow to us. Hands on her hips, Wendy commands an answer. "Well? Where is the last victim?"

Tasha swipes again with one paw at my feet. With no response from me, she drives both paws into the snow.

"Right under me." I stab my second wand into the snow.

"Are you sure?"

"Yes. That's an alert. Tasha, dig!"

She feeds off my excitement. She dive-bombs an invisible mark on the snow with a ferocious pounce. Tasha double-digs with both paws. Spittle flies from her mouth. She digs her way to the tiny opening three feet under the snow. I see a hand appear.

"Okay, the test is over," Wendy states in a matter-of-fact voice. "Dig that girl out."

"Did we pass?"

"Go reward your dog at your first hole. They're digging her up now. We'll meet at the bottom of the mountain with your results."

Meeting up later at a restaurant, I treat Wendy and my evaluators to an Aspen slope-side lunch, hoping to earn doggy points by thanking them for their volunteer hours in travel and setting up the test site. Before Wendy will reveal our results, we discuss our performance. Wendy notes that Tasha alerted on the first subject thirty seconds into the test and the second subject at ninety seconds into the test, plus returned to the subjects several more times.

"That can't be true! I didn't see it."

Years later, I'd remember something I'd heard from a SARDOC handler. "It's humans that make the errors, not the dogs. Pay attention to the first few minutes, and a dog's behavior will tell you everything."

With Wendy Wampler's stamp of approval—"You and Tasha are now the fourteenth SARDOC avalanche team in Colorado,"—I leap from my seat and high-five my evaluators. Tasha, asleep at my feet, jumps up on my legs when she hears my voice escalate to yips and hollers. I grab her front paws, and we dance in circles. While I run to the pay phone to call Poodle Lady then Doug, I leave Tasha alone to gobble up the prime rib sandwich I left for her.

Tasha and I join the ranks of a certified canine avalanche team, and we are the only team within a three-hour radius of Crested Butte. We are ready to save lives. Steve and Odie were not so lucky.

The next day, during a ski patrol morning meeting, I stand in front of my coworkers, summoning the courage to make an announcement. The assistant patrol director hushes the dozen patrollers in the room, a few of whom avoid my eyes.

"Sue just returned from Aspen Mountain with good news."

Still feeling elated from my road trip, I dampen down my enthusiasm, so they won't think I'm bragging. I stand, my short stature lost in the sea of brawn. I clear my throat.

"Guys, I just want you to know—Tasha and I just passed our avalanche test. We're officially certified, the only certified avalanche team within a hundred miles." I emphasize "only" and "certified" and remind the dog handlers in the room why Crested Butte should consider adopting SARDOC standards like other patrol organizations in Colorado.

Silence crushes me. My eyes scan the room for a smile, a nod of approval. Something. Instead, patrollers lean forward to buckle boots. Their voices rise to discuss boundary closures, daily housekeeping duties, and who had some action last night.

Not one person says, *Nice work, Sue*. I had prayed they would say, "Maybe you and Tasha could come up sometime and show us what you've learned." No one cares, not even the uncertified dog handlers on patrol.

Since 1950, avalanches have killed twenty-six ski patrollers in the US. At least eight of those fatalities occurred in Colorado. The risky nature of the ski-patrol profession warrants tools like certified avalanche dogs. Kept on-site, dogs increase chances of survival.

Deflated at the response from ski patrol, I clomp out of the building, slamming the door, to go check closure signs.

CHAPTER 13

Wilderness and Rescue Medicine

Spring 1997
Snowbird, Utah

Tasha sits at my feet, her attention flitting around the other people. Standing in a circle of strangers with their canine partners at Snowbird Ski Resort in Utah, I clutch my two-week-old avalanche certification in one hand and Tasha's leash in the other. *Screw my local patrol. I'm with the big guns.*

Twenty dog teams from ski patrols all over the western United States rim the circle at the Wasatch Backcountry Rescue Avalanche Rescue Dog School. Over the next week, five instructors from the US and Canada will teach us about avalanche-dog tactics, alerts, problem solving, dog psychology, case studies, automobile burials on highways, and helicopter deployment. Additional lecturers include ex–Royal Canadian Mounted Police dog-handlers and a holistic veterinarian.

Considered one of the most avalanche-prone ski areas in the nation, Snowbird and Alta host the premiere canine avalanche dog seminar every other year. Avalanches have buried cars, buildings, and the lone two-lane Little Cottonwood Canyon road that snakes up to the resort from Salt Lake City. I find it odd that none of my Crested Butte patrol colleagues are here with their dogs, attending this premier program. The chilly, blue-skied, spring morning lights up mountainsides that are riddled with avalanche scars, some running down to the parking lot where we stand.

"Drop your dog's leash and walk toward the center of the circle," shouts a former patroller turned Salt Lake City Sheriff's Department deputy. The no-nonsense man looks as if he has crates on his shoulders. He stands alongside his large male shepherd.

I gulp. Overstimulated Tasha swivels her head back and forth, devouring the commotion: strangers, a new place, kibble crumbs, fresh butts to sniff, snow to mark, loud squeaky toys—all on top of an eight-hour drive the night before and sharing a motel room with Poodle Lady and her new boyfriend.

Weeks before, Poodle Lady called. "You gotta go with me to Snowbird, girlfriend. All the leaders in the industry will be there. I'm going, but with my new sweetie, Peetie."

"Peetie? What the f—?" Surprised, I held my breath and didn't ask questions. I wanted to say, *what the hell happened to your marriage?* But she switched subjects and urged me to ask my search-and-rescue team for a little cash.

Without hesitation, Aspen Mountain Rescue flipped the full bill for Poodle Lady. My team gave me $75 to cover the $800 cost, barely enough for gas. At least I had the courage to ask. When I confronted them later about sending a group of SAR guys to a technical symposium, they justified their spending as necessary. Mine, not so much. With their token support, Tasha and I hopped in our truck for the five-hundred-mile road trip to Snowbird. Doug stayed behind, unable to attend due to work commitments. To save money, Tasha and I share a room with Poodle Lady and friend for the night, then we move out. I figure if Poodle Lady wants me to know what happened in her marriage she'll tell me. (She never did on that trip. We were too busy learning how to save lives.)

Now, in the snowy morning light, the deputy has commanded us to drop our leashes. The other handlers respond, releasing the grip of their leads. Leashes fall to the snow. The dogs stay as handlers migrate to the center of the circle. I stand frozen, gripping Tasha's leash, afraid that she won't stay. *Why can all these handlers trust their dogs, and I can't?* I pass on the activity, shame flushing my face.

"Call your dogs," the deputy commands. Dogs rush toward their owners, wagging their tails. The exercise repeats, the handlers walking further away each time until they reach a hundred-foot distance. Tasha and I watch from the sidelines before finally summoning the spirit to join the exercise.

Tash, don't let me down. "Sit. Stay!" Dropping my hand from her leash, I shove my palm at her face and back up slowly, step-by-step, locking my eyes on hers. Tasha swivels her head, first right, then left, then right, then left. She processes the information, looking at me.

"Here!" I slap my palms on my ski pants.

She darts toward me. Her tail wags. But instead of stopping, she runs past me.

That little shit. I lunge for her lead but miss.

"Tash, here." In a quiet voice, I try to summon her back, slapping my hands on my thighs again. I look around to see if the instructors noticed my error. Tasha finds a glove, clamping it in her mouth. She stares at me, begging me to play.

I run to grab her leash, but she cuts to the left just out of reach. The cat and mouse game lasts for what seems like an eternity. I call. She ignores me. I chase. She cuts away. Finally, I stomp my boot on her leash, pummel my body weight on her, knocking her to the ground, wrench the glove from her mouth, and drag her back to the circle. Sweat drips down my face. Covertly, I scan the circle, hoping no one witnessed the mishap. With my hand clutching Tasha's leash, I pull her in tight to introduce us.

"My name is Sue, and this is Tasha. We're a certified avalanche dog team from Crested Butte."

I can only imagine what they think. *Yeah, right. She can't even get her dog to obey.*

Several days into our school, I discover my avalanche certificate is the equivalent of graduating from elementary school. I have a long way to go before finishing college. My lack of mentorship and naïveté have led me to underestimate what is required to become highly competent in avalanche deployment.

Nearly a decade later, I've come to understand why ski patrol wanted competent line patrollers first, before they handled dogs. I can also see why SARDOC insisted handlers join patrol and SAR teams and take avalanche courses. I had to get fluent quickly in something I knew very little about.

It's what Malcolm Gladwell talks about in his book *Outliers*. He asks the question: What makes high-achievers different and the most successful? He claims it's the ten-thousand-hour rule. Most people have ten, twenty, thirty years to become fluent and reach the ten thousand hours of training. Like other working dogs, Tasha's time was short and so would be her tenure as a search dog. There I was, pushing and shoving my agenda on everyone else, juggling what felt like a dozen unknown balls in the air, trying to become fluent in dog, Spanish, avalanche, group dynamics, small-town politics, and my own language of love. I could see now why all the training rules were in place. They were all saving me from myself.

Our avalanche school even digs into canine nutrition. "Feed your dog raw, clean food, all the good food us humans eat," lectures the homeopathic veterinarian. "If you eat chicken and green vegetables, so should your dog. Avoid turning them into begging dogs by serving it separately, in their own bowls."

Looking at Tasha, I see my big bad supermarket bag of dog food helping her bulk out.

"What do you think the alpha wolf eats first from a deer kill?"

I shrug my shoulders with no clue.

"It's the gut bag. That's where all the digested grasses and grains are. Feed your dog similar food. Make sure the first four ingredients in your dog food are real food. Watch out for the word 'meal.' It's poison."

She argues commercial, mass-produced dog food contains the four D's: diseased, dead, dying, or disabled meat. That meat gets mixed in a giant vat to create dog food. I want to puke. I curse myself for my lack of education.

I vow never again to feed Tasha cheap, bulk dog food. As my partner, she deserves the best. No wonder Poodle Lady always packs prime rib. Doug and I agree to change to a healthier diet in the coming month.

The next day, Tasha and I join three other dog teams at a station called, "Drives, Socialization, Obedience, Temperament." The deputy with the Salt Lake City Sheriff's Department addresses us. He strides across the snow with arms and legs stiff like a robot.

"You can't train a dog in your ski boots, people. You've got to be able to run around, get down in the snow, and get on your dog's level. Go get your regular boots. And when you come back, we're training in motivation."

Returning with Sorels on my feet, I grouse to Tasha that she doesn't need motivation, as she's the trailing and digging machine. But for avalanche searches, I learn she needs to bark, especially if I can't see her in a blizzard. Cowering below the six-foot-three instructor, I pose the barking problem.

"Can you teach Tasha how to bark? I can't get her to speak."

"That's easy."

"Easy? I've been trying to get her to speak for three months. I don't get a peep from her."

"What does she love, ma'am?"

"The schlong." I whip out her foot-long, orange toy, which I'd stuffed in the back of my pants. Dangling it, I tease Tasha before handing it over to the deputy. Tasha lunges at the man, clawing his ski pants with her front paws. He allows the behavior to escalate by holding the schlong over his head and whirling it through the air. Tasha jumps higher on the deputy.

"See, she won't bark. Speak. Tasha, speak!"

"Hold your dog. Your dog will be barking in one minute. Ready? I'm going to go run out of sight. When I yell, release her."

The sheriff waves the schlong, screaming gibber as he runs away. Tasha freezes, quivering under her thick winter coat.

"Send her," the voice blurts from the nearby trees.

I release my grip. Tasha tracks the deputy's path, cuts right, and dives into the woods. I wait. And wait.

"Woooooof!" A one-time, solid, loud bark. A bark that means business.

"Jump, jump. That's it." The sheriff amps up the teasing.

Tasha barks again.

The deputy rewards her, and they play tug with the schlong.

We switch the game, making me the runner. After teasing Tasha with the schlong, I bolt another direction into the woods. The deputy releases her. Tucking the schlong close to my body, I slam my face down onto the snow to wait for her full assault. I hear her panting, then feel her pads on my back and head. Even after she knocks my hat and goggles off, I play dead. Knowing the toy sits beneath me, Tasha shoves her nose into my jacket. I wait. More nudges ensue.

"Speak! Tasha, speak."

She resists. A whine follows more nudging.

"Sue, hold your ground. Don't give in."

"Wooooooooff."

I reward her with schlong play. Her one woof can serve as another alert.

At a seminar the next day, a short, full-bellied ex-RCMP named Dewey speaks about the complexities of multiburial, multiday, multiagency avalanche missions. The man seems so atypical of search-dog handlers, like an oversize Chew Man. But his experience proves otherwise.

"I've been on an avalanche so big it took days to find the group of people buried in less than ten feet of snow." He relates one group who had stopped for lunch during a cross-country ski outing. The avalanche barreled down the mountain, burying all of them. He narrates a series of photos identifying the complexities of the mission. On top of that, the skiers were all eating tuna sandwiches. He asks, "How do we know our dogs aren't chasing tuna sandwiches flung out of the skiers' hands?"

I think about how Tasha and I might approach that scene. I imagine a wall of snow roaring down the mountainside, leaving behind a mishmash of broken trees mixed with avalanche debris and buried skiers. He prompts us each to describe our search strategy.

"Strategy? Aren't avalanche missions pretty straightforward?" one handler asks. "They can't be that complicated. Guy in the snow. Scent rises, right?"

Dewey shakes his head. "In deep burials, human scent can be carried upward, downward, sideways, on the timbers, only to surface a long distance from the buried victims. Then the wind pushes it. Human scent catches in tree branches, willows, and tree wells."

I rivet onto Dewey. The nuance of scent movement fascinates me and I will dedicate my entire career to understanding it.

"When you prove yourself and show your work, then you'll get called. Don't be afraid to control a scene. You must be in charge. You're the only one who knows how your dog works," he finishes up. "We work for the Canadian government, but you work for your own fielding agencies. You may have the best dog, but if no one knows about you, you're never going to get deployed. If you love this stuff, you're gonna have to go sell yourself."

Sell myself! I carp under my breath, abhorring the idea of hawking dog-team skills like a slick used-car salesman. *The last thing I sold was a box of cookies in Brownies.* But after the reception I got from ski patrol after our certification, I recognize the wisdom of his advice.

I leave Snowbird with a newfound appreciation for the work ahead of us. Utah's avalanche program is light years ahead of Crested Butte's. Now I'm tasked with convincing the rescue community to call us.

❈ ❈ ❈

Spring 1997
Crested Butte, Colorado

A day at the clinic treating more than thirty patients with an assortment of ailments—including double wrist fractures, a boot-top crack, an outbreak of herpes simplex viral infection on the lips, and a couple of "I don't feel so good" patients—wears me out.

With minimal time to pee or eat, my patience wanes to the verge of fraying. Two-year-old Tasha lies on the waiting-room carpet with her head between her front paws. "I know. It's been a long day."

Hours beyond her normal feeding time, she has already hounded me by nibbling her front teeth up and down on my lower pant leg, as if she is fleecing me or eating corn on the cob. Her ferocious appetite and ability to find anything that even resembles food sends her once-trim teenage body traveling toward full-figuredness. She senses the difficulty of the day.

I look up to our last patient. The young woman coughs up frothy pink sputum into a plastic bucket. By my second season at the clinic, I've seen the same symptoms plenty of times.

Tasha's tail thumps the floor once, as she watches me turn back to work on the woman. On this day, Dr. Tom is away in Aspen performing surgery. He's left a new practitioner in charge—Scott Smith, a physician's assistant recently arrived from the East Coast and with years of rescue experience, is eager to join our search-and-rescue team.

Standing at the door of the coughing woman's room, Scott plans to give her Tylenol for what he diagnoses as a cold or bronchitis. He intends to send her home to her ski condo for the night. I foresee tragedy.

"Scott, wait." I grab his arm before he enters the room. My voice crackles as I summon the bravery to tell him something he might not want to hear. After all, I'm an EMT, not a physician.

"Yeah?" He squares his shoulders.

"Um … ah … I know we've had a big day, and it's late. But …" I pull him toward me, so the patient can't hear my words. To reassure myself, I eye the patient's chest X-ray hanging in the light box. Healthy lung tissue on X-ray normally looks black. This woman's tissue is snow white, and the lungs are full of fluid. She lives at sea level, but she's skiing at eleven thousand feet. If I don't say something, she will drown in her own fluid tonight at her condo.

The sudden raspy cough, pink frothy sputum, fever, weakness, and rapid heart rate confirm my diagnosis: high-altitude pulmonary edema (HAPE), an illness we frequently see at the clinic. HAPE happens at high altitude. The only cure is transporting the patient to a lower elevation. The oxygen I have been giving her isn't helping. The woman must go to the hospital in Gunnison, seventeen hundred feet below the clinic.

I face Scott. The ubersmart, driven perfectionist now carries a streak of Napoleon complex on his tense, short frame. My experience in the clinic doesn't measure up to his tenure as a physician's assistant, his decade of ski trauma work, and his position as curriculum director at the largest wilderness medical organization in the world. He has preached to thousands of students the dangers of HAPE, yet on this day he fails to recognize a classic example in the coughing woman.

From behind the wall, the young woman sits up to cough. Her inhalation rattles from fluid stuck in her chest. She gasps, coughs again, and falls back into the gurney.

"Scott. That lady can't stay here. We need to call her an ambulance and get her to Gunnison. She's got HAPE." There, I said it. I mustered courage to intervene. I hold my breath for his response.

In the silence, Scott scratches his head. Glancing at the X-ray, he spins from me toward the reception room. His footsteps circle the clinic floor. Tasha's eyes follow, and I prepare for a thrashing. I just questioned his authority, his position, his knowledge. I'm dead. Or at least soon to be unemployed.

He faces me. "You're right, Sue. I've been teaching this stuff for years, and I couldn't see it in front of me. How could I have missed that?!"

The air leaves my body in one big exhale, and my shoulders lower as tension dissipates. A weak smile twitches my mouth.

Scott adds, "You just saved her life."

Near the completion of season two, at the end of another long spring-break day treating forty patients at the clinic, Scott approaches me. Our working relationship, honed by treating hundreds of patients together, has relaxed into an easy camaraderie. While training together on the same search-and-rescue team, he shows interest in my search-dog work, unlike the lackluster response from a majority of my teammates.

Scott lobs a question at me. "How would you like to become a wilderness-medicine instructor, like me?"

"Me?"

"Yeah. I think you have potential."

"Wilderness medicine? What is it?"

"We teach students how to think critically in unconventional settings."

In the late 1970s, Scott got introduced to wilderness medicine—how to manage medical emergencies in remote, dangerous, or difficult terrain, when 911 is not coming to rescue you—while working for Outward Bound in Maine. He met a physician who'd designed a curriculum for guides working on the Hurricane Islands in Maine, since standard first-aid courses did not contain procedures appropriate for the wilderness environment.

With emphasis on the function and structure of the three major body systems, he developed a teaching program for Wilderness Medical Associates, an organization he founded, which has become the largest wilderness medical-training organization in the world. Scott writes me a letter of recommendation to Wilderness Medical Associates with an off-the-cuff approach: "Sue is a calm, cooperative, sober, and alert intern, who has no spine pain and no spine tenderness. I think she would make a perfect instructor for our program. I would like to make this official and have her apply for a position as assistant instructor."

I read the note and laugh. "Okay, I'll do it."

"Don't worry that you don't know how to teach. I'll be your mentor. After all, I write the curriculum."

Several months later, students pack a classroom for our weeklong wilderness-medicine course. I'd bought a new blouse to teach in—a white-and-blue plaid, long-sleeve shirt, rolled to my elbows. I think I look sophisticated. But as Scott is starting to talk, my lovely cotton blouse is already soaked with sweat. I sit in the back, listening to Scott talk medicine as fast as the campesino men speak Spanish in the field. The students scribble notes to keep up with his machine-gun-fire-fast lecture about the function of the spine. Lying at my feet under the table, Tasha pants just as fast.

Scott walks as speedily as he talks, to and fro, hands in his pockets, head down, in front of the twenty students. His articulate words, punctuated with a large vocabulary, spill in a flawless lecture style, refined by fifteen years of teaching to everyone from homemakers to doctors, open-water sailors, and combat medics.

My inner voice expresses doubt. *How on earth am I ever going to retain this information, let alone teach it?* All new instructors are required to attend a course before they are hired. Scott waived my requirement because he teaches me daily at the clinic. But, I've been dragging my feet, ducking the duty of standing up in front of the students, talking with the authority I doubt I possess.

"Enough is enough." Scott finally calls me on my multiple excuses. "Get up there and talk like you do when you lecture at the SAR cache about search dogs or how to read a topo map. You light up when you talk about scent behavior and Tasha or navigation."

"I do?"

"Yes, of course."

Two minutes before lecture time, I force myself to march to the front of class. Blood from my head sinks to my feet as I flip on the first overhead slide. I cower, wishing to be an invisible wallflower. My voice falters and my hands clench white. I detail the musculoskeletal system and how to manage injuries. My hour-long session stretches ahead into eternity. Like my students, I eye the clock, yearning for the end. When the hour finally ticks its last minute, I know I'm a failure as a teacher. Scott says nothing—he doesn't have to.

The next day, Scott films me as I teach. That night, I take the video home to watch. From my first step in front of the class to the end of the lesson, I portray the opposite of Scott. Instead of confidence, I look scared to death. Instead of speaking clearly to the class, I mumble. My eyes stare at the floor or the slides, never at the students.

Watching myself on the video, I shrivel like a dried flower. *I can't let that happen again.* I grit my teeth with determination to improve.

In teaching several more courses over the next months, my skills inch upward, and my students no longer stare at the clock, nor roll their eyes in boredom. Tasha doesn't bother anyone and serves as our mascot, taking naps during lectures and roaming the hillside during field scenarios. By the end of the year, Scott and I form Crested Butte Outdoors, LLC, a business teaching students to understand how the body works and manage medical emergencies. We work together as business partners, coinstructors, and volunteers with Crested Butte Search and Rescue. As our business booms and CBO gains in popularity, we begin to earn decent wages and spend days together in the classroom.

Doug agrees to mentor me in Bookkeeping 101, as he has been managing a million-dollar gold-exploration budget, and since he has a vested interested in CBO's financials. After a few months of coaching me, his patience wears thin. When he notices my errors, he shoves me away from the keyboard and sits down. "I already told you sixteen times how to do this."

"Sorry," I say under my breath. Feeling like an incompetent human, I retreat to the living room and curl up next to sleeping Tasha. She acknowledges me by licking my sweaty hand. I curse myself for not being as smart and disciplined as Doug.

From the desk he roars, "I don't want you taking that ski guiding job either, until you can figure this shit out, and you need to get your taxes done!"

His hectoring and my self-pity pattern repeats itself for months, until one day I take action. I buckle down, hire a bookkeeper to teach me, in detail, how to operate the accounting program, and eventually, I figure it out. But I had to do it on my time, in my way.

Recently, I asked a dog handler / bison wrangler who works on Ted Turner's New Mexico ranch what twenty years of using cur dogs to move bison had taught him about life. While we drove in his pickup through the 150,000-acre ranch, he shared his thoughts with me. "Sue, there is a fine dance between me, my dogs, and the herd of bison. You see, the bison will move, they go wherever you want them to go with ease, as long as you don't put too much pressure on them. If the pressure is too great, the bison will stop, stare you in the eye, and stand their ground and not move for days."

Sometimes I feel Doug behaves like a pack of curs circling too close to me. My instincts teach me to stop until the pressure subsides before I move forward.

Over time, Doug eases up, and I learn to manage all aspects of my business. Doug doesn't apologize, but his dedication to my success makes me shine as a competent businesswoman in the eyes of Scott and the community. Scott believes I "have potential," words I'd never heard before. All my skills are piggybacking on one another.

Doug continues to lend a hand in my endeavors, creating a business web page and internet exposure. However, between shifts at the clinic, ski patrol, and teaching, Doug and I share less time together. He insists we take the honeymoon we'd never taken (backpacking into the Bob Marshall Wilderness), that I sign on for several more shifts with him in the Dominican Republic, and that I demand Doc Tom increase my wages. "Just walk if he doesn't give you the salary and respect you deserve."

So, I work up my courage and ask.

Doc Tom delivers the well-deserved wage increase. I accept the part-time job as an assistant ski guide at a backcountry lodge, which boosts my confidence as a fledgling avalanche professional.

My girlfriend Kathy from Boulder and dear friend of Doug's since college would tell me later, "That's what I loved about your relationship with Doug. He stuck up for you, gave you courage to go get what you deserved. I remember him telling me he'd never allow your field helpers to disrespect you. He even bought you a life insurance plan, in the event he was killed on the job. My husband never did that for me."

It appears I'm on top of the world. Inside, I sometimes feel like a lone bison encircled by my own pack of curs.

News of a female ski patroller getting blown to pieces from a hand charge at Montana's Big Sky Resort increases my discomfort with the bomb work, and ski patrol seemed to have little interest in helping Tasha and me train. So, while I stay rooted with Dr. Tom, I quit patrol. Scott opts to sign on at a competing clinic and hires on with ski patrol. It doesn't matter though, I intend to carve my own avalanche path with one foot still in the mud and the other in the snow.

CHAPTER 14

The Real Deal

Spring & Summer 1997
Crested Butte, Colorado

Doug and I head to the Sierra Madre Mountains in a remote part of Mexico, on a gold-exploration project. Because I don't trust Tasha to obey Kathy, Amy, or the neighbors, I check her into the dog kennel. She clocks three weeks cooped up; my mom-guilt mounts.

After a long flight home, we touch down at the Gunnison Airport. My frazzled, travel-weariness mixes with relief at being home. In the Mexican mountains, bullets from drunken men riding horses had nearly nicked us, causing us to take cover in a stone hut at our camp. Stepping off the plane, I breathe with relief.

At the kennel, with wide-open arms, I greet Black Dog. "Tasha! No more doggy jail. You're free." Attempting to abate my guilt, I hug her hard.

First, she ignores me. Then she smothers me with wet kisses. Leaping into the car, she plops her trembling fifty-five-pound body on my lap and then bounces between Doug and me, tickling our faces and hands until her tongue turns white. Her paws leave grimy smears on my tan travel pants.

"Easy girl. It's okay. Phew … you stink." I push her away. Her breath and flat coat smell of a dirty, damp cellar mop, mixed with the slobber of other dogs, stale urine, and hormonal sweat. If she could talk, she'd say the same about me.

She insists on riding on my lap for the fifty-minute drive. I pet her the entire way. She nips me, or what I call "fleaing me," a recognizable, repeatable behavior. I can't tell if it means she's excited, nervous, or anxious ... or loves me. Her nips don't draw blood, yet they're firm enough to pinch my skin.

Tasha springs to her feet to stick her head out the window when she recognizes the downshift of the engine and the double right-hand turn toward the condo. Ears flapping in the wind and half her body dangling over the car door, she growls to warn the neighborhood coyotes she's back home.

"Sue, keep Tasha on lead when we get out of the car," Doug warns. "She will take off on you." I stare out the window with Tasha, and he repeats his caution.

I ignore him, even though I know—because his blood pressure was high and he'd been complaining of super achy joints—that he's at his wit's end with his job. "Look, Black Dog. We're home." To keep Tasha from jumping out, I roll up the window as Doug parks the car.

"Sue, keep her on lead." He enunciates every word in a distinct command as he marches with two bags into the condo.

With Doug out of earshot, I argue back. "But, honey, she's been cooped up for so long. She won't run away." How could I be so foolish? Is this denial or stupidity?

Off lead, under the starry night, Tasha and I walk side by side to the end of our driveway. The altitude brings back my usual dull headache and shortness of breath. Tasha sticks close, stopping to sniff the lawn. With the leash and collar dangling in my hand, I saunter to the street, stretching my legs. I figure she'll just do a quick pee on the lawn, then lollygag into the condo.

At the street, I look back to the lawn. No dog. I search in multiple directions: at the willow-tangled drainage, across the road toward the ski hill, and east toward the dumpsters. I squint, trying to spot a black dog running through the inky night. No streetlights, no moonlight, not even a porch light casts a yellow glow into the dark.

"Tasha, here dog. Come. Tasha, come here!" I call. No response. Seconds turn to minutes. I pace up and down the driveway. "Tasha, come!"

Increasing my stride and search perimeter, I cup my eyes with my hands to peek into the ditch paralleling the driveway. I see and hear nothing: no willows moving in the ditch, no toenails clacking on the asphalt, no swish of a wagging tail. Nothing. I glance at my neighbors' door, which I know Tasha can nudge open to sneak into their pantry for food, but the door is closed.

I imagine my neighbors scolding me with sarcasm, "The lady with the search dog can't find her dog. Again."

"Tasha, bad dog! COME HERE!"

Nothing.

My calls turn to yells. Panic sets in with a surge of adrenaline. My heart rate increases. This is what Lawrence Gonzales refers to as the second stage of lostness: *anger*. I remind myself that the words "come here" only mean "blah, blah, blah" to Tasha.

I change tactics. "Cookie?" *Bargaining*! That command usually catches her attention because it means cheese or beef jerky. Her food obsession once induced her to jump on a friend's antique sports car to reach cat food on an adjacent workbench. I found her standing on his workbench with her head in a ten-pound bag of cat food. Hours later her belly was as tight as a drum. I got in big trouble for that one as I tried to rub away the toenail marks on the car with my finger.

"Tasha, if you don't get back here right now, I am going to kill you."

Still no response.

Glued in place by fear, I hear the echo of Doug's stern, scolding words: *You're so irresponsible. You think this is funny. No wonder you have so much conflict with everyone. You think you're above the law.*

Too embarrassed to ask Doug for help, I hop in our Toyota station wagon. I race through the neighborhood yelling out the window, "Tasha, here!" I zigzag on mountain roads in the dark night, looking for a black dog.

Panic takes over, and I imagine the worst: Tasha being hit by a car, stolen by someone, or eaten by coyotes. The hole in my stomach grows larger with each passing minute. My anger mutates into fear, and a tear trails down my cheek.

For the first time in my life, I feel what it means to have a loved one missing. Now I identify with families of avalanche victims and lost hikers in the mountains. The quote by John Walsh of *America's Most Wanted* comes to mind: "It's the not knowing where they are that kills you."

My emotions hover between disorientation, that helpless feeling of my partner missing, and anger, where I want to ring her neck. Books I've read tell me there are five stages of loss: denial, anger, bargaining, depression, and finally acceptance. I'd bypassed denial.

I've lost control of my team. *I am a bad dog owner. I should have never let her run free. I should have listened to Doug. I'm a bad wife.* Then, I shift to blaming her.

"That's it, when I find you I am putting a shock collar on you." I beg and bargain, "Tasha, please come home."

Hopelessness oozes into me as another twenty minutes tick by. I squint through tears on each road I drive. *Depression?*

After forty minutes of searching, I find her at the end of a cul-de-sac, halfway up the mountain. She stands under a streetlight, appearing to eat grass. Stopping the car, I jump out and grab her by the scruff of her neck, dragging her back to the car. She continues to chew the contents of her mouth.

"Bad dog! Load up."

She swallows and jumps into the back seat of the Toyota, smacking her lips, looking straight ahead, out the front window, and tucking her hind legs tight under her body.

Silence permeates the car. With anger returning in full force, my face feels as hot as a burning woodstove as I drive down the mountain. But by the time we enter the driveway, my shoulders relax, and I turn my head to look at Tasha.

I melt. "My bad little rotten Tasha, you scared me. I thought I'd never see you again. Don't ever do that again."

Her tail thumps once as she smacks her lips one more time.

"I forgive you."

She burps. Her belly gurgles. She gags once. Retching signals something moving from her stomach, up through the esophagus, and into her mouth. Projectile vomit spews onto the carpeted floor and seat. I scoot away to avoid the splattering barf.

Parking the car, I pinch my nose at the foul smell of kennel stomach … with added permutations. Somewhere along her journey, she managed to eat poo—human excrement. Its distinct odor fills the car.

I should have known. Tasha still has the taste for human waste. Even as a puppy she demonstrated a hankering for poo when she nearly tore open a fresh warm diaper with her razor-sharp puppy teeth.

I click on the car's interior lights. A brown slurry of crunchy peanut butter–looking feces soaks into the carpet and the fabric seat.

Of all the poop piles in the Crested Butte area, Tasha finds and consumes that one, probably a donation from a hiker. But then I look at Tasha with another thought: *At least she has the ability to find human scent.*

I unroll all the windows in the car and pray it doesn't rain.

A week later, I drop five hundred dollars on a shock collar.

I have not seen a dead person since attending an open-casket funeral as a child, when my elementary school crossing guard dropped dead. My mom made me go.

Not wanting our first exposure to be on a real mission, after a quick call to a funeral home I lead Tasha into a morgue. Trepidation at viewing a corpse roils through me. But in the morgue, we might both recoil at a human corpse.

Tasha and I peruse an old man lying on the gurney, my shoulders dropping into place from their tense perch. The man is stiff, yet warm to the touch inside his coveralls. He wears a half-crooked smile. His face scruffy.

"Paws up, Tash," I whisper. I couple the command with a flick of my wrist.

She puts her paws on the gurney. After one whiff, she jumps away, finished. No fear, no shivering, just another new smell in her growing data bank.

A few months later, I lay eyes on another corpse at the funeral service of our geologist César, who suddenly collapsed in the middle of the night at our Dominican field house. Years before, when I'd caught him wandering through our dark field house, fully dressed and wearing his headlamp, from 3:00 a.m. 'til sun up, he'd explained why:

"Suzanna, a few years ago, six men entered *mi casa* in Santo Domingo in *la noche*." He tossed in a few Spanish words and huffed in a big breath. "*Mi esposa* in bed next to me and my three little girls and boy sleeping in the other room, *los ladrones* tiptoed up the stairs, shoved the knife in my throat, tie me like hog. Told us if we yelled out they would first torture my wife, then kill *mis niños* one at a time and make me watch." His wide brown eyes stared into mine. Tears flowed down his cheeks. "No breathe, no move. I listened while they take everything from *mi casa*. They take my car. Since that day, I jump from bed at three and can't get back to sleep. I chained a watchdog to our front porch for protection."

Now he is dead. The diagnosis: *ataque al corazón,* a sudden heart attack.

And, like he had promised, he was installing iron bars in the windows and doors when it happened.

❧ ❧ ❧

Summer 1997
Red Feather Lakes, Colorado

Jenny from SARDOC invites me to a multiagency training mission near Rocky Mountain National Park, a once in a lifetime chance to find a cadaver.

On the road again, Tasha and I drive for seven hours over three mountain passes, toward Fort Collins. I justify the trip, planning to knock off some support dog handler requirements in order to propel myself into statewide, year-round wilderness deployment under SARDOC. Patti Burnett had told me, "If you want to make a live find, you better certify in wilderness too. Your odds of making a live find for lost people in the woods are so much better than finding an avalanche victim."

The weekend will pair a one-day search mission with a day of crime-scene training—one of four weekend trainings each year that focus on different search environments like water, buildings, and wilderness. On this weekend, fifteen dog teams will deploy to search a twenty-mile area for a woman missing for the past seven months. Stranded in an unexpected November snowstorm at Red Feather Lakes, the sixty-six-year-old woman walked away from her vehicle and disappeared.

Anticipation of a real mission shoots so much energy through me that I must force myself to ease off the gas pedal to arrive in one piece. "What do you think, Tasha? Did the lady walk away from the car like her boyfriend claimed, or did he toss her out the door and leave her for dead?" I wonder what the woman's remains will look like after seven months.

Tasha ignores my speculation and thumps her tail on the seat. I knead her soft ear.

After spending the night at Kathy's house in Boulder, we pick up Jenny and her dog, Tassie. The seasoned dog handler will evaluate me while I support her and Tassie. As my truck crawls over bumpy dirt logging roads, we aim for Red Feather Lakes, sixty miles northwest. Weaving through the woods, we cross small creeks, climbing higher into the Roosevelt National Forest to a broad basin containing the lakes rimmed with timbered mountains. No wind with broken clouds bodes well for an afternoon of June sunshine.

One hour later, we reach a makeshift staging area alongside the dirt road. An RV trailer acts as a command center with support personnel milling about with clipboards. Most wear bright orange vests with glow-in-the-dark emblems identifying their roles as Safety Officer, Incident Command, or Logistics. With authority, they instruct trucks pulling horse trailers where to park, organize dog teams and ground pounders, and corral men on ATVs. The scene almost looks like a state fair, except that everyone sports the professionalism of caring volunteers. The effort to find a corpse flabbergasts me. I hope if I ever go missing, the same effort will come forward before I'm dead.

Standing near the command center, I spot Poodle Lady with her search dog.

"Sweet! You get to field your dog." I raise my hand to high-five her, but halt midair at her tight expression.

"Nope. They won't let me field my dog. I am so pissed."

"Why not?"

"The coordinator claims I don't have cadaver experience. Crap on that." She paces a few steps, boots pounding the dirt. "Not only did I go to the top cadaver-dog seminar in the nation, but I was called to look for victims of a serial killer who may have buried them in his backyard. My dog found some human remains. They're just pissed I did that without their consent."

SARDOC, like most organizations, functions with its own regimen of rules, hierarchy, and politics. I also rail against their hoop-jumping requirements for me, needing to demonstrate today that I can navigate unknown terrain even though that's a basic skill required for my gold-exploration work. But now Poodle Lady seems to have encountered the same inflexibility. I shake my head in sympathy.

"So, what are you going to do?"

"I'm not going to make a big stink right now. I'm gonna keep my mouth shut and walk alongside Bob and be his support person. My dog has to stay in the car." Poodle Lady marches off in a huff.

Because Tasha is not yet certified in wilderness air-scent or imprinted on human remains, I leave her behind in my truck, in the shade of the evergreen trees and under the eye of a volunteer. Only cadaver-trained or cadaver-imprinted teams will be deployed. The dogs have either passed a human remains cadaver detection test or have been exposed to human remains. Their job is to find the dead.

Last month, when I trained with Poodle Lady, she showed me her stash of body parts kept in a military ammo can. We exposed Tasha to the smells of a human skullcap, an old tooth, and somebody's blood. I keep the secret under my baseball hat for now.

I rejoin Jenny, who has Tassie ready to work. Certified in air-scent, water, and avalanche, Tassie has had her fair share of cadaver exposure, too. With only avalanche certification, I mull over the time-consuming challenge of acquiring multiple certifications like Jenny. She breaks my reverie by handing me a 7.5-minute topographic map, the standard detailed map used by searchers—a reminder that I must tick off my navigation-skills requirement on this mission. My confidence expands at my chance to show Jenny my outdoor navigation skills.

Before departing to search for the missing woman, I demonstrate careful collection and proper packing of a scent article, by now a habit to me. As we hike, Jenny periodically asks me to show her our location on a map. I locate us with flawless accuracy and update incident command with our coordinates.

Walking through the heavily timbered terrain, looking for the woman's remains, I demonstrate my knowledge to Jenny as part of my test. I explain why we started on the downwind side of our area. I guide us on a grid zigzagging from boundary to boundary through our one-half-mile by one-half-mile search area.

She likes what she hears and continues to test me. "You will be asked by IC to determine POD." Jenny refers to the *Probability of Detection*, a term used to describe the likelihood of finding a person in an area under the right conditions. She explains in this search we'll use a grid method, wind, temperature, terrain, contamination, our knowledge, the health of the dog, and a gut feeling to come up with a percentage to represent the possibility of finding the woman.

Jenny's affability and down-to-earth sensibility opens the door for me to vent about the SARDOC hoop-jumping. "Look, I'm a geologist. I navigate for a living. I work with maps all day long. I plot things on maps—rock outcrops, drill hole locations, and stream samples. I can't believe you guys are asking me to prove I can navigate. I can out-navigate all the people here."

I bite my lip to hold back more damaging words, but I want to shout my irritation. *I find this request from SARDOC offensive, just like the time I had to show Wendy Wampler I could hike up a hill with a forty-pound pack! It's like asking a doctor to demonstrate he can put a bandage on a patient or requiring a teacher to recite the ABCs as a competency test!* But I don't go that far.

"A geologist? Wow. I want you on my team. Navigation is always hard for me."

I skew my eyes at Jenny in suspicion before recognizing the genuine tone of her words. As a member of the standards committee, Jenny supports the rules. Since the organization takes on handlers with few or no outdoor skills, testers must ensure procedures are followed to prevent injury or worse for dog handlers, dogs, and victims. I happen to be one of the more outdoorsy new members. But the rudimentary requirements still chafe.

Suck it up and shut up. Get over your ego. I remind myself of my weaknesses—understanding the science of scent and handling a dog.

As Tassie sniffs around, holding a stick in her mouth, I watch her work and continue to complete navigational tests for Jenny, plotting our location on the map. More hoops to jump through, more *t*'s to cross.

Tassie fails to find an animal bone, a scrap of clothing, or a piece of trash. Walking over the young shoots of budding spring plants, I wonder if hundreds of hours of volunteer efforts were for nothing.

When we return to incident command, we hear a radio call from one dog team. "It's her."

With permission, Jenny and I dash for our vehicle wanting to be the first to investigate before the scene gets cluttered.

After a short drive down the dirt road and a few minutes walking, we arrive at a serene scene. Patches of clothing lie on the ground with fragments of skeletal remains. The backside of the woman's black cotton jeans and red long-sleeve shirt spread across the fresh blades of spring grass as if she had just lain down to rest. One white shoe and her purse are tucked near her side. She perhaps sat down against a tree to rest before curling up to sleep. Hypothermia set in, and she took her last breath.

"Can we go find the rest of her?" I whisper out of respect for the woman. Jenny agrees, wanting to use the opportunity to imprint her dog on human remains.

Leaning into Tassie, Jenny gives her the special cadaver command. Her dog finds a stick and leads us toward a small drainage. Piece by piece, Tassie finds a few more bones. Not many—a chewed portion of a humerus; a smooth, round, intact cranium; broken vertebrae; and smaller bone fragments. Predators must have carried body parts toward the shelter of the willow and brush drainage. From there, smaller critters dispersed her farther away. Through the deep thickets of the drainage, other searchers approach, including Poodle Lady and her crew.

"Be careful not to disturb anything." We tiptoe to avoid potential crime-scene evidence.

While waiting for the coroner and sheriff deputy to arrive, we string crime tape between trees. A search dog bounds toward us with a human bone in its mouth. The handler shrieks at her dog.

I look at Jenny. "Automatic flunk?"

"Oh yeah. Picking up human remains is one of the biggest violations a cadaver dog can make."

I smile grimly. *Tasha would never do something like that—NOT!*

Back at our vehicle, Jenny gives me the thumbs-up. SARDOC support person, check.

Now I can assist dog teams on real missions throughout the state.

Tasha and I have increased our odds of making a live find.

CHAPTER 15

Searching for the Lost

Summer 1997
Mount of the Holy Cross, Colorado

Five weeks after the discovery of the skull and bones at Red Feather Lakes, twenty-three-month-old Tasha and I wear more tread off my truck's tires to return to the mountains near Fort Collins for another evaluation, another tick mark necessary for advancement toward wilderness air-scent certification.

"Another seven-hour drive for a one-hour test?" Doug fumed to me earlier that morning while I packed the truck. "It's going to cost *me* another three hundred dollars by the time you get home," he added as he strapped his helmet on for a mountain bike ride with Big, who'd moved part time to Crested Butte with Amy and the two kids.

I ignored his slam and slinked away to the kitchen to make a sandwich for the road, "Saving money, dear," I huffed to Tasha, who had been at my heels all morning, and tossed her a chuck of cheese. Caught off guard by Doug's comment, I should have defended myself by saying, "Really? You don't think I contribute to this family?" But, I kept quiet. I think he acted out because I'd be gone for a few days. I had learned to ignore his comments.

The night before, while making elk burgers on the BBQ, I tried to explain to Doug the importance of this trip. "I've finally rounded up a team of SARDOC evaluators willing to assess Tasha's air-scent abilities. Her task is to locate a subject in a quarter-square-mile area, in complex terrain, without a trail." Over the summer, I'd switched disciplines with Tasha from *trailing* to *air-scent*, a technique better suited for the two of us, since she can work off leash. I had watched Patti and Wendy's dogs work without leashes, and I wanted that for Tasha—nose in the air, problem solving and running in wide-open spaces. For the past two years, she'd proven to me she could track scent on the ground like a hound chasing a coon. I just had one worry. Tasha had the propensity to take off, to do her own thing. Would she come back when called?

At Fort Collins, we take the first pretests for wilderness air-scent. I celebrate passing the football field–size area test with one hidden victim. Tasha came back like a loyal soldier. Phew! We squeaked by on that one. But even more training and testing loom in the months ahead. I must glean all the nuggets of wisdom I can from Jenny and other evaluators.

In the midst of conversing with my evaluators, pagers squawk. "Search-dog teams requested for tomorrow to look for a missing sixty-eight-year-old hiker, last seen near the top of Mount of the Holy Cross," an unrecognizable voice announces from a pager.

"Can I go?" I blurt out like an eager school kid. "I'm approved for support. This is what I've been working so hard for." I beg and plead with my eyes.

Silence ensues. Glances dart between the evaluators. Lack of response begins to deflate my enthusiasm.

"Absolutely you should go," Jenny pipes up. "But just know, Tasha is ineligible." Avalanche certification doesn't qualify Tasha and me to work wilderness missions.

The next day, adrenaline pumps through my veins. Inside a Black Hawk helicopter, hovering below the jumbled rock summit of the 14,005-foot Mount of the Holy Cross, I sit next to search-and-rescue legend Ann Wichmann and her dog, Jenner. When I look at Jenner, a momentary guilt pang reminds me of Tasha, whom I left restrained by a woman at incident command as I walked to the chopper with my backpack, boots, helmet, and goggles. I yearn for her to finish her wilderness certification, so she can go on missions, too.

In the mountains of Montana on my first backpacking trip. (I'm on the far right.) 1976.

While working as a survival instructor, I run to greet the parents of a student after we've spent twenty-one days in the Arizona desert. 1986.

Six-week-old Tasha sleeps after an exciting elk hunt. Conifer, Colorado. 1995.

The last great Colorado ski town: Crested Butte, Colorado.

Taking a break in the Dominican Republic. Early 1990s.

Fieldwork in the rock-exposed drainages of the Dominican Republic. Early 1990s.

Sunlight Ridge after an avalanche. This is near the location that buried the three boys, killing one of them, in Mt. Crested Butte in 1989—the story that inspired me to start training Tasha to save lives.

An avalanche probe line searches for a missing hiker on South Arapaho Peak. 1999.

Eight-week-old Tasha chilling on our hotel room floor after her first plane ride. 1995.

Doug and me, trying to hold rebellious Tasha as we stand in front of our condo and Mount Crested Butte, Colorado. 1995.

Poodle Lady, Cassidy, me, and Tasha playing at the Pacific Ocean during Cadaver-Dog Boot Camp. 2001.

Tasha watches intently as a training victim walks away in the snow.

Fish and the Crested Butte Search and Rescue Team training in the winter. Crested Butte, Colorado. 1996.

The infamous Headwall ski run, where a woman lost control, bounced through the trees on the right, and nearly killed herself. Crested Butte Mountain Resort. (Note the recent six-foot avalanche crown in the center of the photo.)

Safety first! Handing off an avalanche beacon and radio while burying a friend in a snow cave for training. Crested Butte, Colorado. 1996.

Tasha learning to ride a snowmobile. Mt. Crested Butte, Colorado.

"Dig, Tasha, dig." Crested Butte, Colorado.

Training Tasha in a rappelling harness in Colorado Springs, Colorado. 1997.

Photo © Scott Warren

Patrolling Star Pass during the Elk Mountain Grand Traverse ski race from Crested Butte to Aspen. Late 1990s.

"Go find, Tasha." Summer backpacking trip in the Maroon Bells–Snowmass Wilderness between Aspen and Crested Butte, Colorado. 1997.

Defiant Tasha hanging on to all her power, self-rewarding with a stick during a January swim in the thirty-five-degree Slate River. 1998.

Mission-ready. Playing with Tasha's favorite toy, "the Schlong," while we wait. 1998.

Photo © Chris Ladoulis

Tasha showing our friend Kathy Tureck how to find me buried under three feet of snow. Mt. Crested Butte, Colorado.

Determined, Tasha makes an avalanche find.

How to safely travel down the mountain with avalanche dogs so their paws don't get cut on the skis' sharp edges. Crested Butte Mountain Resort.

Jenny's search dog, Tassie, locates a human skull during an extensive search for a missing woman. Red Feather Lakes, Colorado. 1997.

Teaching wilderness medicine to a group of Sherpas in the high country of Nepal with Ama Dablam peak in the background. 2005.

Search-and-rescue volunteers line up to search for an avalanche victim during the South Arapaho Peak Avalanche Mission. Continental Divide near Nederland, Colorado. 1999.

Divers scour the bottom of the Gunnison Reservoir near the location of Tasha's alert. Gunnison, Colorado. 2001.

Tasha returning from a retrieve with her favorite toy. Crested Butte, Colorado.

Photo © Chris Ladoulis

Patti, Tasha, me, and the Colorado Avalanche Information Center Forecaster looking down on the staging area during the search for a buried snowmobiler on Hancock Pass. Continental Divide, Colorado. 2003.

After a successful alert, Tasha watches as rescuers dig out the arm of a missing snowmobiler. Hancock Pass, Colorado. 2003.

Search-and-rescue volunteers probe the avalanche debris, hoping to find the missing snowmobiler. (Tasha later located the snowmobiler fifty meters from this location.) Ptarmigan Pass, Colorado. 2003.

Tasha and me, flown to the foot of the avalanche debris, searching before other team members arrive on La Plata Peak. The victim was found below my feet one hour later. Continental Divide, Colorado. 2004.

Holding Tasha close after her discovery. Whitehouse Mountain, Ouray, Colorado. 2005.

Somewhere on this towering slope—Whitehouse Mountain outside of Ouray, Colorado— is the body of a plane-crash victim, buried under tons of avalanche debris. 2005.

Ouray Mountain Rescue Team preparing to short-haul the body to a one-hundred-foot cable that hangs from the helicopter. Whitehouse Mountain, Ouray, Colorado. 2005.

The helicopter lifting the victim. Whitehouse Mountain, Ouray, Colorado. 2005.

Tasha and me waiting after our mission on the flanks of Whitehouse Mountain in the June morning sun, for the return of the helicopter. Ouray, Colorado. 2005.

Tasha and me, ready to board a Huey helicopter at the base of Mount of the Holy Cross. Vail, Colorado. 2005.

Tasha searching avalanche debris on Kebler Pass Road. Mt. Crested Butte, Colorado, is in the background.

Tasha searching avalanche debris that struck condos in Mt. Crested Butte, Colorado.

Tasha's last days working as an avalanche dog at Eldora Ski Resort, Colorado. 2007.

Almost retired, Tasha kicks back at the Hotel Jerome in downtown Aspen, Colorado.

Congressional Record

United States of America

PROCEEDINGS AND DEBATES OF THE *108*TH CONGRESS, FIRST SESSION

House of Representatives

PAYING TRIBUTE TO SUE PURVIS AND TASHA THE SEARCH DOG -- HON. SCOTT McINNIS

(Extensions of Remarks - June 19, 2003)

HON. SCOTT McINNIS
OF COLORADO
IN THE HOUSE OF REPRESENTATIVES
June 19, 2003

Mr. Speaker, I would like to pay tribute today to a woman and her dog who willingly give their time to provide assistance to others. Sue Purvis and her search dog Tasha of Crested Butte, Colorado volunteer to help locate victims of avalanches. In doing so, they help bring closure to victims' families and perform a public service to their community.

During one week in March of this year, Sue and Tasha were called to the scene of two avalanches. The first trapped a 33-year-old man who had been caught in a slide while snowmobiling. Some 30 rescuers searched unsuccessfully for several hours before calling in Sue and Tasha. Together, working with another canine search team, they found the man's body within half an hour.

A few days later, the pair received a call involving another snowmobiler. This time, the victim triggered a massive slide 10-feet deep and several hundred feet wide. The slide packed so much power that the debris field was 20 feet deep and contained chunks of snow and ice the size of a van. Despite working by themselves, Sue and Tasha found the man's body buried in six feet of snow about an hour later.

Mr. Speaker, when Sue and Tasha venture off into the Colorado backcountry to search for victims, they often enter very unstable and dangerous snow conditions. Still, they do so willingly to help bring closure to the victim's families as quickly as possible. That unselfish spirit of neighbor-helping-neighbor is what helped make this country great, and I am truly honored to have the opportunity to honor Sue and her amazing search dog Tasha here before this body of Congress today.

Earlier that spring, I had met Ann at a Colorado Search and Rescue Board Conference. The fit, large-framed, middle-aged woman was nearing retirement from her twenty-year service as a ranger in Colorado, where she started working search dogs. She lectured to a room full of search-and-rescue professionals about the infancy years of SARDOC and her search efforts after the Mexico City earthquake.

God forbid I'd ever have to work Tasha in Mexico City. I knew that third-world life all too well, including the week I spent at a geology conference in Mexico City with burning eyeballs and a cough. Then, the toxic brown cloud had been from pollution rather than a disaster.

Forgetting thoughts of Tasha, I gaze at the endless miles of rugged wilderness below and am thankful I can tag along to experience flying into a wilderness area where helicopters usually aren't allowed. *This woman could be anywhere.* I shake my head. The enormity of the task at hand overwhelms me. Katy, a retired schoolteacher from New Orleans, had been missing for three days.

A thousand feet above the tree line, one helicopter skid settles, suspending us over a three-thousand-foot precipice of talus rock on the flank below the blocky summit pyramid. I look at Ann for confirmation, "Here?" I point to the edge of the flat, Volkswagen-size boulder that's supporting the skid.

"Yes," she nods, with her quiet demeanor and years of confidence written in the lines of her soft face.

I clutch my backpack, and the three of us ease out of the chopper and onto the rock, perched on a ridge supporting the summit rising one thousand feet above us. Cowering below the spinning rotors, I shove my head into my jacket for safety against the hurricane-force winds that blast us until the Black Hawk spins away and dives toward the valley floor, where searchers scour the forest.

On the precipitous mountainside, under the midsummer sun, I collect my wits, ready to support Ann and her dog. My job is to navigate us safely down the mountain and help Ann detect any alerts from her dog. My stomach agitates in a soup of fear, elation, and the need to impress her.

We stand near the point last seen, where Katy and her hiking partner, both flatlanders, became separated. The friend summited the peak while Katy plopped in the boulder field to wait. But the pair never reconnected. Missing for seventy-two hours in a place where summer temperatures can dip to near freezing, Katy could be alive or dead. She could be nearby waiting for rescue or have slipped and fallen to her death as she struggled to descend.

"These ladies made it way up here?" I ask Ann while juggling thoughts about where we start and what to do if we find a body slumped between two rocks.

"Unfortunately, sometimes the flatlanders aren't prepared for the demands of climbing down once they've gone up. The missing woman could be anywhere in a ten-square-mile area."

Ann checks Jenner, her black Lab. The leggy dog, long and slender, sports bulging muscles and a classic pointed face and snout. Her coat shines bright like fresh oil. When she leaps, she reminds me of an antelope bounding through the field. The contrast between Jenner and Tasha spikes embarrassment through me. Short, squatty, rotund Tasha looks more like a sumo wrestler than a sleek search-machine. People frequently judge her appearance, asking why she's so fat. "She can't be a search dog," they pronounce. I defend her like a protective mom. But that's both genetics and developed behavior. I promised myself to keep her on a strict diet of mostly raw food and expensive kibble, but she has an insatiable appetite and will gorge on anything, dead or alive. Plus, she can manipulate *all* of her caregivers, including my parents, the neighbors, Poodle Lady, Kathy, and Amy to stuff her face any time we turned our backs.

My mom would tell me years later about her time granddog-sitting Tasha at their home in Michigan while we were away in the Dominican Republic. "Tasha would nudge me with her wet, cold snout in the arm at 6:00 a.m. But only a couple of times. She'd stare me down with those big, dark-brown eyes until I got up. Then she'd follow me to the kitchen and wait for me to prepare her food. She'd never leave my sight until your dad woke up. Then the two of them would putter around outside the rest of the day. By 3:00 p.m. the entire cycle would start again, poking at me while I watched my soap opera in the recliner."

Dad said Tasha never left his side or their wooded acre lot, never wandered away. "It was tough, you know," he'd tear up, "when you'd take her back home to Montana. We loved it when you left her for the summer with us. She was our granddog."

Once again shoving Tasha out of my head, I begin our three-thousand-foot descent down the nearly vertical mountain. Ann gives Jenner the search command.

No trail exists, hence the reason so many people get lost or are never found on this massive boulder peak. In the confusion of fatigue, dehydration, disintegrating weather, and exhaustion, hikers go down in all directions, thinking they know the route back. But the Mount of the Holy Cross monolith bulks so big that once they descend, off the rocks and into the forested valley floor, they sometimes perish in the woods, never to be seen again.

Determined to avoid letting us get turned around, I pull out my topographic map. My GPS flashes coordinates that don't match my map. Panic wells in my stomach. *Shit! Where's Doug when I need him? He'd surely get me out of this mess.* Perhaps I depend on him way too much for everything. Perhaps I haven't changed the GPS map datum since my last trip to Mexico. My GPS says we're somewhere else, but I know where we are on the map. Standing on the mountainside of irregularly shaped boulders, some the size of vehicles, I go with my gut and disregard my GPS, throwing it into my pack. *Trust your maps and compass.*

We descend, hopping from one rock to the next, peeking into the giant cavernous holes to see if a lady wearing red lies curled up in one of them.

"Katy!" The name echoes back off the rocks.

Jenner bounds from rock to rock like a mountain goat. Ann cross-trains Jenner with the Colorado Task Force 1 Federal Emergency Management Agency (FEMA) team, which has to jump onto piles of urban rubble and tiptoe around barbed wire and broken glass. FEMA is the only organization that has national standards for urban canine disaster work. Ann and Jenner are one of less than a hundred certified teams. FEMA dog teams only train for the live find—rescuing a living person in disaster zones. If Jenner alerts on food, cadavers, or animals, she'd fail her FEMA test. I doubt Tasha could make the FEMA cut. She'd snatch a half-eaten hamburger on a trail while in pursuit of a human.

As we climb down for the next five hours, I can only think how difficult this would be for stubs-for-legs Tasha. I send up some small thanks that SARDOC has strict rules: "No noncertified dogs!" Now, I understand why. Tasha isn't ready for this, and in my overzealousness to work her in this terrain, she could split open her toenails and little pads, crack her leg bones as she claws her way from one rock to another, cripple herself, or maybe even get killed. This is far too dangerous for a two-year-old dog, still growing into her developing bones.

Ann and I watch her dog sniff the air for any sign of the missing woman. We yell out but hear nothing except our faint echoes and the voices of other searchers across the valley. I pick Ann's brain about training, testing, and a career as a search-dog handler. I want to know everything. She tells me about her training in Europe and a decadelong career of wilderness missions in Colorado.

"What is your dog doing? Why?" I repeat the questions ad nauseam.

Ann fills me full of scent-movement theory. "Human scent rises as the sun warms the earth." With hands flapping in the air, she continues. "Scent sinks or moves downhill as the night cools. Scent moves in the air like water flows downstream in a river."

Once we reach the valley floor and the adrenaline wears off, fatigue sets into my achy legs. I rub my temples to relieve my dehydration headache. Jenner never shows signs of fatigue or frustration.

"Now what? Do you think she is alive up on the mountain somewhere?" I seek Ann's thoughts as we navigate our way through the creek bottom to the main trail.

"Your guess is as good as mine. That's a tough place to survive after eighty-some hours. We're limited in what we can do up there."

I look behind my shoulder at the massive mountain we just hiked down. In my naïveté, I assumed that Jenner and Ann, the superhero team, would find her. I had envisioned Jenner catching Katy's scent in the boulder field and bounding away. When we arrived we'd find a black, wagging tail, Jenner with his head down in a hole, licking the warm hand of a very dehydrated lady wearing a red coat. If Ann and Jenner, the consummate pros, couldn't find her, who else could?

Despair settles on me. I slump with the weight of our failure on my shoulders. I'd never thought about failing to find a person; I just figured we would.

Ann senses my sadness. "Sue, searching with my dogs is my passion. Sometimes we have success; other times we don't. I've been doing this for a very long time. It's the nature of the beast."

She wraps her long arm around my shoulder to shore up my languishing spirits. "I think you will be a great search-dog handler. Stick with it." Her steady, infectious reassurance puts me back on track.

Bound by a similar passion, the two of us and the loyal search dog walk another ten miles back to the trailhead. We continue to call out and search, hoping to find Katy along the way.

We spot no trace of Katy. Nor did anyone else, not even a clue. When I arrive back to mission base, I thank the woman who watched Tasha.

"Tasha whined, barked, and pulled the table across the room when she watched you board the Black Hawk helicopter. She wanted to go so badly," she reports. "Otherwise, she was a good girl."

Six days after Katy went missing, incident command prepares to suspend the search. One last helicopter flies out. Scanning the massive ocean of rock, the searcher glimpses red fabric in the black rocks high on the mountain. With the helicopter hovering close, he detects part of Katy's arm sticking out from under a rock. One crewman and a rescuer jump out. They transport Katy to the hospital, saving her life. Days later, she appears on one of the network morning shows, telling the world that she never heard rescuers, not even once in her six-day ordeal.

I watch her interview, stunned that she could not hear the reverberating *thud, thud, thud* of a helicopter overhead. She had entered the fourth stage of lostness: *depression*. Now I understand why she was not participating in her self-rescue. Was she ready to give up and die? Cochrane, the Incident Commander in charge of this mission and our evaluator for our Mountain Rescue Association test in Crested Butte, didn't give up.

Later in the summer, the article written at Dinosaur National Park when Tasha first learned to rappel off a cliff hits the newsstands. *Smithsonian* magazine features Tasha and me as a puppy team in training. Poodle Lady and her dog make the cover shot. Soon after, a film producer named Ross tracks me down via telephone, wanting the lowdown on search-and-rescue dog teams for a movie idea. SARDOC calls immediately, when they catch wind of our conversation, and tell me that Tasha and I would *never* get certified if we gave any more interviews or talked with any of the Hollywood types who come calling. I understand that SARDOC speaks for SARDOC, but I also understand that they are controlling the narrative to the point of being irritating. Their pettiness highlights the competitiveness that exists even within the search-dog community. Not surprisingly, Poodle Lady and SARDOC part ways not long after she made the cover.

CHAPTER 16

Challenges and Temptations

Spring & Summer 1998
The mountains of Colorado

In the wee-hour dark of a chilly April night, a dull throbbing headache coupled with a fast heart rate remind me where I am. Tasha and I crawl from the toasty sleeping bag we share with Doug in the Friends Hut, a backcountry ski cabin at 11,300 feet in the Elk Mountains. Sandwiched between Doug on the right and Scott on the left, I feel like the rose between two thorns. We are crammed together into this hut serving as the support crew for the first Elk Mountain Grand Traverse. The others won't roust themselves out of bed for another hour. They'll both serve as medical and rescue support at the hut while Tash and I hump it to the windswept pass with the avalanche team. I had convinced them to volunteer, along with a half-dozen other SAR members, for the backcountry ski race that started at midnight.

A few hours ago, a gunshot launched ninety-six backcountry skiers on the forty-mile race from Crested Butte to Aspen. Avalanches, stream crossings, wind, sun, and high elevation on the traverse conspire to wallop skiers with risks, ranging from crippling blisters to death.

My duty with Tasha requires I leave now with three avalanche forecasters to ski to Star Pass, an hour's vertical climb, and the most avalanche-prone section of the course. I'm both honored and scared for my life and Tasha's this morning. Earlier in the winter, a SAR member asked me to stand guard on Star Pass with Tasha. Without hesitation, I quickly said yes. His offer made me feel so validated and respected, a first in a long time. Not only would we respond to avalanches, but I could practice my wilderness-medicine skills. There wasn't a more extreme race than this. But in my haste, I didn't consider my physical challenges or Tasha's, especially since I had just returned from a trip to sea level, and she'd sat at Amy's house for two weeks, just being a couch potato. I figured I could muscle my way through anything without the proper preparation. Call it ego or stupidity, it's the stuff that kills rescuers.

Grabbing my pack, I say my goodbyes. "Pray for us," I whisper to Doug and kiss his cheek.

I nudge Scott. "Hey. I'll call you on the radio if someone gets into trouble."

This was the first time my husband and business partner had spent significant time together, and now they lay side by side like they've been best friends for decades. I had arranged for Doug and Scott to join me as a "get to know each other" trip, so Doug wouldn't feel jealous every time I worked with Scott. Doug was used to having all of my attention in the Dominican Republic. Now he had to share me with a bunch of men in macho professions: patrolling, search and rescue, medicine, and now avalanche technician.

As Crested Butte Outdoors Company blossomed, Scott and I spent more time together. Doug's hackles would rise every time I came home and called him Scott. Likewise, Scott had shared with me that he'd go home and call his wife "Sue," and she was feeling suspicious like Doug. I hadn't given the "me in the middle" jealousy thing much thought until Doug said something to me one morning while we were skiing. Out of nowhere, he growled, "You're paying Scott way too much money. We do all the work running the business. All he does is show up and teach."

I felt sucker punched. I hated talking about money, and I didn't want to rock a boat that was sailing just fine. Besides, I still had a lot to learn from Scott. It'd be several more years until I became fluent in teaching wilderness medicine. Doug knew I made an agreement with Scott that we'd split everything fifty-fifty. So, I didn't say anything to Doug that day. I changed the subject. Avoidance was my friend. And denial kept me from seeing how Doug's and my lives were diverging while Tasha's and mine were emerging.

Flipping on our headlamps, I curse myself for being out of shape and slide one ski in front of the other, unable to see our destination— only the avalanche forecaster before me. The frigid air pierces my throat, and my head still throbs. Our headlamps light up the wind-scoured route, the tracks from the forecaster's scouting missions over the past few days.

As the support team to monitor avalanche hazard, facilitate technical rescues, and render first aid, we must reach the pass before the first skiers, and well before daylight. Within ten minutes, sweat drips from my forehead, and my breathing is labored as we ascend a ridge. Tasha's red collar light blinks, marking her position as she runs to check on each person. Picking up the rear, an avalanche-forecaster-in-training yodels as he places glow sticks along the course to light the way for the oncoming competitors.

Getting to Friends Hut required a thirteen-mile climb on skis, going up several thousand feet in elevation. Doug, Scott, and I fastened ski skins, one side with mohair and the other with sticky adhesive, to the bottom of our skis to help us climb uphill. I cursed my thirty-pound pack, full of too much dog food and too many first-aid supplies. I missed Julian, the part-time pig farmer who always carried my pack in the Dominican Republic.

Doug and Scott had shared war stories and laughed all day, which gave me joy. I had struggled to stay in the packed single-track, as stepping off it sunk my skis into deep snow. Tasha had battled the path, gaining purchase by stepping on top of my ski tails. I swatted my pole backward at her with a loud, "Off!" afraid the metal edges of my skis might slice her leg.

Eight hours after we started, I'd collapsed through the front door of the hut, nauseous and dehydrated. I'd vomited once from the altitude.

Recognizing the first signs of Acute Mountain Sickness from oxygen deprivation, I'd treated myself with two liters of water instead of a celebratory whiskey. Then rest and, a few hours later, food.

Above the tree line, a clear night sky blazes with stars while gusts of wind cut sideways, whirling glass-sharp snow crystals across my face. As I stop to catch my breath during the climb along the ridge, I call Tasha. I demand she heel and keep pace at the tail of my skis.

I peer back down the valley toward Crested Butte. Two headlamp lights bounce between the trees, miles below the hut. Skiing in teams of two, competitors carry enough survival gear for twenty-four hours. I check my watch: 3:35 a.m. *Sheesh*. No one anticipated such fast racers.

When we crest the ridgeline, more headlamped pairs, looking like distant car lights, dot the valley. Pressure to reach Star Pass snaps my attention back to the ridgeline. I dig my metal edges into the near-ice hard pack, hoping they cling. The knife-edge ridge plummets into dark emptiness in both directions. With Tasha off leash, I put up with her stepping on my ski tails to prevent her slipping into either black abyss. I shine my headlamp on the ski tails in front of me to keep pace. Only the yodeling from my teammate tempers my fear.

Just before diving into our orange nylon tent-outpost at the pass, I spot the headlights of two racers cresting the ridge. By the time I waddle out of the tent with five layers of clothing, the first team reaches us.

Both sides of 12,300-foot Star Pass cross highly exposed avalanche paths—the most dangerous, remote portion of the course. The pass sits just under the marathon's halfway point, around the twenty-mile mark. My forecaster companions have spent the past week digging pits, looking for the instabilities lurking in the snowpack that might cause a slope to avalanche. To mitigate danger by eliminating the strain, they ski quickly across a slope to release tension from the new snow, a technique known as ski cutting.

Once the racers ski beyond the pass, they'll cross into no-man's-land until they reach the support crews near Aspen Mountain. In this extreme endurance race, Star Pass is the point where the weak part from the strong, where those struggling will turn back.

When the two male athletes arrive, I look like a roly-poly Pillsbury Doughgirl next to them, the frigid wind still cutting through my hefty layers. They wear skimpy Lycra cross-country racing suits. Frozen snot clings to their faces. Their lightweight touring skis and small backpacks aid their speed. Without dawdling, the pair gives us a quick greeting. I attempt to monitor their condition.

"How are you guys doing? Come in the tent, so I can check you out. You can get a bite to eat."

"No thanks. We're doing great," one of them pipes up while the other looks behind his shoulder into the darkness, checking for competitors' headlamps. They ask for directions.

"Drop in right over the cornice. Stay left and high." One forecaster points to the flashing strobe light that's attached to a single ski stake at the top of the cornice. "Be ready for the drop and traverse high."

The two skiers leap over the edge, vanishing into the dark night. I shrug my shoulders at the forecaster. "Guess they don't need me today."

I turn back to the ridgeline to see a second team of lights not far behind. To take care of Tasha, I clip her to her leash. "Good girl, Tash. I'm keeping you close today."

The second team skis into camp, also wearing Lycra and cross-country racing gear. They inquire when the first team came through the pass. I adapt my medical assessments to accommodate their need to get moving in the subzero predawn winds.

"How are you feeling?"

They both give me thumbs-up as they swallow liquid sugar from packets. With a big smile, they drop over the edge, the night swallowing them.

Thirty minutes later, as a sliver of light emerges in the east, the first Crested Butte team comes through our station. "Look!" One points to Tasha. "An avalanche dog. How awesome." The skier pats Tasha on the head, forgetting for a moment about his frost-nipped feet and hands. Like the others, he questions how far behind the first-place team they are. They, too, waste no time chitchatting and plunge over the lip.

"Sunrise is almost here," notes one of the avalanche forecasters. "It'll heat up the east-facing slopes on the pass, shooting the avalanche conditions up. Remember our 8:00 a.m. deadline: everyone needs to be through here by then."

I look at my watch.

Ninety minutes left.

The sunrise arrives in golden splendor, lighting up the ridge and its single-file parade of racers. The bright reds, greens, and blues of their clothing contrast against the ominous, vast, white mountainous backdrop.

From our vista, the shuffling racers appear small. Some teams ski together and others split, having one partner ski on to our checkpoint to wait. Once at the pass, the biting wind and their desire to finish the race force them onward. With a few minutes to spare, I peek over the cornice. The four-foot ledge drops on rock-hard snow, demanding that the skiers land sideways, digging in their metal edges for grip.

As teams pile up at the tent, the avalanche forecasters help me by conversing with some of the racers—half avalanche condition discussion, half jokes. We all listen for lack of lucidity as an indicator of exhaustion or altitude sickness. Pulling off their gloves, some racers kneel to pet Tasha. She licks the salt off their exposed hands.

One racer appears without his gloves or hat. I gape at him as he skis up.

"Howdy-doo," he grins, striding on past. As he skis off the cornice, he shoves his bare fist into the snow to regain his balance. A minute behind, his partner arrives.

"What's with the gloveless, hatless wonder?"

His partner laughs. "He's been skiing eight years without either. He's a real tough mountain man." He shuffles off in pursuit of his buddy.

One forecaster shakes his head. "Those guys are either on acid or 'shrooms."

One team arrives decked out in costumes: one skier in a black-and-white Dr. Seuss hat, while the other flaunts a superhero cape. Beards and mustaches come through, frozen with snotty icicles. A handful of female teams appear, as if they had just walked two blocks to the store. By the cutoff time, thirty-eight teams have crossed the pass. Only one skier sits down in our tent for ten minutes to catch his breath.

Just as the last racers jump off the cornice at Star Pass, the radio confirms the winners skiing across the finish line in Aspen in eight hours. Ten teams never show at the pass. Via radio, we call to Scott at the Friends Hut, who assumed the role of Incident Commander. He confirms their whereabouts. Some dropped out with equipment failure. Some quit from exhaustion.

No injuries, no catastrophes to handle. Experience without tragedy.

Tasha and I join Doug and Scott at the Friends Hut. Hugs and high-fives circulate amongst our collective group of volunteers. As we ski down the fifteen miles to our truck, I snowplow with Tasha trotting between my legs and my hand cinching on her harness. Her position between my legs prevents me from skiing into her. When the slope moderates into flats, I lift Tasha, straighten my skis, and let both of us sail together across the snow in joy.

As Tasha and I settle into a rhythm on a flat road ski in the last three miles, I ponder the past twenty-four hours. Doug and Scott now seem more like allies than enemies.

I feel more comfortable now, knowing the terrain I'll be working in and the players in the avalanche community. Most could now serve as vocal advocates for our work. Being asked to serve as the medical officer and avalanche dog team for the race inches us up in my estimation. It was the real deal, much more than the contrived testing situation for the avalanche certification. I proved to my SAR team that I am not some Jane Doe working on the twenty-fourth floor of the ARCO building in Denver, saying I have an avalanche dog, but that I'm living it, breathing it, doing it.

A ring of five cardboard refrigerator boxes form a circle at a Fort Collins training session, where the trainer challenges Tasha and me to a test. Each of the boxes hides something, but only one contains the match to the scent article. With gusto, I take the challenge, keen to prove Tasha's scent discrimination skill.

I hold the scent article, a sock, to Tasha's nose, letting her get a good whiff. With Tasha on lead, we parade past each of the boxes. When she ignores the first box, I surmise it is empty. At box two, she sniffs the edges of the box, lifts her nose, and lets out a two-second whine, similar to when she can't reach something. She trots past box three, but she attacks box four, jumping and barking.

"That's it. That's the matching sock."

I pull Tasha away to smell box five. With a longer stop, she sniffs and paws at the dirt, but moves away. When we finish the loop around the boxes, the trainer asks me for my verdict.

"So, which one hides the sock's owner with the sock's mate?"

With my shoulders squared to the trainer, I point to box four, where Tasha jumped and barked. "That one."

"Well, let's see." The trainer opens the box to reveal a juicy hamburger and french fries.

"Agh. Food. It's always food with you." I lambaste Tasha who looks at me as if she did nothing wrong.

"Pay attention to her whine," the instructor advises. "She's trying to tell you something."

We find the matching sock in box two.

"Back to Red Feather Lakes, Black Dog."

Once again, I bundle us into my truck for the seven-hour drive, but instead of me searching without Tasha, the two of us will test for certification in wilderness air-scent. Since no evaluators live around our home turf, Tasha and I must test with the disadvantage of travel and unfamiliar terrain. This time, Doug goes along to be my navigator, responsible for keeping track of our location, just as I did on the mission with Ann and Jenner.

I had pushed for a late-May test date to coincide with Doug and I departing for a honeymoon backpacking in Montana, a trip long overdue. Even though we've traveled some of the finest white-sand beaches in the DR, we never took time out for the two of us—he'd always be fishing, reading, or working on something. Unfortunately, even in late May, Red Feather Lakes is buried under two feet of snow. My shoulders drop. Wind-crusted snow increases the difficulty for Tasha. To complicate the search test, a cold front pushed through Colorado that morning, gusting with high winds.

Hunkering into my jacket, I greet Jenny and her husband, my lead evaluators, who have hidden a stranger for Tasha and me to find. Since no one wants to dilly-dally in the cold, we launch right into the test.

In lieu of a scent article, I open the victim's car seat to give Tasha a whiff. "Here, Tasha, check out the scent here." She nabs a quick sniff of the driver's seat. It's been fourteen months since we passed our avalanche test on Aspen Mountain, and nine months since I switched from trailing to air-scent training. I pray we're ready.

We slog into crusted snow that collapses with each step. The crust holds us for a second until our full weight forces postholing—Doug to his knees, me to my thighs, and Tasha to her chest. We labor with sluggish movements, Tasha taking a slower-than-usual charge.

"You can do it, girl."

Racing down the east flank of the Continental Divide, forty-mile-per-hour gusts hammer us. Tasha fights the wind, chasing the subject's scent to the edge of exhaustion. Her white tongue falls nearly to the ground. I make her drink water often.

Once refueled, she charges forward again, pursuing the invisible odor of the hidden subject. With the wind, the scent bounces, rolls, boils up into the trees, and clings to depressions. Tasha pushes on.

As we struggle into the second hour of the test, in search of the hidden subject, the crusty snow rubs Tasha's pads raw. Her energy wanes. Yet she powers on against the wind and snow. In fear for her safety, I'm eaten away by her efforts.

Jenny calls the test two hours later. I force air into my lungs, my warm exhale disappearing in the wind toward Kansas. Back at the trailhead, Jenny analyzes our performance.

"You've done a fabulous job on all the technical components of search: navigating, map location, strategy, working terrain features, handler and dog endurance, communication, respect for us and your dog, consistent dog-alert recording and reading." Then she sighs.

"So, tell me, where do you think the subject is? Show me on your map. If you had to send new dogs in, where would you send them?"

I look at Doug for support. His eyes avoid mine. I feel his unspoken words: *Don't ask me. This is your test. You're the expert.*

Mustering confidence, I shove my pointer finger back and forth between two areas on the topographic map. "Based on all of Tasha's alerts ... here." I stab at one of the spots.

"Okay then," she says. "Test is over."

They return one hour later with my results.

My intuition tells me I failed.

"Even though you scored ninety-nine out of one hundred we had to flunk you. Sorry. Tasha didn't find the subject. A high score in doing everything right means nothing when you can't locate the victim."

"But—"

Jenny surmised Tasha literally walked ten feet from the subject—upwind on the first pass. Tasha did not smell her because the wind pushed the scent in the opposite direction.

During the long miles to Montana, I battle a sickness in my gut. If our test had been a real mission, Tasha and I would have left the victim for dead. I reach my hand to the back seat of my pickup to pat my exhausted ball of black fur on the head.

"Tash, we can't let that happen ever again."

A FEMA dog tester once told me, "You die a slow death as an evaluator, watching a dog fail." But I am reminded flunking is not so much failing as it is just a part of the process toward certification. Testing scenarios become our biggest teachers, and sometimes failure is the most valuable thing that can happen.

❄ ❄ ❄

After fourteen days backpacking in the Montana wilderness alongside grizzlies and elk, plus Doug developing hypothermia after we got caught in a weeklong storm, we return for a second attempt at passing the wilderness air-scent test. Three new evaluators meet us at a campground in the mountains near Estes Park, Colorado. Granite rock outcroppings break up the heavily timbered slopes, still covered with a foot of snow. Unlike the gale-force winds of the last test, the twenty-degree sunny morning wafts with only mild breezes. Perfect weather conditions for testing.

Once the testers give me a map of the area, I plot my strategy. To take advantage of the westerly wind, we drive a quarter mile to the southeast boundary of the testing site. I note a terrain trap in the middle of my search area—a shallow, low scrub depression that will trap scent—so, I avoid it. Exuding confidence, I give Tasha a whiff of the subject's ball cap. "Go find."

Within one minute, Tasha locates a set of footprints. With nose to track, she sprints, disappearing into the thick forest.

Crap, I should have kept her on lead. After four uncomfortable minutes standing alongside my tester, my shoulders drop at another failure. "This is unacceptable." I throw my hands up in frustration. "Can I borrow your radio? Hey, whoever is hiding out there, can you tell Tasha to find Sue?"

I stand in the snow waiting, tapping my hand on my thigh. One minute later, Tasha's bell tinkles, and she appears. She runs back to me, pasty white tongue hanging low. Too tired to jump, her nose nudges my thigh, telling me, "I found her!" She turns around to lead me back to the subject curled up next to a rock in the snow.

I fight for justification and certification. "She found the victim in two minutes. Once I prompted her, she came to me with a stellar refind. Then, she took me back to the subject. She did her job."

"Tasha backtracked on the footprints. That's trailing, not air-scent." the lead evaluator reasons.

I object to how the test was set up. "But those footprints were yours from escorting the victim to her hiding location. You had the victim's scent on your prints from hanging out together for two hours in the car before setting up the scenario. That's time enough for your scents to comingle. You shouldn't have contaminated the site."

"Doesn't matter."

"But she used all the tools in her toolbox. Give her some credit. She's a pro at following footsteps, a pro at searching. She smelled the minuscule scent of the subject on your footprints."

The examiner holds his ground. Perhaps he just needs to save face, having botched the setup for the test.

Tasha, Doug, and I pile into the truck for the seven-hour-long drive home. Tasha sleeps. Fuming, I rail on about incompetent test setups. I bitch so much that we don't even get sleepy driving. When Doug suggests it's time to quit testing and be happy I have an avalanche dog, I glare at him.

I won't give up, even if it means months more training, more road trips, and labor camp in the Dominican Republic.

The stuffy Crested Butte Search and Rescue cache room shrinks in the hot August evening. Why we're all sweltering inside baffles me, but I listen to the instructions for our team's mock-search training scenario at Kebler Pass. Teenage Tasha is maturing into an obedient dog, so I let her roam the room to greet team members before I kennel her in the truck. Earlier, my team had hidden a person in the woods for Tasha to find.

Stink Face drones on, and my eyes dart to the carpet to check Tasha, but she isn't there. I shrug off her disappearance, assuming she's headed to the clear waters of the Slate River to cool off. After all, Labs love water.

Several minutes later, as we huddle like a football team, a clumping sound heralds the return of the sixty-pound Lab plodding up the stairs. I hope she has already shaken off the water instead of waiting to come inside to fling water droplets on everyone.

Instead, she enters covered head-to-toe in foamy, chocolate milk–like sewer water. Her three-inch-long whiskers dangle with the goop of poop. The stench of sewer accompanies her in an invisible cloud around her glistening, sludgy body. Only her eyes and the crown of her head are the familiar black.

Retching, I hold my breath, eyes bursting wide. In unison, my team-mates all turn together, their mouths gaping. Tasha prances into the middle of the circle, tail wagging, while frothy foam blops flick into the air. Her mouth hangs open in a grin.

The nearest people jump back with both feet to avoid the swat of her tail. The stench infuses the room. In anticipation of Tasha shaking herself, we dash for fresh air.

Tasha follows. We spread across the parking lot to avoid her. When I turn to Doug for help, he shakes his head. "This is your problem."

Grabbing a pair of medical gloves from my truck, I drag Tasha by her slimy collar to the river. In water to my midcalf, I wash off her sewer sweater. Still half covered in sludge, I let her go and return to the truck to take her home. By the time I pull my gloves off, Tasha dives back into the sewer pond for one last swim.

She spends the rest of the week sleeping in the garage, while I try to forget yet another stellar impression she's made on my team. If I'm not careful, Doug might have me join her out there.

"This guy could be anywhere." I point out the obvious.

Doug concurs.

Gloomy clouds and light rain settle over the 275 square miles of the rugged West Elk Wilderness in Gunnison County. At a remote trailhead, my search-and-rescue team prepares to look for an overdue thirty-year-old bowhunter from the Midwest. His hunting partner contacted the sheriff's office yesterday, saying that they split up days ago at their campsite.

Harold, an aging deputy in charge of SAR operations for the sheriff's department, meets us at the point last seen: the hunters' trailhead campsite. He knows Tasha and me by name because he, the sheriff, and a few deputies had attended a SARDOC wilderness weekend I hosted near Crested Butte a few months ago. Harold and crew spent the morning listening to Wendy Wampler and other leaders in the organization preach philosophy and theory. The department had been so impressed, they'd spent the rest of the day with the dog teams. The sheriff later announced that they had secured funding to train a shepherd for police, tracking, and narcotic work—a first for Gunnison County. And, I'm sure, a ten-thousand-dollar-plus proposition. Harold had even given some of his time to hide in the woods and play victim for Tasha.

"Good to see you again." Harold reaches out and shakes my hand. I want to profess to him right here and now that Tasha still isn't wilderness air-scent certified. Which means I can't deploy her.

But, instead of confessing, I change the subject. "My gut tells me the missing guy is not here," I tell him. "I suspect that these two flew in, rented a car, bought some camping supplies and a new bow set from Walmart, and drove dirt roads to the middle of nowhere to hunt elk." I motion around the campsite. Missing the accoutrements of a developed campground—toilets, picnic tables, and trash cans—the location features only a small grassy plot big enough for a tent.

"Yes, something doesn't add up. Looking at the evidence in the rental car, I think this guy could now be in ROW," the deputy says, referring to the rest of the world. "He could be at the bar, home sleeping, or heck, even in Vegas."

I nod, then slap Tasha's bum. She sits and then slides to her belly.

"First, if the men were truly camping here, like the friend reported, the campsite would show signs of use: flattened grass, perhaps a makeshift fire, and bits of trash," he adds.

I explain Tasha's unique ability to scrounge for human "leftovers."

If they spent time here, Tasha would find anything they dropped on the ground including hot-dog buns or discarded steak bones, and she'd zero in on their feces nearby. Two men can't camp for days without leaving a pile behind. If they camped here, Tasha would find the evidence.

Despite suspicions about the hunter's whereabouts, we're excited to deploy after the long car ride—and after several months without a mission—and my team readies to hike up the trail for at least a workout. They bustle about, stuffing backpacks with water bottles, extra food, and clothing. They zip on gaiters to keep the mud out of their boots. They examine topographical maps spread on truck hoods.

"Well, Sue, are the two of you going to go find this bowhunter?" Harold grins at Tasha.

Tasha bounds to her feet and jumps on his pleated blue pants. I tug her back.

Tempted to field Tasha, I long to be a hero after so many failures. The only thing missing besides our certification is a *real* mission. We'd receive fame and glory for locating the missing bowhunter. I could tell ski patrol, "I told you so." I could prove to the sheriff's department and my local search team just how fast and efficient canine teams can be. I could show Doug that all the money and time spent is a life worth living, and that I can make a living doing this. All of that mattered to me then.

But the SARDOC policy manual dictates the terms of our involvement. Noncertified dog teams that field themselves without permission risk suspension. We might save a life, but simultaneously flatten our dreams of certification and credibility. The organization had reprimanded Poodle Lady for violations including fielding her dog without their permission.

While the sheriff's deputy waits for my reply, Tasha sniffs the air. Her airplane ears stand erect. She tugs on her leash as the team sets out up the trail, toward the wilderness. I look for Doug to answer my moral dilemma. Instead, he slings his pack over his shoulders and marches out. On the drive to the trailhead, he'd already spelled out his position. "This is your program, your destiny. You decide."

I watch my team walk away. *Quick, Sue. Make a decision. If you decide right now, it won't be too late to catch up.*

Why not snub SARDOC rules and regulations? The law enforcement agencies and my search team don't care about certification status, or whether Tasha is a trailing or air-scent search dog. Many sheriff's deputies, feeling pressure from the media, the family, or their boss, will use any untrained dog rather than none at all.

But SARDOC does care. And so do I. Fielding a qualified dog does matter. If I field Tasha, the credibility of search dogs in general can be irreparably damaged if we, an uncertified dog team, fail to perform effectively.

As I wage battle with myself, I sense a loss either way—with fielding Tasha despite SARDOC or holding her back even with a life at stake, to play the game according to the rules. But above all, I do not want to risk my canine-search career. I summon honesty.

"I can't deploy her. I must follow the rules."

"I respect that," says Harold.

Watching my team disappear into the mountains, I bow my head.

While the old deputy and I wait, we chat about search dogs. I describe Tasha's training and her love of human excrement. "You know, if that hunter's story is really true, Tasha would find their poo."

With no command, I guide Tasha around the campsite. She sniffs bushes and marks her turf like she does on the way to the clinic. She finds nothing.

While Harold and I wait, I take the opportunity to tell him about our training, mission experiences, and all the things she finds including money, expensive sunglasses, and a $1,500 revolver in a leather case, which she'd dropped on our porch when I let her out unattended to pee. I even share our failed test stories. By next month, I promise him, three-year-old Tasha will have completed her third and final wilderness test. I brag we'll be the first search-dog team in Gunnison County history to work in both wilderness and avalanche. I hand him my business card reminding him to call me the minute someone goes missing.

Later, our search team reports back they hadn't found one clue, not even a footprint. Harold makes several calls to dispatch and learns the missing person is home. He admits he was at the campsite with his friend, but they got in a fight, and while his buddy was hunting, he hitched a ride to the airport and flew home. Our guy was in Vegas after all.

CHAPTER 17

Worst Avalanche Disaster in a Decade

Winter 1999
Gunnison County, Colorado

Back in the Dominican Republic hordes of people smother me, but I resign myself to straddling two worlds for Doug, trading breathing space for crowds. Clean mountain air for smog. Snow for mud. Cold for heat. Open windows for iron bars. No fence for AK-47-armed guards. Freedom for feeling caged. I'm doing this for you too, Tasha. I try not to think about her, as I know Amy and the boys are taking her for long walks, scratching her back by the fire, and feeding her well. I count the minutes that remain of my three-week work shift as I sit for the umpteenth time in a traffic jam, ten blocks from a stoplight in Santo Domingo. Power is out. Horns honk. Exhaust builds. The tropical sun could fry an egg on the hood of our new pickup. Eight barefoot children with dirty sponges mob our vehicle. Youngsters beg for pesos, others wash the truck. On instinct, I lock the door and roll up the window. Doug's arm muscles tense, and he jerks open his door to push the kids away.

"*Vayase!*" Get out of here.

They back off, but the minute he slams the door they swarm again like flies. At my window, three beggars dangle junk necklaces for sale. Because the traffic lights have no power, we inch forward with our swarm until we can shoot through the intersection to be rid of them.

Safe.

❧ ❧ ❧

By the time I return to my Crested Butte life, a blanket of snow covers the ground and months have elapsed since *finally* passing our wilderness air-scent certification. Two years have passed since our avalanche certification. My pager never goes off, and I wonder if the work is all for nothing. I read in the SARDOC newsletter that my colleagues are deploying monthly. My gear is piled, unused, next to Tasha's bed. Tasha lies on her side, head hanging off the edge with one paw dangling to the floor, on her new double-thick canine orthopedic mattress, big enough for two Saint Bernards. Doug scolded me when the dog bed, half the size of a twin bed, arrived via UPS.

"Our campesinos would kill to have a bed like that for their whole family." He adds the $150 bed to the long laundry list of expenditures for my volunteer-search-dog career. To date, I've invested my entire Dominican yearly salary on gear and gas and more than a thousand volunteer hours. But I don't tell that to Doug.

I curl up with Tasha on her mattress. "You're a good dog."

Her tail thumps. Her front teeth nibble on my triceps, a nip I attribute to love.

"Ouch, you little stinker." I push her muzzle away and descend into a fit of coughing from a viral infection I'd picked up at a recent shift at the clinic. "No walkies today. I'm sick." She drops her head onto her paws. No wonder I'm sick. Traveling inside of an airplane with all those germs from sea level to 9,500 feet doesn't help.

Lately I've been stressed. Doc Tom, the surgeon, is fighting with the family practice doctor who owns the other ski clinic about what ski patrol sleds get delivered where. Tom argues all orthopedic injuries should be brought to his clinic when he's in town. Both ski patrol and management are stuck in the middle of the feud, which makes my relationship with Scott strained. We work at the opposing clinics. And to makes matters worse, each time I come home from a trip, Tasha snubs me for about a day.

As an early February snowstorm rages outside, I stare at my avalanche pack next to Tasha's bed. Without working on ski patrol, I put in more hours at the clinic. I miss working on skis, staying fit. The walk to work past the chairlift reminds me every day that Tasha isn't allowed to train at the resort. Even after I petitioned ski patrol management based on passing our avalanche certification, the director still banned us from training on the ski slopes unless my entire search team accompanied us. *Impractical for a dog team that needs to train most days.* We make do with practicing in the six-foot-high snowbanks around our condo.

I did the right thing by certifying with SARDOC. I now have a chance to work my dog outside the confines of Crested Butte. And to work year-round. Entire careers sometimes pass by without a ski-patrol dog team ever working an avalanche.

But we're only biding time.

On a recent morning, Poodle Lady telephoned me with news of Aspen's first avalanche fatality of the season. If only the victim had taken an avalanche course, he'd have known that when perfectly shaped snow-flakes fall from the sky and blanket the mountains in early November, the cold, clear nights that follow can change the crystals to depth hoar. Then, when consecutive storms drop perfect champagne powder, the depth hoar layer becomes hidden. This is where poorly bonded snow lies concealed, creating an unsupportive snowpack. All the slope needs to avalanche is a slab formation on top of a weak layer, a trigger—like a skier—and a steep enough slope. Most people don't know this. I never did until my avalanche mentors showed me how to dig deep to look for snowpack instabilities.

I've sorted my gear to be ready for an avalanche. My pack contains essential gear for Tasha and me to survive overnight in blizzard conditions. A foam pad, an oversize garbage bag for emergency shelter, fire-starting material, a down coat, and a collapsible shovel and probe pole are all tucked inside the pack. Wands with colored flags to mark Tasha's alerts in the snow fill an outside pocket. Another pocket holds two rolls of white medical tape and a small container of blood stopper powder for Tasha's pads in case they get cut on ice or by my ski edges. The schlong, her vest, and two avalanche beacons—one for me and the other for her—complete the supplies. Food and water must be added at the last minute.

Pulling a blanket over us, I doze into my stuffy head stupor, soaking up heat from her. The phone wakes me into coughing spasms. My eyes itch and my nose drips. But I pull myself together enough to answer.

"Gunnison dispatch?" Why on earth is the sheriff's office calling me on the phone instead of summoning my search-and-rescue team via pagers?

"The sheriff is requesting you and your dog to respond to an avalanche at Cumberland Pass. At least four skiers are buried."

That grabs my attention, even through the viral fog in my head. While dispatch fills in details, I wobble off Tasha's dog bed. My shift of mood causes her to stand at attention, eyes following my movements. As I grab my avalanche pack, her ears perk forward. "Doug," I shout. "Get dressed. We got a mission."

Racing to fill water bottles and stuff food in my pack, I recall Patti Burnett's account of the 1987 Breckenridge avalanche, the worst in Summit County history. Outside the ski-area boundary, the avalanche caught nine skiers, burying four completely. It was Patti's first mission with her dog, Hasty, and the rescue and body retrieval proved taxing, stringing out over three days. The extensive search required one helicopter, four snowcats, sixteen snowmobiles, two metal detectors, a ground radar unit, a command trailer, two ambulances, one hundred thirty probe poles, two tents, two generators, hundreds of searchers, dozens of rescue teams, and several canine teams, including some from Utah, to find all four bodies. In all, over six thousand man-hours had been devoted to finding the victims.

Loading the truck, I muddle in panic. *Cumberland Pass! This is the real deal. Four people!* I take several deep breaths to steel myself. The sheriff called me. He didn't call my team. He didn't call ski patrol. He called Tasha and me.

Another coughing fit wracks my throat.

As Doug and I toss gear into the back of the truck, I give thanks he is home, rather than in the Dominican Republic, to be both my navigator and giant security blanket. We load anything we might possibly need: skis, snowshoes, Telemark boots, big packs, small packs, dog food, ropes, goggles, tent, sleeping bags, fuel, and food. I worry about how to keep Tasha's water from freezing.

We race away from Crested Butte without our search-and-rescue team, stopping briefly at the cache for radios, our only means of communication once we get on the road.

"What's Stink Face going to say when he finds out we took two radios without his permission?" I ask Doug between a sniffle and a cough. The team had made it plenty clear that I couldn't take a radio home or use them for training. And now this forces us to waste precious time detouring to pick them up.

"I'm sure they're monitoring the radio. They all know what's going on. They'll be pissed."

"Resentful, I'm sure." I say as I scrawl quick words, placing the note in place of the radios.

"Ask the sheriff if he'll give us a radio."

"Really?" Sinking into my truck seat, I know I lack the courage to ask for radios. But I smirk with pride knowing the sheriff believes in us. Over the years, as I've integrated with key agencies like the sheriff's office, my local team has punished me by not giving me a radio to use. Radios represent power. Carrying a radio is key to learning about a scene. They want to withhold that power and keep me in the dark. They are holding me back, and I know it.

With Doug accelerating on the two-lane highway out of town, I blow my nose so much my nostrils turn raw. Using napkins from the glove compartment on my nose, the wads pile up on the floor. Tasha curls up on the bench behind my seat.

Confronted with the real thing, I replay our hours of training for avalanche burials—digging hundreds of snow caves to bury CEOs, friends, and anyone willing to brave a tomb under four feet of snow. Once, with frigid night closing in on us, we buried a local lawyer too deep. As darkness approached, Tasha couldn't pinpoint his scent, nor could I locate him. We lost him for a while, scaring the crap out of me. An hour later, we found him, terrified. After feeding him chocolate for his shivering, he cracked a little smile. Doug scolded me, and the lawyer never volunteered again. Nevertheless, we had at least one hundred practices under our collective belt, with Tasha finding many people in less than one minute.

The truck rocks back and forth through the East River Canyon curves. I pump imaginary brakes with my feet as Doug negotiates icy patches on the road.

With apprehension at how to refer to us, I call Gunnison dispatch for the first time on the radio. "Crested Butte Dog Team en route. Could you please update us regarding the avalanche and where we should meet the deputy?" I smile at Doug, feeling proud I didn't fumble my words. I sound professional and to the point.

"Stand by." Dispatch has no new information on the avalanche but asks us to meet a sheriff's deputy ten miles north of Gunnison. Dispatch advises us that the Western State College Search and Rescue team has already arrived on scene, one hour east of Gunnison.

We pull over to the side of the road at the appointed meeting place, and I cough up phlegm. Spitting it out the window, I wonder if I'll be able to breathe stomping around at twelve thousand feet in elevation. Cold air rushes in. I zip my jacket up to my chin.

Dispatch updates us. The Western State College Search and Rescue team traveled six miles by snowmobile to reach the reporting party. Dispatch requests that we wait. Despite my viral infection, I pace circles around the truck. Time is crucial in avalanche burials. After two hours under snow, very few people survive. By the time we arrive with Tasha, more than three hours will have passed since the avalanche buried the four young men.

After what seems like an interminable wait, dispatch updates us again. "Stand down. Searchers have accounted for all four victims. Three dead. One survivor."

Stand down? My head hangs in disappointment.

One lone survivor who was completely buried next to a tree dug himself out. He located the other three friends with his avalanche transceiver. They were found dead beneath three to six feet of snow.

Unneeded, Tasha and I could return home and climb under a warm blanket to nurse my cough. But I want to see the command center to learn how things are done, and to expose Tasha to the chaos, the smells, and the situation. Hoping to talk to the rescuers, I want to discover what happened and why. I ask the deputy for permission to proceed to the staging area over one hour away. He agrees.

On the way up the narrow canyon, we pass a fast-moving ambulance on its way to the hospital. I wonder if it's transporting the survivor.

We arrive at a solemn winter trailhead. Emergency vehicles and a hearse line the plowed two-lane road. Another ambulance sits parked with the engine running. My friend Harold the sheriff's deputy and a few emergency-service personnel stand alongside their vehicles with their hands in their pockets, pacing in the fading evening light.

Cold stings my body. I gaze north toward the ominous-looking Continental Divide, wondering what it would be like to be up there. Low-hanging clouds hamper my view of the windswept fourteen-thousand-foot peaks. The SAR team that snowmobiled to the avalanche site over an hour ago had not yet returned. We wait for the arrival of the three avalanche victims. Two men huddle inside the ambulance with a medic treating them for hypothermia. They were not involved in the avalanche but had been skiing with the group of four, and they had responded first.

After gaining permission to speak to the two men, I enter the ambulance with Tasha and sit across from them. Both shivering men, pale and thin, stare at the linoleum floor. When Tasha nudges one, he reaches over to pet her.

I offer hard candies. "I am so sorry. You doing okay?"

One man wearing a blue knit ski hat stares forward, avoiding eye contact. I sit in silence. Tasha licks his hand. Hidden behind a beard and mustache, the blue-hat man cracks a smile. Interaction with Tasha brings him out of his stupor to relate his story.

He and his buddy had been taking a break from towing one another with snowmobiles up the mountain. "We headed back to the cabin to pack up our gear, to head back to the trailhead," the blue-hat man recalls.

"That's when we thought we heard something and noticed a cloud of sparkling snow in the air. When I went to investigate and saw the avalanche, I raced back for my friend. I searched while my buddy left to get help. The lone survivor had an air pocket. He was buried against a tree and able to dig himself partially out. I couldn't see anyone else."

Tasha's tongue licks his hand, no doubt full of salt from his sweat.

He swallows, then shakes his head sideways. "I used my beacon to find the others. They were deep, really deep. Took forever. I think their snowmobile got stuck on the slope. And as they dug the machine out, it sank deeper and deeper into the bottom layer." He gestures using his arms. "The entire slope shattered like broken glass." From the top of the ridge, near the Continental Divide, the entire snow slope ripped to the ground. The avalanche tore down fifteen hundred vertical feet, and the debris field filled with blocks as big as houses.

"They had all taken avalanche courses, too." He tells me this as I exit the ambulance, hearing the first snowmobile arrive. The machine pulls up to the hearse towing a rescue sled carrying a body wrapped in a tarp. The coroner approaches the sled. Tasha, Doug, and I follow. We stand around the tarp-wrapped corpse of one of the victims. Dropping to one knee, I whisper cooing sounds into Tasha's ear. The coroner pulls back the tarp to identify the victim. Fearing the worst, I squeeze my arms around Tasha's neck and brace myself to see a dead body, possibly mangled and bloody.

But the young man lying in the toboggan seems peaceful, his face tan from the sunny Colorado winter. His eyes shut, he looks like he is napping rather than dead from an avalanche. The coroner notes that he died of cardiorespiratory arrest—suffocation. I survive my first glance. Tasha stands by my side, disinterested.

Two other victims arrive at the trailhead, packaged in the same manner. The coroner escorts the two young men from the ambulance to the sleds. Blue-hat man identifies the first victim as Mike. He mentions the man's hometown—it's my hometown in Michigan. I never knew him or his family.

Mike wears a red shirt and sandy blond hair pokes out from under his ski hat. A round, white plastic object stuffed in his mouth looks like snow. I bend over to peer closer. It is an oral pharyngeal airway, used by medics to aid in opening an airway for breathing. The rescuers used CPR and basic airway techniques to try to revive him. But the force of Mother Nature had extinguished all life from Mike and the other two skiers.

The coroner pulls back the tarps around the other two victims and asks the young men to identify each of them. Swallowing hard, I hold back my tears as the bodies are loaded into the black hearse.

Several weeks after the avalanche, I receive a call at home from Mike's mother.

"Your sister is a friend of mine. She told me you and Tasha responded to my son's avalanche."

"Yes, and I'm so sorry." I cringe, wondering why she is calling. "How can I help?"

"I need to know why they didn't start CPR on my son."

My innards clench in a knot as my chest deflates. Silence ensues. She sniffles back tears.

"I'm sure they tried." I couldn't explain the white plastic airway device left in their mouths were proof. She didn't need to know those details.

Soft heaves of crying fill the phone for a minute before she can speak. She says, "I just saw a show on television where people in Europe were buried under the snow for several hours and survived."

I'd heard of the European avalanche. The unique conditions slammed the victims into a building where air pockets helped them survive, but they still suffered physical trauma. Fumbling with words, I try to explain why the Europeans survived when her son didn't.

"But did they do everything possible?"

I inhale a mouthful of air to muster up a soothing voice, but stammer anyway, "*Ah … duh … bah …* Ma'am, don't worry. The rescuers did everything they could."

After I hung up, I thought that I should have told her more. I could have shared the facts that the Colorado Avalanche Information

Center tags the Cumberland Pass avalanche as the state's worst avalanche accident in a decade.

I could have shared the stats that 75 percent of people die of asphyxia and the other 25 percent from trauma. I could have explained that most avalanche survivors are dug out by people traveling with them, not by rescue teams arriving hours later. At less than fifteen minutes of burial, 92 percent survive. The chance of surviving drops as more time passes. After thirty-five minutes, survivors drop to 30 percent, and after one hundred thirty minutes of burial, only 3 percent survive. I could have told her that virtually no one survives burial beneath two meters of snow because the pressure of the snowpack on the chest prevents breathing.

I could have talked about hypothermia and told her that burial in snow reduces the body temperature. Studies indicate human bodies cool at a rate of one to three degrees centigrade per hour in avalanche burials, but some estimates have increased the cooling rate to four to six degrees C. In any case, an avalanche victim with a body core temperature under ten C can't be saved.

With her son being buried so long, the chances of surviving had plunged to minimal. After the snow settled around him, his burial depth would have meant there was tremendous pressure on his chest. His mouth may have been full of snow, and even if a small air pocket had formed around his face, a few breaths could have formed an ice mask around the pocket, preventing further oxygen from coming in, smothering him in his own carbon dioxide. Meanwhile, his core body temperature would have spiraled.

The odds were stacked against her son. Nothing would have saved him, not even the nose of the search dog.

For days, the raw pain in the mother's voice haunts me. Families can come to terms with loss, but only when nagging questions about their loved one's death have been answered. When an accident happens, the family wants to reach out to somebody who's been in the field. For rescuers, compassion for the family is paramount.

I resolve to respond better to the loved ones of future tragedies.

At our next search-and-rescue training, I face my team. Stink Face huffs about not getting called immediately and demands the sheriff notify the Crested Butte SAR team leader before Tasha and I deploy. I ignore their demands and leave it up to the sheriff. My team doesn't rail at me for taking the radios. Nevertheless, Doug plunks down over a thousand dollars for our own set of radios, which frees us up to operate as the sole avalanche-certified dog team in Gunnison County.

CHAPTER 18

Death in the Field

Summer 1999
Gunnison County, Colorado

"If that girl dies because they didn't call us earlier …" My fist slams the dash. The noon July sun blazes into the canyon with sharp shadows tucked under cliffs. Tasha pants in the back seat. I fume as Doug drives the truck through the narrow canyon bounded on one side by steep rock walls and on the other by the Lake Fork of the Gunnison River. "This is the absolute worst time of the day to call a dog team. Don't they know that?"

Doug reminds me that the National Park Service is Incident Commander, not the sheriff's department, that the NPS had never met Tasha and me, and was used to calling upon law enforcement dogs in other counties.

"Don't these agencies talk?" I shout as I roll down the window to peer up a slot canyon, one of fifteen we pass. "If she's up in one of those canyons, her scent would pool down here along the road. If we were here at daybreak, Tasha would have found her by now."

Five hours ago, the cool, morning air flowed down each canyon like a raft in water carrying the scent of the missing young woman to the road. I slap my hands together to emphasize my point. "Air currents are reversed. We'll have to hike uphill in the heat to pick up her rising scent." I reach behind the seat to pet panting Black Dog.

"I know, I know," Doug answers. "They should have called us last night or early this morning."

The way he speaks sounds more like pandering to shut me up. As we near the missing woman's camp, a police car from a neighboring county approaches us.

"They called a street cop and his bloodhound for a wilderness search mission?" I go into a slow burn, sending heat to my face. "Doug. Stop the car."

The police car stops alongside us. The porcine man reaches through our window to shake Doug's hand.

"You the dog handlers from Crested Butte?"

I butt in. Jumping from her position in the back of the cab, nearly four-year-old Tasha crawls into my lap. "Yeah, nice to meet you. I'm Sue," Tasha stands with her pads on my thighs. I grimace as her tail whacks my face. "So, tell me," I shout above the noise of both motors running, "what was your strategy? What did you and your dog do?" I say, knowing his dog didn't locate the woman.

"I worked the area around the tent and the camping zone."

Duh … don't you think the family did that over the past day? I struggle to contain my outrage at his incompetence, doubting his bloodhound could even discriminate between scents. Plus, with the man's portliness and lack of athletic prowess, he has no business hiking in the canyon country cliffs. I stroke Tasha. Her fresh mountain-dog smell calms me.

Wanting the glory, to be the hero, to save this woman's life, the officer wasted prime conditions for searching, working *his* dog in the cool morning. Now, I get to work black Tasha in the midday heat, the most futile of conditions for scent. I hide my sneer of contempt behind Tasha.

At the campsite, we pull alongside search vehicles, the National Park Service, a sheriff's deputy, and two search-and-rescue teams: one from the college and mine. Meeting the new faces, I keep my mouth shut about being called so late and after the policeman and his bloodhound. Tasha greets incident command in her search vest, sporting her new wilderness and air-scent patch.

"This is a waste of time. She's not going to be on this trail," Doug complains.

"I know, but it's so dangerous to be scrambling in those cliff bands. We've got to get up high where the scent is rising." As I sling my pack on my back, I power every movement with vexation. "We're rookies. They're the cops. They're not thinking about scent and how it's moving all day." Marching uphill, the "what if" questions nag me. I chew on her whereabouts. That loss of time is crucial if she's hurt. To be effective with Tasha and large search areas, we must wait until tonight for the air currents to shift. But by then she might be dead.

Doug rolls his eyes at the situation as we trudge up the trail. Tasha's harness bell jingles as we hike to the top of a flat mesa. Dodging prickly pear cactus and hot rocks, Tasha pants, her dry tongue hanging low. No scents attract her interest.

How will I get the word out to all these different law enforcement agencies to call qualified, certified search dogs early—late at night or at first light?

One hour later into our hike, a low-flying helicopter requested by the park service whips by overhead. It drops out of sight, but we hear the thud of the blades as it hovers between the missing woman's campsite and us. A few minutes later, incident command radios that a body has been spotted below a cliff band.

The search-and-rescue operation shifts to a body recovery problem— my first. Racing back down the trail and returning to the campsite, I approach Rudy, our team leader—a strong competent Aussie who left his career as an accountant to become a ski bum and mountaineer—who will organize the technical rescue.

"I'd really like Tasha to see the body."

Rudy stumbles for words.

I fight for my position. "She needs the exposure." Reading hesitation in his face, I plead, "You know, to a cadaver."

Minutes after a thunder and lightning storm passes over with its afternoon fury, Tasha and I scramble along with a handful of my teammates. We climb six hundred feet uphill, through jumbled rock fall and into an ashy gray slot canyon. Panting, Tasha heels a few paces behind me, her hips swaying, tail half-mast.

Catching my balance, I shift my leather lug-soled boots on the unstable talus. I pause to glance back at Tasha, who hops off lead from one loose toaster-size rock to another. My chest heaves as I keep pace with my superfit counterparts in a silent march with heads down. Fifteen minutes into the hike, I note that Tasha has shifted into work mode, rather than playing, and her nose is in the air. She smells something.

We halt in the boulder field where the lifeless body lies face up. This young woman looks different than the peaceful old man in the morgue or the young men caught in the avalanche. The woman's back arches over jagged rocks, with her arms spread-eagle and legs akimbo at unnatural angles. Blue-black bruises mar her skin. Her body bloats, swollen like an overinflated inner tube, straining and tearing the seams on her clothing and popping buttons off her shirt. The ninety-degree temperature coupled with the direct sun beating down into the slot canyon has ballooned her to twice her normal size. She looks one-third human, two-thirds alien.

Her face bears a different look from the faces we saw in the rescue sleds near Cumberland Pass. The young woman's bloated, pale face contorts.

Tasha and I inch closer. We both inhale a new scent. Dead bodies emit odors different from living people. I stare. There it was … the stuff I'd read about. The natural process of death and decomposition. The postmortem bloating, the off-gassing of cells. The stench of the decaying human body. The textbooks had described it well. But they failed to note the simultaneous interplay of fascination and revulsion that lures me to move closer.

With Tasha next to me, I kneel beside the young lady, not really knowing what to do. "It's okay, girl," I coo to Tasha, motioning her to approach the body. I scan for the details of her fall in her injuries. When my pupils lock onto the woman's half-opened, fixed eyes, I gasp. The horror-struck expression sealed on her face confirms she knew she was falling to her death.

Tasha creeps forward with her front and hind legs bent, stretching her neck, uncertain, hackles standing erect. She sniffs. Her nose hovers millimeters above the woman's taut skin. Standing back to avoid gagging on the stench, I whisper, "Good girl. That's decomp."

Tasha shifts her gaze toward me, her skin stretched in concentration across her skull, eyes wide, and lips drawn back. I read comprehension of death in her eyes.

Dividing into two groups, Doug's crew sets up a low angle scree-evacuation belay station, while Rudy's crew moves the woman into a body bag. After stepping away from both tasks to find shade for Tasha under a small tree, I watch the crew struggle with the body. The contrast with the avalanche deaths strikes me again. Dug up within hours after their death, before rigor mortis, the avalanche victims' heads bobbed side to side with the sled movement. Due to the elapsed time since the young woman's death yesterday, her stiff body fails to slide neatly into the body bag. The crew must push it in and hold it down to close the bag.

Tasha jumps into my lap the minute I sit on a boulder to watch my team lower her body down the slope in a rescue litter. I stroke Tasha's forehead for comfort. The young woman will be delivered first to the coroner and then to the family.

I wonder if Tasha and I had been called yesterday, could she have been rescued alive? How can I convince authorities to call us first, before it's too late?

CHAPTER 19

All Certified and
Nowhere to Go

1999–2000
Gunnison County, Colorado

As aspen leaves spin shots of gold in the fall wind and after hiking with Tasha the past three hours, I race up the stairs to the condo to check the answering machine. No flashing light. No messages. Three months have gone by since our last mission.

"Crap." I scratch Tasha's ear. "We're four years into this. At this rate, you'll retire before we get to save a life." She senses my frustration and shoves her nose into my arm to nibble on my shirt. You'd think since we're the only certified team in Gunnison County that the phone would be ringing off the hook.

Tasha looks at me as if she could voice the same complaint.

Eighteen thousand dollars out of pocket, thirty thousand miles on the road, and nothing to show for it, Tasha and I face an uncertain future. Between monthlong stints in the sweltering Dominican Republic, I volunteer with the local ambulance and work part time at two clinics. I expected ample missions to find lost hunters, missing children, overdue hikers, and buried skiers. Instead, we wait and wait. We'd been called twice since her avalanche certification two years ago.

Flipping through the mail, I zero in on the SARDOC newsletter. It lists mission briefings from the past quarter—nineteen wilderness missions, including water searches. The certified dog teams stay busy near population centers—the Front Range with Denver, Fort Collins, and Colorado Springs; and the I-70 corridor with Vail, Frisco, Glenwood Springs, and Grand Junction. Tasha and I weren't deployed on a single one. Gunnison County only has ten thousand residents, and far fewer people to get into trouble.

With many of the Colorado dog handlers having partners, spouses, or friends working in law enforcement or leaders on search-and-rescue teams, they're guaranteed callouts on missions. Not me. I pout knowing Doug can't help me, especially from two thousand miles away. Even the SARDOC dispatchers, located seven hours away, have forgotten about us.

I wave the newsletter in Tasha's face. "Can you believe this? We're the team that needs to be out there."

Tasha lunges her snout into me again. She nips up and down my sleeved arm.

If we want to work, I'm gonna have to go knock on a few doors. I need to be like Jehovah's Witnesses or the Amway lady. Who would have thought I'd have to go sell myself and my dog?"

I stare at the avalanche paths outside my window for a minute, then grab Tasha's chin. "Who better to call upon than the source itself?"

A few days later, I prance into the Gunnison County sheriff's conference room with Tasha on lead in one hand and my computer bag in the other. Tasha wears her search vest, adorned with her WILDERNESS AIR-SCENT patch on one side, her avalanche-certified badge on the other side, and her CRESTED BUTTE SEARCH AND RESCUE patch on her back. I eye the Gunnison sheriff's patch, hoping to collect one more. I wear pressed khaki pants over low hiking boots. My orange Crested Butte SAR jacket covers a pinstripe button-down shirt, tucked in. My hair is pulled back in a ponytail from my tan face, spruced up with red lipstick and a stroke of mascara. My shirt is wet from sweat as I stand before a handful of men.

The gaggle of law enforcers from police and sheriff's departments sits around the table in blue uniforms with silver badges and arm patches. Packing handguns, batons, handcuffs, and mace on their hip belts, they lean back in disinterest.

I clear my voice. "Hi guys, thanks for having me here today." Tasha lies at my feet, yawning in the stifling indoor air after sniffing every boot, pant leg, and hand that reached down to pet her.

After the deputy introduces me, I pop up the first slide and lob a challenge with a smile. "Guys, take a look at the photo. You're probably wondering why I came all the way down from Crested Butte to throw up a black image on the wall." I scan the room for a laugh.

Nothing. So, I get right to the point.

"What would you do if your five-year-old daughter was lost in the mountains in the middle of a dark night, and a winter storm was brewing?"

No response.

"The Gunnison Sheriff's department is responsible for all SAR missions, right? So, who do you call in the middle of the night?"

"Well, Sue," one pipes up with sarcasm. "We'd call search and rescue and a dog team."

"Excellent answer. Did you know dogs comb an area three times faster than humans, saving sheriff's time, resources, and money? Let's look at the amazing capabilities of search dogs." I recite the list of scent-dog facts using my slides: their ability to discriminate between the scents of different people, the power of their scent receptors, and that dogs can even smell scent through water.

"Really?" An officer leans forward. "A dog can find someone in the water?"

"Yes. Remember, Gunnison has one of the largest reservoirs in Colorado."

"The largest," one adds. "With several drownings per year. We usually call Wendy Wampler for those missions."

"Get this." I flip another slide. "Dogs smell like we see. Where we could not smell a gram of human sweat in a ten-story building, a dog can smell that one gram of sweat three hundred feet in the atmosphere above that building."

"Is that why bomb dogs can smell ammunition residue on a coat?" a policeman asks.

"Absolutely! That's why it's taken me three years to train Tasha. It's not just about a person and her pet hiking through the mountains. This is a serious business with thousands of hours of training behind us. We can find people submerged in the water or body parts hidden in shallow graves."

I direct them back to the black slide and remind them about their hypothetical lost child. This time, the men lean forward in their seats in rapt attention.

"The black slide is night. What happens to scent at night? It flows like water in a river." I explain the movement of scent like Ann and Jenny had taught me. "The best time to call a dog team is at daybreak, when the scent flows downhill, or in the evening, when the air is more stable."

I flip to my next slide, which shows the outline of a mountain. "Normally, law enforcement calls dog teams during the day because they perceive daytime as safe. But remember, that's when scent rises to the mountaintops. We need to be called during the morning or evening, when scent drops to valley bottoms and roads, where navigation is safer." I explain that our certification tests included daytime, nighttime, and multi-subject, to prepare for real-world scenarios.

My presentation continues another forty-five minutes, and we relax into productive conversation about working together. They, too, are devoted to buying a police dog and hope I will assist in training. I have Scott to thank for giving me the confidence to stand up in a room of professionals and teach what I believe. I wind up my pitch, the men express appreciation, shake my hand, and thank me. After I pack up, I march into the sheriff's office.

"Hey, Sheriff Wilson. I have two requests." I hold up the SARDOC manual in my hand. "Since there seems to be some confusion between all these agencies—four search-and-rescue teams in the county: National Park Service, sheriff's department, Crested Butte Marshal's Office, Mt. Crested Butte Police, Gunnison Police—wouldn't it be nice to all be on the same page?"

"Sure thing. We'll adopt SARDOC's standards," he says with a smile.

Then I ask him for one last favor.

Opening his lower desk drawer, he tosses the patch across his desk and reaches for the manual. "Thanks for such an educational pitch. We'll be calling you."

In the next several months, I bring the Dog-and-Sue Show to my local police department, National Park Service, and neighboring county sheriff's departments.

"Dogs can find people in water?" Heads cock to the side, quizzical looks plastered on faces. "Really?"

Even after I share stories and slide shows about canines on water missions with dive teams, people still doubt. To demonstrate the power of a dog's scent skills with water, I organize a training session on Blue Mesa Reservoir, Colorado's largest lake, with the dive teams from the Gunnison County Sheriff's Department and the National Park Service. Based on several water trainings with SARDOC teammates on rivers and alpine lakes, I feel confident to tackle today's demonstration on my own.

On a hot, windy July day, four dive team members, Tasha, and I motor on an open aluminum rescue boat out of the Blue Mesa Reservoir marina, thirty minutes west of Gunnison. Tasha lies on her belly, front paws dangling over the bow of the boat above the small chop as wind blows her ears back, her nose lifting in the air. Over the past summers, Tasha has turned into a real water dog, learning to ride in our raft atop our camping gear for multiday trips into the Gunnison Gorge.

The dive team dons scuba gear, turning them into alien creatures. Tasha moves in for closer sniffs of their neoprene suits. She likes anything related to the water. Jon, a supervisor with the park service, pats her head with his rubber hand, cooing, "Good girl, Tasha. You going to come find us?"

Tasha pumps her tail sideways.

I hope today's training will educate law enforcement that dogs can help divers pinpoint bodies underwater and get us called to drownings earlier. For decades, wilderness-medicine textbooks referred to only two successes with cold-water near-drownings, the resuscitation of a five-year-old Seattle boy submersed for sixty-six minutes and a European woman underwater for forty-five minutes. Both were proximal to trauma hospitals. There are no reports of wilderness near-drowning saves. Most victims die after a few minutes underwater. Maybe someday, especially with all the cold, high-altitude lakes in Gunnison County, Jon, Tasha, and I could be the first dog and dive team to recover a drowning victim and pump life back into him or her. But that would require water certification, still yet on my horizon.

Dogs and dive teams form symbiotic relationships. Because cloudy, deep water limits visibility, divers feel for what resembles a corpse. Dogs can home in on the scent to reduce the size of a search area in water.

I hold quivering Tasha in the boat as three divers scoot to the edge of the craft to secure fins and breathing masks. In sync, the three backflip overboard. Tasha peeks over the gunwale, ready to lunge off the boat after the divers.

"Whoa, girl. You're not slipping away from me. Sit." Her butt hits the deck.

Collecting information for the search-dog log, in the event I ever testify in court, I whip out my water submersible Kestrel weather tool and record the outside air temperature at eighty-five degrees Fahrenheit and the water surface temperature at sixty. But the water ten feet below the surface is forty-five degrees, cold enough to seize exposed human muscles in twenty minutes. Life jackets keep potential drowning victims up in the warmer water layers.

The driver sets an anchor while the men descend. Tasha fixes her eyes on their rising bubbles. "Keep your eyes on the bubbles, Blackie."

Her stare into the water doesn't waver. She trembles.

"Good dog." I reassure her, knowing she'll lunge belly first at any command that sounds like "jump."

Ten minutes later, I see the divers' heads bobble and arms rise to the surface, our prediscussed signal to let me know they're ready. They submerse again. I release my grip from Tasha and whisper, "Go find!"

With a running start, she spread-eagles off the front of the boat, belly flopping onto the rough chop of the water, and swims for sixty feet. I keep a long leash on her, so I can yank her back if she entangles with the divers. Dog paddling like a canine on crack, she swims toward the rising bubbles. When she picks up their scent in the bubbles, she whines, then, snaps her jaws as if to bite the scent.

"Aha. That's her alert. Good girl!"

One diver pops to the surface with her schlong. The two others rise. With her prize toy clamped in her mouth, Tasha's thick black tail steers her body in a victory lap around the divers. Then, aided by my cupped hand behind her neck, she hauls herself out of the water and onto the boat's rear platform.

We practice the drill multiple times. On one drill, she beelines in the right direction, but halfway to the bubbles, the wind changes. She loses scent and, with no information, swims in concentric circles.

"Go over," I cast my arm to the right like a cheerleader. She turns to look at me. I repeat. She heads toward the bubbles. "Good girl." Directly over the bubbles, she whines.

After endless sessions swimming from the boat, I call a rest. While Tasha curls up to sleep, I eye the shore to demonstrate one last thing. My green ammo box holds the stinky, unidentifiable decomposed juices of Kimmy—a woman who had been found after several months dead, wrapped in a bed sheet in a laundry closet—a training aid I obtained from a friend. I stuff bits of the sheets in a PVC pipe with holes and cap the ends.

After the boat drops Tasha and me onshore, Tasha bolts up and down the beach investigating new smells and ignoring what I am doing. As the men watch carefully from the boat, I pluck the PVC pipe with Kimmy from my ammo box. With fishing line, I anchor the plastic pipe offshore in two feet of water and place a wind flag in a nearby willow to show me the wind direction.

To allow time for Kimmy's scent to rise, the men pick Tasha and me up and motor around the reservoir. I use the time to educate the NPS and sheriff's department teams about optimum conditions for dogs to search. "Nighttime or early morning, when the air is stable and nobody is around to add in more scents." I use an analogy to make my point: "You wouldn't ask your teenage kid to take the college entry exam on the prairie, baking in the ninety-degree afternoon sun, with the wind whipping test papers around and thirty people milling about. Similarly, dogs need calm winds and quiet water to stay focused."

Upon return, I notice the wind on the boat bears a different heading than the wind on my shoreline flag. I ask the driver to zigzag into the wind, toward the flag onshore. Kimmy's scent funnels right at us. The driver shuts off the motor as we drift.

At forty feet offshore, Tasha lifts her nose and whines. Before I can reach her harness, she launches off the boat, spread eagles into a belly flop, and swims to shore. She sprints up the shore, homing in on the submerged pipe. Before reaching it, she flips in a reverse to rush a patch of willows, then runs back into the water near the pipe.

"Go find!"

She noses the water. I jump into the water to join her, pointing, to help her find the submerged pipe. Tasha nosedives into the water, snatching the pipe in her mouth.

"Good girl! You found Kimmy." I reward her with a toss of the schlong.

Jon beams, recognizing what dogs can do. Another deputy, on the other hand, stares ahead expressionless. Maybe he's upset I'm taking away divers' glory? Or he's in cahoots with Stink Face? But using a dog might help bring closure to a grieving family.

Packing up Tasha, my ammo box, and life jacket, I head for the truck. My training aids are simple. I have no motorboat, scuba gear, team radios, county-owned truck, wet suits, or thousands of dollars in training money like these volunteer divers do. Their agencies pay for it all. I realize not only do I have to educate law enforcement agencies, but I've got to go beg for support.

Poodle Lady tells me, "If you don't ask, you don't get." She holds the gold star for charisma. Before I know it, she's trained me to push Tasha in a shopping cart inside the Gunnison Walmart and present a request for goods to the manager. Within a week, a GPS is handed to me. Marmot, the outdoor clothing manufacturer, ships Doug and me jackets after I write them a lengthy letter showcasing Tasha's accomplishments. It won't be long before Marmot anoints me as a Brand Ambassador. Backcountry Access (BCA), an avalanche rescue gear company, ships beacons, probes, and shovels and scholarship money. Ortovox, BCA's competitor, sends me a matchbox-sized beacon for Tasha. I design a harness for her with a zip pocket. I seek out a top dog food manufacturer and twenty-pound bags pile on the front door.

Doug is delighted.

Now all I need is a mission.

CHAPTER 20

A Dog's Nose

1999–2000
Boulder County, Colorado

"Holy mother," I yelp to Doug when we respond to an avalanche two days before Christmas. Ten months have passed since we responded to the Cumberland Pass avalanche that killed three college students. Looming in front of me, the conical South Arapaho Peak rockets up to 13,397 feet on the Continental Divide. Staring up at the monstrous peak, I should feel nervous. But I don't. We have trained so much; only anxiousness to get to work and find the missing hiker pumps through. Finally, a chance for Tasha to find someone and for us to prove ourselves.

A week earlier, only skiffs of snow pocked the range, but for the past six days a storm has pummeled the mountains, leaving several feet of fresh snow. Hundred-mile-per-hour winds have scoured the upper summit bare, exposing chiseled rocky formations. Standing there, I feel like a mouse crouched in front of a giant fortress.

From the peak, the spine of a ridge shoots toward us. In the lee of the ridge, a dozen steep, narrow avalanche chutes peel off. Rubble from recent slides clogs every chute. The Boulder County incident commander tries to direct my gaze to the hiker's point last seen, but because of the distance and angle, I can't locate it.

A week ago, under blue skies, two young men in hiking boots tagged the summit of South Arapaho Peak. On their descent, the storm blew in. Unprepared for the change in weather, they descended the ridgeline, battling hammering winds and disorientation from blowing snow. They dropped off the lee side of the ridge. The survivor reported his buddy had been trailing right behind him. But when they stepped off the ridge, a slough of snow had carried the hikers downslope. Thirty feet below, the leader crawled out, but not his buddy.

During the week's snowstorm, sixty avalanches have tumbled across the mountain range. Twenty-two were logged the day the young man went missing.

The survivor, who wore a court-ordered ankle monitor, claimed he looked for his buddy for hours, then gave up and descended to report his hiking partner missing in the avalanche. While the incident commander is responsible for verifying the reporting party's story, Doug and I speculate about the possibility of an argument, abandonment, even murder.

Rocky Mountain Rescue, the local Boulder search-and-rescue team, had reconnoitered at the trailhead with snowmobiles and their avalanche backcountry team at dusk to look for the missing hiker. But snow was accumulating an inch an hour. As the rescue crew slogged through midthigh snow, smaller storm slab avalanches had caught several of them. The incident commander called off the mission due to the extreme avalanche danger. The storm raged for five more days while the Boulder County sheriff and Rocky Mountain Rescue team leaders planned to go back up the mountain when the cantankerous weather abated.

Excited, I depart once again without my team, but Doug joins me. After driving to overnight in Boulder, we meet up with search-and-rescue teams on the first clear, sunny morning following the storm. At the trailhead to South Arapaho Peak, four-year-old Tasha, Doug, and I find the incident commander and a gaggle of probers, snowmobilers, backcountry skiers, and a few dog teams from other ski patrols. Avalanche technicians from Breckenridge Ski Resort plan to mitigate the hang fire danger of additional slides by lobbing bombs onto the slope where we'll be searching.

With the sun beating down and masking the below-freezing

temperatures, I don my avalanche pack, helmet, and skis to be towed behind a snowmobile to the avalanche site. The cold winter wind funneling off the Continental Divide seeps into every exposed crack, finding its way to my skin.

Tasha pants with excitement as I outfit her in her working vest with the bell. We coax her onto a snowmobile to ride in front of the driver, who uses his arms to keep her in place. I grab onto the towline behind the snowmobile, and Doug hitches behind another machine.

The parade of snowmobiles plows through deep powder snow to a staging area below the avalanche path. Tasha dismounts, running in circles and jumping on rescuers.

"Tasha, come here. You're going to slice your paws on the metal ski edges. They're razor-sharp."

She ignores me.

I click out of my skis, sinking thigh deep into the snow to wallow toward her. Clipping her leash onto her vest, I drag her back to my skis and command her to sit while I prep for the climb.

Avalanche technicians and a few support personnel join Tasha, Doug, and me—the first team on site. Tasha trails behind me, post-holing to her chest with every step. In her effort to stay up on the snow, she tries to crawl on my ski tails. As usual, I shoo her back to protect her from the metal edges.

At the base of what appears to be a medium-size avalanche, enough to bury, injure, or kill a person, I gaze upslope to assess the terrain. A narrow couloir descends from the ridge, fanning out into a debris field the size of a small grocery-store parking lot.

Tasha and I move off to a safety zone while the Breckenridge avalanche technicians and an older certified avalanche dog climb to the ridge. They sling a two-pound hand charge onto the upper chute. Ninety seconds later, the bomb detonates. A small avalanche spins downhill.

As the new avalanche comes to a stop, the radio erupts with yelling from the patroller. "My bomb just scared my dog. He just bolted over the ridge and into an avalanche chute."

A surge of anger roils through me. "He just threw a bomb in front of his dog?" I vent to Doug. "That's so irresponsible. I hope the dog doesn't get caught in another avalanche."

"But, Sue," Doug reminds me, "while he's retrieving his dog, Tasha will work the scene first, without distractions."

I give Doug a small smile, realizing the truth of his words. After six days with no one on scene, Tasha should have a clean zone to pick up scent. If the hiker is here, she'll find him. Here's our chance: she's in prime shape, has a brain of the thirty-year-old person, and is entering her fifth season.

After the avalanche technicians throw a few more bombs, they declare the zone safe enough for us to work. Unleashing Tasha to proceed, I shove the missing dog out of my mind to focus on our search job.

With a breeze wafting across the slope, I opt to work Tasha on the right side of the avalanche debris, in order to put her downwind of the potential scent cone. That should allow Tasha to home right in on the missing hiker's scent. I plan for us to search uphill, to where the avalanche started.

With Tasha anxious to bound from my hold and licking her chops, I give her the signal to start: "Go find!"

She darts off upslope, her bell tinkling. Her nose hovers two inches above the snow as she runs up the right-hand flank. Her tail wagging, she stays on task at a fast clip, forcing me to scramble to keep up with her. Doug follows. Both of us slide six-foot metal probes into the snow as we go to check for snow depth.

"I'm hitting ground at about a foot. How about you?"

"Hard to believe it's this shallow."

"With so shallow an avalanche, Tasha should smell the guy quickly." Anticipation of Tasha soon picking up a scent keeps my eyes glued to her.

Tasha speeds further upslope, nose to the snow. She works like a computer gathering data, only instead of bytes, she sorts scents. As I watch her, I realize that searching for scent is similar to searching for gold. Where we collect parts per million of geochemistry to find gold, Tasha smells certain parts per million of a decomposing body. But, where the lab reports the amount of gold bits to us, I must watch Tasha for any indication that she has struck gold. Her behavior will tell me if gold is buried in the avalanche or not.

After a few minutes of following Tasha, we reach the icy surface above the debris, where the avalanche tore everything away. Tasha slips on the ice. We try to kick steps, but our plastic ski boots fail to gain a purchase on the slick surface. I analyze the situation.

"We don't need to go higher, Doug. The guy will be in the lower debris rather than on this sheered surface."

Tasha's behavior indicates that she has finished working.

Tasha follows us onto the outcrop and sits as if waiting for the next job. She no longer sniffs. She looks from Doug to me.

"Doug, she's done. There's no scent." In the back of my mind I question whether or not she'd alerted on the cadaver.

"I agree. She should have picked up something."

"The guy isn't in this avalanche. If he were here, she would have picked up the scent on that first pass and done her double-dig alert. I'd bet a hundred bucks that he is elsewhere." Now what? I must march down to the IC and tell him our guy is not here, but that takes courage. I swallow the thought of doubting my dog.

From the outcrop, we look down on the avalanche, now bustling at the toe with a line of probers marching in sync, shoulder to shoulder—poking right, poking left, poking center—to leave no space unchecked. They advance in unison as a wall. Another dog team starts working just above the probers. The dog seems to show interest on a swell of debris. Radio chatter confirms interest in the mound, and a request for spot probers to investigate follows.

"Did Tasha miss the scent?" Horror at the idea of failure hollows a pit in my stomach.

"Go check that site," Doug responds.

We down climb the rock band back to the debris. Tasha trots with us. We pass the ski patroller who'd lost his dog. He skins back uphill with his dog dragging behind, head hanging down, tail between his legs—the opposite of a dog searching for scent. I breathe a sigh of relief that he found his dog before an avalanche caught the gray-faced golden retriever.

"Doug, that dog has shut down. He's force-marching his dog up that icy slope."

"Why don't you go tell him?"

"He's not going to listen to me." I shrug my shoulders, giving in with the excuse that they may do things differently at the ski resort. But the scared dog haunts me. After working our way downslope, we near the mound. I whisper in Tasha's ear, "Go find."

She lifts her head, her muscles tense, her eyes widen, and she runs toward the spot with the probers. Tail wagging, she circles the probers, her nose four inches above the snow.

I bite my lip, doubting Tasha's nose. We start to probe, while a few shovelers dig small holes.

Tasha homes in on us probing. She throws her nose in a hole. She sniffs, pops her nose out, and stares at me. I can't decipher what her stare means, but she doesn't double-dig. I walk away to let her determine a course of action. She follows me.

"Nothing seems to be here. The snow is aerated, chopped by probe pole holes that can release scent." Tasha's behavior tells me the guy is not here.

I want to triple check our work before making my pronouncement to the incident commander. With Tasha, we descend to follow the line of probers up the hill. I advise the probers against eating, drinking, spitting, chewing, or peeing on the avalanche as those actions can leave scents that may confuse search dogs. But the probers ignore my advice when they peel aside to rest.

Tasha checks every hole. No animation. No barking. No double-digging. Nothing.

After thirty minutes of following the probers, Tasha finds nothing. We pull her off the debris to rest her fatigued nose. To hide from the glaring sun, we hunker under trees for shade. I take off Tasha's working vest, give her water and kibble. The incident commander in the field joins us.

"Did Tasha find anything?"

"This guy isn't here." I shake my head. *There … I said it.* "He could be two hundred feet over in the next avalanche chute, but he's not here in this one. I recommend you search somewhere else."

"We'll consider it." His words ring businesslike, but lack conviction. He departs to speak with a few probers.

"Crap, Doug. What if the guy is here, and I just told IC he wasn't?"

"Stop doubting yourself."

"Tasha didn't pick up anything. That's the only conclusion I can reach." Tricky business, this life-and-death game.

After skiing down to the snowmobiles, we hitch rides back to the trailhead, where I locate the sheriff's deputy to hand him a hand-drawn map to illustrate the work Tasha performed. I circle where the other dog team showed interest.

"Tasha's behavior tells me the guy isn't in this avalanche. I suggest you look somewhere else."

"Thanks for your time. I appreciate it." He snaps the map onto his clipboard, with the same dismissal as the site commander.

My faith in Tasha's nose wavers in the next several days as we follow the South Arapaho Peak–search news via SARDOC channels. More dog teams deploy. A second and third round of probers comb the avalanche debris. The dollars, volunteer hours, and resources mount daily.

After more than a week of searching that included ten avalanche dog teams, the sheriff determines the missing man is not in the avalanche path we searched on South Arapaho Peak. Tasha and I are vindicated. Days earlier, her nose confirmed that conclusion. If the incident commanders had listened to me, they could have saved taxpayer dollars, spent on six different agencies, and the time of hundreds of volunteers during a holiday week.

A few months later, Crested Butte Ski Resort received a thank-you note from the sister of the missing man. She writes, "This has been a very difficult time for my family. But it's the care and concern of the people like you that make the situation a little better. I really appreciate all that you have done for us."

This note confirms what I've always believed. The public perceives all avalanche-dog programs the same. Unlike Canada, where one entity—the Canadian Avalanche Rescue Dog Association (CARDA)—certifies avalanche dogs, there is no such thing in America. Any ski patrol, county, and SAR team can set their own set of standards. The business is unregulated. Ski-resort personnel did pass the letter on to me, otherwise I'd never have come to know how Tasha, Doug, and I affect the lives of others.

Four months later, Tasha and I return as support for the third Elk Mountain Grand Traverse. This time, instead of returning to the Friends Hut after the race, Tasha and I go for it. We launch off the cornice like all the other racers and follow them to Aspen. We would volunteer for four years, total, before I retire her from the event.

In summer, six months after the avalanche, hikers find the missing man a couple of miles from the avalanche site. An autopsy confirms he died of exposure rather than an avalanche. I shake my head at the wasted days searching after Tasha detected no scent. But who wants to trust a dog?

The outcome, however frustrating, sends a burst of confidence through me. I can trust my dog. Her nose knows. My biggest battle looms ahead—changing how incident commanders and sheriff's departments weigh the value of dog teams.

I wonder if I'll ever have a voice that is firm enough, loud enough, or confident enough to stand up for us.

❈ ❈ ❈

Spring–Summer 2001
Colorado Springs, Colorado

At the National Association of Search and Rescue conference in the hot, dry plains of Colorado Springs, Colorado, Tasha and I enroll in Andy Rebmann's urban tracking class. He teaches canines to sniff minute particles of human scent across pavement. In the course, I challenge Tasha to track scent on sidewalks, in parking lots, and shopping malls. For several days, between dodging tornado warnings and cramming dogs and handlers inside the hotel conference room, we learn to slow down, to track step-by-step, inch-by-inch, in the sweltering summer heat, with the black tar seeming to bubble under our feet. Five of my classmates hail from the South, with bellies pooching like they'd swallowed watermelons whole and skin sagging to match their leashed bloodhounds. The class teaches me that I never want to track fugitives behind shopping malls on blacktop in the sizzle of summer, but we did learn how to find nearly evaporated scent left by humans.

Besides urban tracking over pavement, Andy's specialty is human-remains detection. Weeks after Poodle Lady had taken a course with Andy, her dog Cassidy found human remains left behind by a serial killer. With what she learned from Andy, Poodle Lady mentors me. From time to time, we tinker with our own training, acquiring a small collection of training aids. In addition to the bloody rags of Kimmy, a skullcap, and a few molars, I collect an amputated finger and a chunk of flesh. I keep some supplies in my freezer next to elk steaks from our fall hunt. I marked the training aids as *biohazard*, to make sure Doug doesn't toss them on the grill.

Because of the difficulty of procuring human-remains training aids, I also purchase synthetic scents from Sigma Pseudo. The Gunnison County sheriff approved funding for me to buy several four-packs of one-milliliter ampules that smelled like corpses—both early detection and postputrifi-cation. I also buy a large bottle of drowning victim–scent tablets to toss in the water to simulate drowning smell.

The aids help me train Tasha by myself, without asking others for help. During walkies to town on the bike path with Tasha, it wouldn't be uncommon for me to slip a tablet in a small creek without her knowing about it. On our way back home, I'd ask her to find decomp and she'd home right in on the source. Sometimes I'd forget her cheese reward, so instead I'd throw her a stick.

A few months later while hosting another SARDOC wilderness weekend at an alpine lake outside Crested Butte, I confide in Patti, the search-dog guru.

"Tasha's career is almost over, and we never get called. We've had no live finds, no avalanche missions where we actually find people. I'm so frustrated," I sulk.

"Patience, Sue," she wraps her arm around me. "Your time is coming. Tasha's in her prime. She's only six."

I pray she is right.

CHAPTER 21

Reeling in Scent

Summer 2001
Gunnison County, Colorado

At two o'clock in the morning outside of Gunnison, with the moon just past full and stars ablaze in the night sky, I escort Tasha on leash to a roadside two-stall concrete outhouse next to our parked truck. A cotton jacket and a shirt drape over a garbage can stuffed with McDonald's wrappers and leftovers. Tasha sniffs for the scent of a missing Western State College cross-country runner who supposedly jumped off the bridge. She pulls hard on her lead, snorting, nose to the ground, bypassing a handful of french fries crushed into the pavement.

"She's on him," I note to Doug. "Otherwise, she would have snatched that food." She tugs me toward the inky black water of Gunnison River flowing under the bridge, where the river dumps into Blue Mesa Reservoir.

A Gunnison County deputy and Jon from the National Park Service block off the two-lane highway over the bridge to provide a clear, safe working space. Opposing one another, their headlights beam bright, illuminating the pavement. Their red and blue rooftop emergency lights ricochet off the volcanic rock wall to the north of the river.

A few hours earlier, fifteen college students combed the area looking for their friend. Last seen partying at 10:00 p.m. on the beach, the runner announced he wanted to jump in the lake from the thirty-six-foot bridge. When friends noticed he was gone, they split up, some heading to Gunnison to see if he returned home and the others searching the shore, leaving footprints between the beach and the bridge. Unable to find him, and leaving a spider web of scent everywhere, the students found his discarded clothes on the garbage can. Unfortunately, a friend picked up the clothes, leaving one more scent for Tasha to sort out.

Glad to have any scent article for the missing runner, I glean information from the friends. "Is there any way he could be somewhere else? Is he playing a big joke on you guys? Could he have run home, hitched to a friend's house?"

"No." Six friends standing in front of me shake their heads.

"He had about four beers, that's it," one young woman pleads. "He really wanted to jump because a few of us had jumped earlier in the day. We tried to discourage him, but he wouldn't listen."

Thanks to Jon calling immediately, we had ideal search conditions. A light downdraft of warm summer wind flows off the high mountains. Only a few law enforcement personnel linger on the fringes of the search zone.

Tasha and I have just a few hours to collect our information as dawn will bring hordes of searchers, including the National Park Service dive team, sheriff's department, search-and-rescue teams, friends, family, and public onlookers gawking from the bridge. In contrast to our wilderness and avalanche training, Tasha must track on pavement and search the shoreline for scent coming out of the water. But after six years of training, Tasha and I had been exposed very recently to the two challenges we face tonight.

First, although a daunting task in the dark, we pull on our tracking-on-pavement skills from the recent urban trailing class with Andy Rebmann. And second, dabbling in cadaver training with Poodle Lady might pay off.

Tonight, because of the moist conditions and cooler temperatures, Tasha seems to pick up scent. Her strong tug pulls me forward. As Tasha drags me onto the bridge, I design my strategy. First, I want to rule out that he ran toward Gunnison, so I coach Tasha to the intersection of the two highways.

"Go find!" I command her at the end of the bridge and unclip her leash. Dressed in her working vest, her bell tinkles and her red blinker light flashes, letting me detect the black dog's whereabouts at night. Her head pops. She weaves back and forth looking for the scent while running toward the intersection of the two highways, where one cop car sits. She darts off the road, smells the bushes, checks the gravel shoulder, jumps off the embankment into the willows, and zips back to the road. She checks out the deputy and comes back to me. After ten minutes, I know the young man didn't run to Gunnison or pass out in the brush, as Tasha picks up no scent.

We return to focus on the bridge, the water, and the party spot. I clip her leash onto her harness. Aiming for the point last seen, the party spot, we search the beach. Tasha picks up the scent, her nose snorting and hovering like a vacuum cleaner on the sand. I release her leash, knowing the blocked road will protect her from cars. She takes off, milling about the party zone. Straining my eyes to keep her blinker in view, I catch up to her as she tries to sort out the scents—perhaps urine, vomit, and spilled booze.

"What do you got?"

Tasha tears toward me, but runs past me, chasing the scent back toward the bridge. Following her, we check out the sand and rock piles below the bridge. Tasha picks up scent but shows no interest in any specific site. After forty minutes, I clip Tasha back on leash and return to the law enforcement officers.

"Tasha's telling me that he's not on land. I think your guy is in the water or long gone. If you want, we'll search under the bridge. But we need to get her on a boat."

The ranger calls for a boat and driver. While we wait, I confess to Jon, "Just so you know, Tasha and I aren't water certified."

"I don't care. I've watched you work. You guys are good. I don't have a problem with it if you don't."

"Thanks, Jon. If he jumped, I think Tasha has a good chance of pinpointing him."

As we all stand around killing time, I rest Tasha and give her water. Doug and I bat around factors affecting a water search, such as wind, current, and water depth. I squeeze down on my puffer, a small plastic bottle. White baking flour squirts out of a punctured hole in the cap and wafts off in the wind. I note the direction.

But as we wait for the boat, guilt creeps in. The threat of SARDOC suspension plagues me, along with images of Wendy Wampler finding out, since this used to be her turf. "Doug, what am I thinking? I can't work Tasha in water. What's SARDOC going to say when they find out I worked a water mission without being certified?"

"They'll probably kick you out."

"But we've done enough water training. I'm close to testing, but with all the driving and pretesting, I haven't had time for the final test."

"I don't know what to tell you."

"I can't give up now." I shine a light on my watch. Four a.m. Conditions are perfect. This is our only chance. By morning, the place will be swarming with searchers.

"Essentially, you're just getting in the boat to see what Tasha does."

"Yeah, you're right. I suppose I can call SARDOC in the morning and tell them I worked this, hoping they'll bless my decision."

"You feel good about that?"

"Absolutely. I know I can't quit now. Tasha is close; she is on his scent."

After the park-service motorboat arrives, Doug, Tasha, and I ride the down current from the bridge. Under the light of my headlamp, I draw a map for the driver of how he needs to cut back and forth across the channel similar to how Tasha runs back and forth when she homes in on scent. I pull out my water buoys, each the size of a sandwich, with forty feet of string attached to a three-pound weight. When Tasha alerts, I'll drop a buoy.

Tasha and I move to the bow of the boat. She crawls in my lap. I wrap my arms around her and stroke her head. My puffer tells me the breeze flows in the same direction of the current.

The driver zigzags the boat upstream in the dark. The featureless water spreads out like an abyss, no starlight dancing across it. The bridge looms above, devoid of people. Tasha and I move to peer over the side, a four-foot drop from the gunwale to the water, not ideal for a water search. Normally, I'd want her nose six inches off the water. With Tasha so high, I worry that she might not be able to reach his scent.

I pull her close to me. "Are you ready to work?" I whisper to her and hold onto her vest to deter her from jumping. "Decomp!"

As we close in on the bridge, Tasha's behavior changes. She scoots to the boat's edge, her nose dipping toward the water. My grip on her harness tightens. She whines.

"She's on scent." I look up, imagining the young man's leap that put him about fifteen feet downstream from the bridge. Tasha's behavior amps up with another whine. She leans toward the water. I restrain her.

"Doug, this is it. Mark this with your GPS." I drop a buoy, out of Tasha's eyesight so she doesn't lunge after it. After the buoy drop, we motor beneath the bridge. Tasha lunges again to leave the boat. She whines and snorts. We drop another buoy. I observe the river movement. "He's a moving target in the current."

We continue upstream of the bridge. Tasha relaxes, a signal that we left the scent cone. I reward Tasha, take off her vest, and give her a snack. She worked hard and located the scent, now marked between the two buoys.

Near dawn we take a break, docking the boat several hundred yards downstream from the bridge. As we wait for the National Park Service dive team to arrive, I push Tasha to check our nighttime work one more time before the masses arrive.

Daylight brings a shift in the winds and increased traffic on the highways. For the first time since we arrived, I can see the bridge, the water, and the beach. As we motor toward the buoys, I squint into the water hoping to see something in the murky green river that deepens to thirty feet in the middle of the channel.

Leaning over the gunwale, Tasha whines again. "Same spot. He's here somewhere."

As we move beneath the bridge, Tasha's head pops up. She whines. I suspect the body is on the bottom where his feet hit the water. Now, ten hours later, his scent pumps straight up the water column, rising upward to be trapped under the bridge. We're in a giant scent trap. The only way out of it is to motor upstream of the bridge.

A few minutes later, a dozen people peer down at us, diverting Tasha's attention. She checks out another gaggle of people on the shore. Her head swivels to the gathering crowds, her focus lost.

"I can't work her anymore now. She has too many distractions."

"Yup. She's done," Doug agrees.

I hand over my map to Jon. "If I were going to send divers down, I'd search right here." Doug supplies the location on his GPS device, smack in the twenty-foot zone between our buoys.

Weary from being up all night, Doug and I drive the ninety minutes home to collapse. Tasha sleeps in the back seat.

But, when we arrive home, there is no time to nap. My message machine holds five phone calls regarding my intensive five-day wilderness-medicine course that's slated to start the next day. I hammer out final instructional details for twenty-two students. Some of these students hail from the Secret Service, in preparation for the Salt Lake City Olympics and protection detail to President George W. Bush. Others are combat paramedics, search-and-rescue members from the west, and a doctor.

With thirty wilderness-medicine classes under my belt—some instructing the Bureau of Alcohol, Tobacco, and Firearms and the FBI—I should be able to prep on autopilot. But the physical preparation demands collecting fresh props. I make a new batch of blood, mixing the red powder with water. I wash the dirty bandages from the last class, replace batteries in the radios, pick up the CPR mannequin heads, and get a new supply of IV bags.

The water mission, still ongoing without me, has no news.

Just before class the next morning, two black Suburbans with dark windows and huge antennas swing into the parking lot at our teaching facility in downtown Crested Butte. As six Secret Service men unload, I catch sight of an arsenal of weapons in locked cages inside the SUVs.

In the first class session, I bludgeon the students, regardless of the fact that they are the men who protect the president and that sit in my class with hidden weapons on their belts. "You're at nine thousand feet. It's high and dry. You need to be peeing every two to three hours. That means drinking lots of water."

Several students nod in concurrence.

"Don't be surprised if you have headaches or feel like you just drank a bottle of whiskey last night. Those are signs of altitude sickness. We recommend for the first three days that you reduce alcohol consumption, limit caffeine intake, eat light meals, stay hydrated, and get plenty of rest."

A few nod, but some look askance. The partiers don't want to give up the alcohol.

"By the way, as we sit here, a mission is underway." I introduce Tasha, who lies on her bed in the corner of the room. I boast about Tasha's work yesterday on land and water. A student from an out-of-state search-and-rescue team raises his hand.

"Dogs can find people in water?"

"Oh, yeah. They can track fugitives across pavement, find the tiniest molecule of nitrogen on a ski patrol jacket, and bust you at the airport if you're carrying pot or fruit. One of these nights, if I don't go back to look for the kid in the reservoir or go shooting guns with these guys, I'll show you my search-dog slide show."

During the week, we practice wilderness-medicine scenarios in the field. For the highlight, we stage a mock search-and-rescue mission at night. The students must find several victims who fell off a cliff and rescue them without conventional urban equipment.

In the evening, I listen to the police scanners and check in with the sheriff's department. The dive team finds nothing, strong currents and low visibility in the water impeding their efforts. With no results, I call SARDOC to report that I violated the biggest rule—that I got into a boat to work my dog on water without being certified. I note that the incident commanders knew we weren't certified on water.

"Thanks for telling the truth. That's fine, I'll let the coordinator know," the representative says.

Off the hook.

News of the search filters in during the week. Three days go by, and the divers exit the water with no luck. On Thursday and Friday, desperate to find the college cross-country runner, the NPS boats troll for the body by dragging nets. The thought of it makes me ill. Sometime during the week, the portly detective from the neighboring county searches the water with his bloodhound. He reports back that his dog alerted a half mile downstream from the bridge, but he can't determine if the alert is for the remains of the college kid, a dead elk, or Native American remains from when the dam's creation flooded the burial ground more than fifty years earlier.

"I'd put my money on Tasha's alert." I rant to Poodle Lady about the bloodhound team's incompetency.

She agrees.

Friday night rolls around with the traditional class finale of cold beers. The Secret Service and I plan to meet up to work at the Olympic Games next year in Salt Lake City.

After betting Doug that the college guy is still missing, I call Jon at NPS headquarters. "I'm done with class now, and we can search tomorrow, day six. What do you think?"

"Sure, let's give it one more try."

"Okay, we'll see you at 7:00 a.m. with a boat." As I joke, I add, "And a body."

With light on the horizon, Doug and I park at the bridge in the same spot where we parked six days earlier. The sheriff, ranger, and law enforcement officers have yet to arrive.

"Let's go pee." I take Tasha across the highway to the beach. She squats and pees, waddling like a duck as she dribbles a route toward the water.

She lifts her nose in the air. Nostrils flare. Her tail goes up. She whips backward to face the bridge. She snorts. She runs the entire length of the bridge, nose lifted, and bolts right down to the water.

"Doug. She's on to something." I huff to follow Tasha, my flip-flops slapping on the pavement.

Halfway across the bridge, I lean over the railing to see Tasha in the water, leaning forward as far as she can without swimming. Her profile

looks like a bullet. She whines. Then, she lets out one loud, "Wooooffff."
Her bark echoes through the canyon.

I squint to focus on the object of her attention, a lump in the water.

"Is that a log?"

"I don't know. An animal?"

"Doug, is that what I think it is?"

We cup our eyes with our hands as if they are binoculars. "Crap, it's
the guy."

By the time we sprint to the beach, Tasha paddles, circling in an eddy,
sixty feet upstream from her original alert. The chest, face, and forearms
barely float above water, puffy and bloated. After Tasha sniffs him, I call
her to shore. Climbing from the water, she shakes.

"Tasha. Is that him? Good girl. Speak!"

Giving one bark, she jams her nose in my pocket for her reward. But
I have nothing with me: no kibble, no schlong. I glance the shore for
something and offer her a spaghetti-thin stick to chase. I throw it and she
snubs the idea in favor of rolling in the sand.

We are stymied as to what to do. We can't retrieve the body, but we
don't want it to float away or sink for good.

In drownings, bodies sink at first, like a rock. In cold, deep water,
bodies may never rise, but in warm, shallow water, they can. At death, they
start to decompose and off-gas, the depth and water temperature deter-
mining the rate. Eventually bodies behave like a helium-filled balloon,
rising to the surface before off-gassing and sinking forever.

"Doug, grab something to bring him in. We need to get him before
he sinks."

After I run to the car for Tasha's search vest and schlong, I watch as
Doug pulls the body toward shore with a long stick.

One foot wears a red shoe. The other foot is bare. The face is swollen,
with half-shut, discolored eyes; and the body has bloated, doubling in size,
ripping pants and shirt open.

After a moment of silence for the young man, I radio the NPS, which
sends two rangers in a boat to retrieve the body. They slide the corpse

into a body bag, haul him onto the boat, and deliver him to a waiting vehicle. Tasha self-rewards by dragging a ten-foot branch she's pulled out from the high-water line. She sashays, bright-eyed, teeth clamped tight, wearing a half smile.

"What happened? Where is he?" hollers a man running across the bridge, his arms flapping, head swiveling.

Assuming he was a searcher who heard the news, I point him to the vehicle.

"I've been here every morning looking for him. This is the first morning I was late!"

I realize this frantic man isn't a searcher, but the father, who demands to see his son. The medic unzips the body bag to reveal the bloated young man.

"That's not my son. That's not my son."

Oh crap. I step back at the denial of grief. "That's your son, sir. We just found him." I speak up, replacing my stoic working mask with empathy.

"No," the father wails and spins on his heels to run back across the bridge. "That's not him."

I stare after the father, absorbing his pain.

CHAPTER 22

Cadaver-Dog Boot Camp

Fall 2001
Seattle, Washington

"Eeewww," I squeal to Poodle Lady sitting next to me. "Sounds nasty." The two of us snicker in whispers while we wait for class to start. "I wonder if we'll meet Priscilla Placenta, Bloody Betty, or Liquefied Lucy," I jab her in the rib. We often make up names for training aids.

"Maybe Adipocerous Adeline," she titters back. "I've heard Andy has Lawn Mower Man, who was chopped by a commercial lawn mower in a city park."

"Eeewww," we chorus together, amped up in anticipation.

In front of us, Andy Rebmann preps to start our seven-day cadaver-dog boot camp in the suburbs of Seattle. Like a pair of blond, perky twins ready to catch candy thrown to us, we perch in the front row of the classroom with our dogs at our feet, my black Lab and her large white poodle. At her prodding, I asked the Gunnison County sheriff for money to send Tasha and me to the course. He coughed up a check for tuition written from the drug bust fund, but the travel came out of my pocket.

At the camp, our classroom is packed with a hulking, buzz-cut Miami Dade policeman with his tough-looking German shepherd, a petite woman from Virginia with a shaggy dog that yaps nonstop, and nineteen other students from around the country with their dogs ready to study Human Remains Detection with Andy. Fresh off the press, his *Cadaver*

229

Dog Handbook textbook details tactics for training dogs in forensic work, based on more than a thousand cadaver-search-dog missions in water, wilderness, and urban environments, plus work in arson, explosive, and narcotics detection.

Pushing his glasses in place, Andy plops his bulk on a chair in front of the classroom. While tossing out concepts on live scent versus dead scent, he regales us with stories about working twenty-six dogs to find human remains: disarticulated body parts scattered in a forest, a serial killer's victim stuffed inside the cavity of a deer carcass, the remains of a woman missing for twelve years, and a six-year-old buried for eighteen years. Most of his stories wrap up with Andy serving as an expert witness in murder trials.

Sitting at attention, I absorb every tidbit. The murder business, so different from my goal of trying to save a life with a dog, makes my eyes bulge more with each story. When Andy dives in to the postmortem process of the human body—including decomposition, skeletalization, disarticulation, and adipocere, a waxlike substance formed by anaerobic bacteria—I scrawl copious notes.

Six years into our search-and-rescue career, I realize that search teams serve as the "cleanup crew," finding dead bodies more often than live ones. To become more proficient, I want to add a human-remains detection certification to our repertoire.

Still from his chair, Andy lobs out the week's schedule.

"We're not training with two-hundred-pound bodies. We will be training on tablespoon to sandwich-size remains. We are teaching your canines to detect the smallest scent source and training you to watch the behavior of your dog. It's 80 percent human training and 20 percent dog training. Remember, your bad shit runs down the leash."

I squirm in my seat. Under Rebmann's rules, I would be under scrutiny, not Tasha.

Andy levels his eyes at us. "If you're having problems with your dog, look in the mirror."

Slinking down further into my seat, I mentally will Tasha to be on good behavior.

"You'll need to have a name for cadaver scent," Andy barrels on from his stool. "You'll need to use that name for your dog to recognize what he or she is looking for. Whatever you call it, you'll need to be consistent with using the term for commanding your dog."

Andy elicits some names handlers currently use. Students toss out *Mr. Stinky, Mort, Find Fred,* or *decomp.*

I snicker, letting the black humor lighten the horror of death. I turn to Poodle Lady to make a joke, but Andy interrupts with further instructions.

"You also need to pick an alert—what you want your dog to do when he or she finds the scent. Bark. Sit down. Lie down. It's your choice, but you'll need to train your dog to do that. Fluency is key here. Accuracy, repetition, reliability."

Andy's point baffles me, due to Tasha's multiple alerts. For a wilderness alert, she makes eye contact, stops, and stares at me, like I'm supposed to read her mind. She rarely does a perfect field trial Lab refind, returning to lead me to the victim. For a water alert, she'll bark. For an avalanche alert, she'll double-dig. Most of the time, I use my whole toolbox to read her. I scrunch my face at what to do for cadavers.

After Andy's introduction to the week's instruction, he hands the next session off to Trudy, a petite cross between Olivia Newton-John in *Grease* and Nicole Kidman in *Dead Calm.*

"Line up outside with your dogs!" she belts in her Aussie accent, handing each of us a plastic clicker that looks like a small garage-door remote.

"What's this for?" I play with the clicker to make noise.

"Well, how do you train your dog when it does something good?"

"I say 'Good girl, Tasha.'" Tasha nudges me for a treat in my pocket. I push her away.

"Ahhh, but this is a faster, better, more precise way to train a dog."

Tasha pads to Poodle Lady, who drops small chunks of prime rib in Cassidy's mouth. Tasha body slams Cassidy out of the way to devour the meat morsels. Poodle Lady plunks a tidbit of prime rib in Tasha's mouth, just as she has done for the past six years.

"Other people can't feed your dog! Why are you letting this woman feed your dog?" Trudy stiffens up to her full, short stature. "I've been watching you and your dog. Who's the alpha in your family?"

The blood drains from my face. I point to blame Poodle Lady with my mouth agape. After all, she has the prime rib. My pocket only holds dry kibble.

"Tasha loves me," coos Poodle Lady, who drops into a cuddle session with my Lab.

"You will never feed that dog again!"

Poodle Lady's face falls.

"Sue, you need to be alpha. Otherwise, both of these two will drive you into the ground."

I gulp and wither inside. Tasha licks the grass for remnants of prime rib. Six years of allowing Tasha to dominate me. Seems like my role in my family is subsidiary to my alphas—Tasha and Doug.

"Tasha needs to respect you, and she doesn't. We have to reverse that. Time to step up, Sunshine. Your turn to be alpha dog." Grabbing Tasha by the leash and me by the arm, Trudy leads us away from the group.

"Sit," Trudy orders my Lab.

Tasha slaps her butt on the ground. In that same instant, Trudy snaps the clicker. "Good girl," she addresses Tasha before turning to me. "Sue, you don't always have to have food as a reward. That's why she's heavy. Verbal rewards work, too. But the key to the clicker is that it can reward faster than the human voice and the physical giving of a treat. The clicker is used to teach obedience, but it can also be used in scent detection. Now, it's your turn."

"Okay. Um. Tasha, down."

Tasha drops her belly to the ground.

I click.

"Your timing is off. Try it again. Click just as she does what you want. Praise can come after."

I repeat, this time clicking just as Tasha hits the ground. "Good girl, Tasha. Good girl."

What I really want to say is "Good girl, Sue." The clicker holds the potential to change years of bad behavior. We practice another ten times with the clicker to reinforce how it works. Tasha learns fast. So do I. As Andy sidles up, I reinforce the clicker response.

"Hey, don't feel bad, Sue," he says. "After thirty years of doing this stuff, Trudy's the only obedience trainer that gives me results. That's why she is here."

To adapt clicker training to cadaver work, Andy sets up eight identical cinder blocks lined up in a row outside our lecture room. Wearing gloves as protection from the biohazard, he inserts grayish-white waxy adipocere—formed by the decomposition of soft tissue in dead bodies subjected to moisture—into a woman's nylon stocking. He then places the nylon into a small PVC pipe, with holes to allow the scent to escape, and tucks it into the hole of cinder block seven.

I walk the line of cinder blocks with Tasha, clicking when the cadaver scent attracts her attention at the seventh cinder block. We each do five rounds to reinforce the cadaver scent. After resting Tasha to prevent nose fatigue, I convince her to give me a clear alert, the same bark she learned in avalanche school.

In the afternoon, after another obedience session with Trudy, we return to a new lineup of cinder blocks. But this time Andy refuses to tell us which block hides the cadaver bone. Tasha must tell me where it is.

"Check," I point Tasha at the first cinder block and repeat the command for the second block. Seven blocks go by with no alert. I scowl at the blocks, wondering if Tasha missed it. On the eighth block, Tasha sniffs, stops, pops her head, turns to me, and belts out one loud woof.

Smiling, I click. Tasha charges my pocket for her reward, but instead of food, I give her a happy dance.

After running through the cinder block routine several more times to reinforce the alert, I watch the Miami officer train his dog to drop next to the cinder block. Lying down protects the crime scene evidence from contamination and the dog from potential harm. When the German shepherd lies down next to the cadaver block, the officer gives a lackluster *rah-rah* reward. The dog seems bored.

At the next station, my name is called. "Sue, watch this!" Facing her toaster-size pooch, Trudy balances a cooked hamburger in one open palm and a cooked hot dog in the other. No buns. After she and her dog lock eye contact, she lowers both hands to the dog's nose level. Neither Trudy nor the dog waver from each other's eyes. "Your dog will do this before she leaves, too."

"No way! My dog would dive-bomb the burger."

"Try it. When you call your dog's name, what do you want your dog to do?"

"Uhhh, good question … Look at me, I guess."

"Does she?"

"I don't know. Sometimes. The truth is, I've never really known what to do with her stare. It's so intense. Often times, I look away because I don't know what she wants. It intimidates me."

"When you call your dog's name, you want your dog to stop her action and look at you. For instance, if your dog is on the other side of a highway with heavy traffic, you should be able to call her name, and she should stop and stare at you to wait for the next command."

"I like that."

Trudy plops Tasha to face me at two feet away. "Sue, put your hands behind your back with your clicker. Then, say 'Tasha.' When Tasha looks you in the eyes, click immediately and say, 'Good girl.'"

Simple enough. "Tasha."

Tasha eyes looks to both sides, tries to angle behind my back, skims at my chin and over my head, and turns away to the side again. *She's looking everywhere but at my eyes.* Then she pulls out all her tricks: sitting, lying down, jumping up, barking. She knows I have a thimble-size piece of meat behind my back. She most likely figures she'll stumble on what I want her to do sooner or later to get that reward.

"Sue, don't say anything. The minute she looks into your eyes, click."

Tasha fiddles a bit more, acting quite human in her avoidance of eye contact. Humans get nervous looking into each other's eyes. So do dogs.

Then, Tasha glances into my eyes.

I click. "Good girl," I chirp several times to congratulate her.

After walking in a circle to release Tasha's tension, we repeat the exercise.

"Tasha."

She instantly looks in my eyes, and I click. I tweet praises like a bird. She lunges at me, and I give her the treat.

"Do this at every opportunity. By the end of the week, you'll be holding food in both hands for a full minute while she maintains eye contact."

"Really?"

"Really."

The next day, we crunch a few dry leaves under our feet as we train at an abandoned lot. Over the week, we've been introduced to human remains from freshly dead to several weeks dead. Today we'll teach the dogs to find cadavers that are buried, sitting on the surface of the ground, or hanging in trees. Outdoors, Andy wheezes on his stool.

"Remains don't always show up where you expect. Perpetrators have stuffed human remains inside dumpsters, buried them in shallow graves, poured cement patios over them, and shoved them in trunks of cars that were then rolled into rivers. Plus, suicide victims hang from trees. What bad humans don't know is that canines can find them."

Some of Andy's descriptions curdle my stomach; others tweak that black humor.

For the first problem, Andy buries the cadaver parts in PVC pipe under a thin gravel pile. After giving Tasha the command, "decomp," I straighten with confidence, knowing she'll nail the scent due to the similarity between rocks and avalanched snow.

She homes in on the scent in seconds. I click. With her paws, she flings loose gravel aside.

"Tell her to knock it off," Andy demands. "She can't dig for the cadaver. That could be a crime scene."

As I run to stop Tasha, she lets out her one-bark alert and unearths the PVC pipe. Clamping the pipe in her teeth, she parades, tail wagging and chin high.

"Drop it," I bark, my face blanching.

She continues to prance with her prize.

Grabbing her, I pry the pipe from her mouth. "Should I reward her for at least finding it?"

"Yep. But next time, don't let her dig it up."

"But I can't dissuade her from digging; that's my alert for avalanche burials. Will I mess her up for avalanche work if I try to keep her from digging?"

"If you're going to work human remains for law enforcement, your dog can not contaminate the crime scene. That's just the way it is."

I shrug my shoulders, unsure that I really want to work crime scenes. While cadaver dog teams can find more work than avalanche teams, the creepiness of homicides makes me cringe.

Later that day, Patty Placenta hangs above the dogs' reach in a rhododendron bush. A tiny portion of a placenta is tucked inside a PVC pipe, which is camouflaged in green to force the dogs to rely on their noses rather than eyes.

"Decomp," I whisper to Tasha a hundred feet from the bush. Moving her into the downwind position of the scent, I watch as she zeroes in on Patty in seconds, narrowing her zigzag through the scent cone. Dropping her nose into the bush, she flares her nostrils with a couple sniffs.

I click.

Tasha lets out a giant bark. I hoot, jump, rah-rah, and give her a handful a kibble.

"Isn't that interesting, Andy? She dug on the buried cadaver but gave me her bark alert for this one."

"Pay attention. You missed her subtle whine when she couldn't reach it. Don't ever dismiss that."

I add her whine to the list of Tasha's inconsistent alerts in my toolbox.

As a light afternoon breeze wafts across the third session's search area, we play hanging-bone-in-the-tree game, using small shards of human tibia and fibula in the PVC pipe that dangles seven feet in the air. Andy shuffles to sit down on a stool.

"We never train our dogs to look up. But I've worked so many suicides where the dog circles the tree, not knowing what to do. If I'd trained my dog to look up, he would have alerted, and we would have found the victim faster."

After whispering "decomp" to Tasha, I step back to let her work the search area as she has many times on wilderness problems. Finding the scent cone, she zigzags to the tree and circles it once. Amping up her speed, she repeats her circle, her eyes glued to the ground. She loops once more, then whines.

"Wow. There it is."

"That means she's close," Andy analyzes her behavior from his seat. "She can smell the scent but is frustrated because she can't find it. Kind of like a baby who can't crawl but wants a toy in sight."

After Tasha pops her nose in the air several times, she hops on her hind feet, slapping her front paws on the tree trunk. She whines again.

"Sue, hit your clicker. Ask her if that is decomp to entice the alert."

"Tasha, is that decomp?"

She whines and jumps.

"Tasha, speak."

She whines.

"Tasha, is that him?"

She lets out a rip-roaring bark. I praise her with cheers.

Andy lowers the PVC pipe from the tree while Tasha watches. When she sniffs the pipe, I reward her with a click, verbal applause, and kibble.

On the last day of camp, I earn one of the four spots to be evaluated and tested by Andy. The other handlers will be observed and tested by his helpers. The final test's search area sprawls across a wooded park with broad lawns sliced by sidewalks. Tasha and I play in the shade while we await our turn.

After twenty minutes, Poodle Lady returns from her test, her head hanging and Cassidy trailing behind, off leash. My shoulders drop when Poodle Lady grimaces.

"I should have known. Cassidy went squirreling."

"You're kidding?"

"I should have known she was chasing a squirrel. I saw her wagging her tail and told the examiner that she found the cadaver, which she hadn't. Automatic fail."

My mouth drops. No words come out. Poodle Lady's failure stabs me with nervousness. *If Cassidy can fail, what are Tasha's and my chances?* My hands fumble as I fasten the vest on Tasha.

"We're doomed. I am asking my dog to find a teaspoon of cadaver scent when for six years I've been asking her to find two-hundred-pound men with plenty of stink. How is she going to find a tiny sliver of scent?"

"Look, you and Tasha will succeed. She works so fast compared to my dog. Pay attention to the first thirty seconds. She'll tell you everything you need to know."

As I walk Tasha on lead to our testing site, all pride from last night's champagne celebration at making the cut filters off in the breeze. In its place, my stomach roils.

"Decomp!" I unclip Tasha's leash, just as I do in the wilderness or on avalanches. Tasha takes off in a charge, the bell on her vest tinkling. She races back and forth across the lawn, searching for scent.

Crap, I should have kept her on lead to control her. She isn't going to stop to find a teaspoon of scent. But I hold my ground to watch.

Tasha zings one way, circles another, races out of sight into the woods, comes back, circles around, and doubles again into the woods. Following her into the woods, I spot Andy sitting on his campstool beneath a tree.

"We're close. Okay, Tash. Decomp. Where is it?"

Tasha whips around, goes to Andy, and then bolts out of the woods.

I wait. Then call her back with another decomp command.

She exits the woods again. She ping-pongs back and forth, in and out of the woods. But no alert. I sigh.

"I think we failed. She's not showing me where the scent is."

"I agree, Sue. She went right by it with no alert."

"I guess she considered you the hamburger and the cadaver the bun. She found you instead of the cadaver."

Andy hands me my evaluation form with a giant *fail* written across it. My heart sinks.

Later that day, I reflect upon what Poodle Lady said. Everything we need to know happens in the first thirty seconds. I question if this could be true of humans? Then I think about Doug and his behavior six years ago on our wedding night at the cozy, historic hotel, a distant, nonintimate encounter. Back then, I brushed it off and blamed his lack of affection on a week of entertaining friends and family and the stress of his job.

Now, Tasha and I face each other two feet apart for an unofficial hamburger and hot-dog test with Trudy. I plan to try for one minute, locking eye contact with Tasha while she ignores the food, but I'll settle for thirty seconds.

"Tasha." I stretch out my arms in an iron cross, hamburger in one hand and hot dog in the other, while I stare right at her eyes. She locks her dark brown eyes onto mine. No blinking. No wiggling. No licking her chops. Neither of us flinches.

"Good girl." I repeat the words over and over in a soft voice. In my head, I count down seconds, but they seem to stretch into hours. During the stare down while chanting the good girl mantra, I lose track of time in order to keep verbally reinforcing Tasha's behavior.

Tasha and I bond with our eyes. In a latch of trust and unconditional love. I feel like I've stepped up a notch, and Tasha respects that. We meet finally on common ground.

"Sue, it's been a minute," Trudy interrupts.

With a huge smile, I inch my hands lower in front of Tasha's nose while still maintaining the eye lock with Tasha. As if connected by steel, her eyes rivet to mine.

"Free." I release her. Jamming her nose in my hands, Tasha devours the meat in two gulps without chewing. Trudy hugs me.

"Awesome. Now that's what I'm talking about. You're the alpha dog now."

Tasha and I dance. I sing. I whip out the schlong. We roughhouse together. Trudy's lessons were worth the price of the trip and they take a lot of the sting out of Andy giving us a failing grade.

Two days after I return home to teach another wilderness-medicine class, the Twin Towers of the World Trade Center in New York fall, and I receive a call to respond. But I decline. It's not my mission.

A few weeks later, an envelope in the mail from the United States Secret Service arrives. Caressing the official letterhead with my fingers, I read:

> Along with my six colleagues, I just got back from the wilderness-medicine rescue course. I just wanted to boast about this incredible course of instruction and the fantastic individuals who provided it. After twenty-five years of public service, I have never been in a more comprehensive or professional class than the one provided by Crested Butte Outdoors, LLC.

I hold the one-page document near my heart. I did it. I am fluent in dog and teaching.

CHAPTER 23

Finding Gold

Fall 2001

Big Blue Wilderness, Gunnison County, Colorado

Freezing rain descends in the dark. Temperatures plummet, warning of an impending October blizzard. Exhaling exhaustion with every breath, I snug my jacket tighter. My hair drips in wet strings on my face as I oversee my twenty wilderness first-responder students, working to problem-solve the week's final scenario. After three hours of slogging through muddy slopes, we wrap up the mock mass-casualty, mountain-disaster simulation and head home. Tasha, too wet for her copilot seat, flops in the truck bed.

I fall through the condo doors with stinky dog in tow. Tasha shakes brown droplets on the white walls. After a hot shower, Doug serves me dinner and together we dive under the down comforter aching to love and to sink into sleep. Just as I doze off, the phone rings, and I peek at the clock: 10:15 p.m. *Crap.*

"Gunnison County sheriff is requesting you and Tasha to respond immediately to help locate a twelve-year-old hunter who's missing in the Big Blue Wilderness."

Law enforcement has done their job. Tasha and I face perfect conditions for a live find. We'll be part of the first group on scene, before the scents from tons of searchers contaminate the area. The young boy has two factors in his favor: his dad marked the last point where the boy was seen, and he immediately called for help.

241

After a three-hour drive on mountainous back roads, with alternating heavy rain and large, wet snowflakes slapping the windshield, we arrive at the hunters' base camp at 2:00 a.m. Strong winds reduce visibility to fifty feet. Doug, Tasha, and I step out of the truck's warmth into four inches of fresh snow blanketing the ground.

The family of the young hunter clusters in a wall tent with a wood stove, while a sheriff's deputy serves as incident command, organizing four members of the Western State College Search and Rescue team to support Tasha and me.

Details unravel from the family, their tense faces piling their desperation on us. The young hunter from Denver, Josh, wears a light jacket and a fanny pack around his waist with a pint of water, a few candy bars, and some matches. He carries a rifle. His ankle-high boots and his cotton pants will be soaked by now.

Before departing the top of the plateau one mile above, the father pointed out the general location of their camp, their destination. The father, older brother, and Josh agreed on an SOS signal, if needed: three rifle shots in a row. Hunting abreast, the team of three walked a hundred yards apart from one another, with Dad in the middle and Josh on the right-hand side. Just before dark, the young hunter disappeared. After two hours passed, the father contacted the local sheriff. The father divulges that Josh lives with his mother in Denver while he lives in Gunnison.

My search antenna jumps—this could be a family kidnapping.

The storm, intensifying in fury, with whiteouts of sideways-blowing snow, elevates the urgency of our deployment. Doug, my navigator for the search, pulls out the topographic map. From 11,500 feet, the vast, meadowed Alpine Plateau plunges down into canyons 1,500 feet deep with volcanic-rock cliff walls squeezing down into thick forests. The father points to a location on the six-square-mile plateau, the last spot he saw his son seven hours earlier. As the dog-team handler, I run various possibilities in my mind for where the young hunter might be.

At 2:24 a.m. Doug, Tasha, and I arrive by truck at the top of Alpine Plateau, along with several other searchers and the father in the sheriff's car. As I open the truck door, the map flies out of my hands. I chase the map, stomping it into submission in the snow. Zipping my oversize parka to buffet me against the forty-mile-per-hour gusts that spiral the wind chill to zero, I reach into my backpack for my goggles and scarf. Tasha cowers behind me for shelter.

While our GPS indicates that we stand on top of the plateau, the darkness prevents us from seeing beyond the glowing circles of our head-lamps. The father verifies the location where the trio started to hunt ten hours earlier.

I slip Tasha into her working harness with flashing neon light and bell. Planning to keep Tasha on a leash instead of working her freely where she might disappear in the vast wilderness, I clamp onto the lead while clipping it to her with a carabiner, determined to prevent potential failure or injury from her running free. I flip her blinking red light on. Her bell tinkles as she shakes. Doug's nod of approval boosts my confidence in the perfect conditions.

I present Tasha with one of Josh's socks. "Tasha, go find!" The gusting wind demands that I yell her command.

Tasha picks up the boy's trail in minutes. At six-years-old, she pulls strong against the leash, her nose pinned to the ground, her tail down and ears back. Her breathing heaves hard and fast. Due to the altitude, my breathing labors, too, as I struggle to keep up with her pace.

The snow curves over lumps, basketball-size rocks, slowing our progress. Several hundred yards later, I pull back on Tasha to allow the other four searchers to catch up. Safety demands we stay together.

I use the lag to watch Tasha's nose working. "I think we need to go this way."

"No, we just came from there," Doug shouts over the roar of the wind. He fumbles with the GPS. "I can't believe you forgot the compass. We need that for backup."

"You're the navigator," I snap back, knowing quite well that I, not Doug, am responsible for every aspect of my search-dog mission. Experience has shown me that GPS units can fail due to dense tree canopies, low clouds, or dead batteries. A compass, my misplaced staple from my search pack, can pinpoint a location faster. Every minute we fuss over our location is another minute lost in the search for Josh. The battle of wills between Doug and me continues until the rest of the crew catches up. As if on cue, Tasha charges away, pulling me back into the search and dropping a shroud over our feud.

After two hours of hanging onto Tasha's lead while she drags me across a mile of terrain, dropping in elevation, she beelines into the shelter of dense timber. With a whine, then a hard tug, Tasha alerts on a footprint in the snow, protected in the large trees from wind drifts. I examine the imprint as if we found gold.

"A footprint." Finally, we have proof of what we've been tracking. "Your nose is amazing, Black Dog." The tension in my shoulders falls away. I swivel toward Doug to brag about Tasha's find, my headlamp shining straight into his eyes, causing him to flinch.

"I'm so glad you didn't let her run loose. She would have been here hours before us and long gone by the time we got here." Doug praises me with a pat on the back and Tasha by offering her a drink from his water hose. She laps up the spouting driblets.

We radio base camp to verify Josh's foot size and shoe pattern. The footprint seems to match the description.

Looking skyward, I hope to glimpse a few stars, maybe the North Star to get my bearings, but clouds prevail. Tasha pulls on her leash, ready to continue searching.

We press on. My headlamp follows Tasha's footsteps while Doug's and the other searchers' lights shine to the sides of Tasha's tracks to illuminate any footprints. Every so often, their lights shine on another footprint in the snow before we lose them again under drifts.

At 5:00 a.m. it's still pitch dark, but Tasha shows no signs of slowing down. Her tug on the leash is as strong as when we started. She drags me down into a steep-sided, narrow creek bed that's clogged with thick forest. We crawl through a snarl of tree snags. Jammed with crisscrossed fallen timber, the bowl-shaped depression hunkers out of the wind. Footprints—perfectly preserved—appear once again.

In the bowl, Tasha's behavior shifts. Her breathing increases, and her nostrils flare. She snorts like a pig, confirming she is either hot on the young hunter's trail or in a giant scent trap, a dog handler's worst nightmare. Due to the depression, I suspect a trap where scent collects. We push forward.

Near the creek, I slide across slick boulders. My boots sink deep into mud. Fallen trees force me to crawl on my hands and knees. Despite the route, I cling to Tasha's leash, trusting her nose.

Doug finds butt marks where Josh slid over a log. Tasha leads us to tracks where he tried to climb up precipitous banks. His scent trail and sporadic tracks zigzag back and forth, up and down. He had wanted out of this obstacle-filled mess. So do I.

When thick willows bar us from going further, we retreat from the haphazard maze. I lead Tasha back to the butt marks. The bowl had collected plenty of scent, which means that the boy had hung around rather than passing through the depression. Tasha just needs to find him.

"Come on, Tasha. That's our kid. Work it out."

As Tasha sniffs around the log, I fear the worst. Josh has been in the elements for nearly fifteen hours. Hypothermia from the storm or trauma from a fall could have already killed him. His potential death collides with my ego, which craves a live find to validate us.

Tasha alters her behavior. Her nose leaving the ground, she lifts her snout toward the night sky. Her short, stubby front legs paw the air. Her shift from tracking to air-scent tells me we're close: I must unclip her to let her find the boy in the scent pool.

I look at Doug for confirmation. He shrugs.

With my hand on the carabiner, I hesitate. If the boy is alive, he might fire his gun in fear at a black dog appearing in the darkness. But letting her go free is the only way we'll find him.

I unclip her leash from her harness, releasing her to work out the scent pool. Like a mom waving goodbye to her little girl as she drives off to college, I unleash my dog. She has all the skills to find the boy. I step back, holding my breath.

Shoulder to shoulder, Doug and I watch as Tasha, under the luminescence of our headlamps, lifts and lowers her head, jumps logs, cuts back and forth, and sorts out the scent. She ping-pongs around the basin. The cold air stills in the basin. Snowflakes fall in silence. Tasha weaves up and down the sides of a steep creek embankment trying to figure out where the scent trail departs from the bowl. I lock onto her, intent on her every move.

Soon, her black body leaves the range of our headlamps. Her red blinking light disappears in the dark. The tinkle of her bell fades.

"Shit. I shouldn't have let her go."

As if Tasha heard me, her blinking red light, moving as fast as a bullet, returns to me. My shoulders drop with relief.

Stopping at my feet, Tasha stares at me, her chin high, her eyes fixed. My headlamp reflects in her dark brown eyes. The other searchers cluster around us, all headlamps illuminating Tasha. Her stocky black frame freezes like a statue. Her loud panting quiets.

I wait. Wanting to elicit Doug's opinion whether she is alerting or not, I pinch my lips together to fight the urge. Tasha needs to direct me, tell me what she wants. The black dog and I lock eyes in silence.

"I'm over here." A small, muted voice whimpers from the darkness.

All of our heads pop up. Our headlamps blind each other's eyes until we deflect the lights off into the woods.

"Josh, is that you?" Two of the searchers shout in a chorus.

"Over here."

With her blinking red light guiding us, Tasha whips around and leads us downhill toward the voice. She drives her wet nose into Josh, curled up in a tight ball. We can barely distinguish his form, his camouflage clothing concealing him under a tall pine tree. He shivers, his clothes soaked. His rifle—never fired—sits beside him.

Tasha licks Josh's face and hands. Then she nags me for her reward. As the searchers move in to aid Josh, I give Tasha a handful of dry kibble. She chokes it down as if she hasn't eaten for weeks. I remove her working vest to let her know that the work is over. Surveying the slope for broken limbs,

I hurl the biggest stick for her. Tail wagging high, Tasha returns to Josh with the stick in her mouth.

After swapping Josh's wet clothes for dry ones, we feed him a packet of GU Energy Gel, an easily digested and long-lasting blend of carbohydrates similar to the consistency of cake frosting. I radio to base camp, "We found him. Tasha found him." Cheers clog further transmissions. "Doug, *we* did it. *She* did it. A live find." I jump into his arms.

He bear-hugs me. "I'm so proud of her, you," he whispers in my ear.

Tears of joy roll onto my face. This was so much better than any letter from the Secret Service. When Josh perks up from the GU, he tells us he's ready to walk out.

On our slow walk to the road, where he'll be met by his father, I quiz the quiet boy. "So, Josh, why didn't you fire your gun when you became lost? Did you hear the three gunshots from your dad?"

"But I wasn't lost. I heard the gunshots and thought my brother was lost. I didn't want to fire my own gun to confuse things."

I elbow Doug. "He's in denial." There it is. The first stage of being lost. Despite the darkness with the wind blowing cold snow, I ponder his adolescent boy psyche. He didn't even go through the other emotions and reactions of being lost like confusion, anger, fear, bargaining, and acceptance. We found him before all that happened.

Stepping onto a dirt road, our faces are aglow with the joy of our accomplishment. Tasha, wagging her tail, chin up and wearing a crooked half smile, drags her ladder-size log to the waiting vehicles. After profuse thank-yous from the family and a shuttle back to our truck, Doug, Tasha, and I drive off Alpine Plateau. As my fingers fondle Tasha's soft ear, I muse over the high standards required for certification. Josh had blended in so well with the forest in his camouflage pants that, if he had not been able to ask for help, searchers could have walked right by him. Tasha's well-practiced nose was required.

In the back seat, Tasha snores. Doug and I glow in that heady mix of exhaustion and elation. I call Scott, my business partner, and scream into the message machine. "Tasha made a live find! I'll be there when I can." I reach for Doug's hand. "We did it." Tears form in my eyes.

We drive into Crested Butte just in time for teaching the last day of the wilderness first responder class. Last evening's mock search-and-rescue mission in the rain seems like days ago.

En route to the classroom upstairs in the fire hall, I pause to greet a few of the ambulance and fire crew. I look for Stink Face but don't see him. I blurt out the night's events, tell them of our success.

"After six years, we made a live find. We just saved a kid's life." I pat Tasha at my side. She wags her tail.

"We heard something was going on," the boss on duty responds. "Henry, go grab me that fire hose and bring it over here." The two men continue with their business as if I hadn't said anything more than "hello." Dumbfounded, I take a deep breath to combat the sucker-punched feeling in my stomach. Why do I need their validation? Snapping Tasha's leash taut, I march her upstairs.

Tasha's nails clack across the classroom. When my students and Scott see us, they jump to their feet with applause. Hoots of approval fill the room. They demand a play-by-play account of the search.

As Scott launches into the debriefing of the previous night's mock mission, I sit in the back of the room. While the response of my students gratifies me, the reaction of the downstairs team irks me. Egos can get huge in the search-and-rescue world. Everyone wants to be the hero, and every time somebody else manages the feat a lot of us wonder, "Why wasn't it me?" I know what Tasha and I accomplished, but I feel empty, depleted. How could that be? I'm not lost. I'm not unloved. I'm not unhappy. The bottom line, though, is that I'm not aware of how lost I actually am.

Our skills are once again validated when we serve as a volunteer avalanche dog team for the Salt Lake City Winter Olympics, using my Secret Service buddies as victims for Tasha's training while we are there. Four months later, fourteen-year-old Elizabeth Smart is abducted from her Salt Lake City home. No one calls us to find her. As the news unfolds about her disappearance, I rant to Poodle Lady about the lack of a search-dog-team federal database. I know Tasha could have found Elizabeth the night she went missing, just like she did Josh.

It's too bad I didn't get my hands on Laurence Gonzales' book, *Deep Survival*, when it was first published. He knows what it is to be lost, and it should be required reading for everyone who goes into the wilderness hoping to find the missing—or who might find themselves *among* the missing.

If I had read it earlier, I might have realized that I was as lost as Josh was, and that, like that lost boy, I was in a state of denial about what was happening in my own life. On the surface, everything looked great. I had accomplished what I set out to do—teaching Tasha how to find someone alive, teaching myself to find my voice, to be less dependent on Doug, to be an educator. Shouldn't that complete me? My business was successful and my partnership with Scott was thriving. Students were flocking in from around the world to fill our seats. Shouldn't that be enough to satisfy my business aspirations?

My marriage looked great from the outside. Friends would see Doug and me sitting close and holding hands at a restaurant and ask, "How do you do it? Work together and play together? You guys look so happy." Amy and Poodle Lady constantly reminded me that Doug was a keeper. And, I agreed: he was a keeper. Yet, deep down, something was wrong about our relationship. But admitting there was a problem was almost impossible for me … because I didn't know what was wrong. So, like people who are lost, I pressed on, chasing after the one mission with Tasha I didn't have under our belt: an avalanche find, alive or not. I'd do anything to keep Black Dog and me on our path—it was the only thing that felt truly right.

But time breathes down on us. Over the next two winters, I continue offering courses and working at the clinic with occasional geology stints in the DR. I had acquired my teaching credentials with the American Institute for Avalanche Research and Education (AIARE), a nonprofit organization designed to save lives through avalanche education.

With missions few and far between, Tasha and I jump at the chance to showcase our avalanche prowess by participating in the Purina Incredible Dog Challenge: Winter Adventure—an avalanche rescue challenge at Vail Ski Resort. Tasha and I make it to the final round, but unfortunately lose the competition to a ski patrol team from Keystone resort because I force an alert. I coerce Tasha to dig where she doesn't want to. Impatience and the need to win gets the best of me. Now I am the pack of cur dogs the bison wrangler told me about, circling and placing way too much pressure on Tasha. Have I been doing that to her all along? After the dog challenge, I tell my mentor Patti, the organizer of the event, "Sorry I let you down. You probably put all bets on Tasha and me."

"I was hoping," she says and gives me a hug, understanding more than anyone all the weeks, months, and years we've spent training. "But, remember, this is just practice. So, you didn't win. Tasha's one hell of a search dog. Trust her. Step back and let her do the work."

With Tasha in her eighth year, I feel like a failure, even though we have made one live find in the wilderness. I still haven't found my real gold: finding someone buried in an avalanche. I question whether or not we can. Tasha's clock ticks. At forty, so does mine.

A few weeks later, as a March storm leaves behind eighteen inches of champagne powder snow piled on successive storm layers, I stand in a dimly lit lecture hall, teaching an avalanche course. Students learn. I throw lollies as rewards for the correct answers. The night is a success.

Driving home from my talk, I peer through an ice-crusted windshield as wind whips snow horizontal. I stop the truck to clean off the glass. As I reach for my gloves, my phone beeps.

CHAPTER 24

Practice Makes Perfect

Spring 2003
Hancock Pass, Colorado

The next morning frigid wind sprays snow in my face as I cling to my snowmobile driver, my arms locked around his waist. Scraping ice from my goggles, I peer around him at Tasha riding on the snowmobile in front of us. She pokes her black head under the arm of her driver to check that I'm still behind her. Doug, Patti, and her dog have joined our small convoy as we traverse a snow-buried road up Chalk Creek to Hancock Pass, a remote saddle at twelve thousand feet in central Colorado's rugged Sawatch Mountains. Sixteen hours ago, a snowmobiler was buried in a half-mile-long avalanche.

I scan the ridges above, lit up with early morning glow. Each one loaded with a snow cornice, threatening to thunder down upon us. I hold my breath as if to prevent other avalanches from careening down to bury us under blocks of immovable snow. Even without digging a pit to assess the snow structure, I see signs of extreme avalanche danger—winds drifting more snow onto cornices and some slopes shot with fracture lines, with rubble below.

Even where avalanches have swept off the top layers, leftover snow clings to ridgelines like loose boulders perched above the snowmobile trail, menacing, lurking with potential to release without warning, to bury us in successive snow slides. As a searcher, I remind myself it's a risk I assume.

251

Still, the hang fire threat chills me more than the cold temperature.

Peering up at the ridge, I see evidence of this past week's abrupt weather changes that make us targets for hang fire: five feet of new snow in the high country, with shifts from cold to warm, cloudy to sunny, no wind to high wind. I glean some comfort that we have an avalanche technician on the snowmobile behind me to keep watch as we search, like the goose with its head up while the rest feed. He can alert incident command if slopes start showing movement. If there is time.

After bouncing eight miles on a snowmobile up a valley corridor toward Hancock Pass, I dismount and kiss the snow, thankful hang fire didn't clobber us en route. Tasha rolls on her back in the snow, her short legs kicking the air. I examine the avalanche above me. It is indeed huge—the equivalent of eight football fields long and several wide. Above the pass, an unnamed mountain rises with a cliffy slab of vertical rock that collects snow as winds rush over the Continental Divide. Wispy clouds whirl, blowing snow to intermittently block the view.

When the avalanche happened, the three survivors scuffed through the debris with their boots and one probe pole to search for the missing rider, but they'd had no clue what to do. In their panic, one guy raced on his snowmobile eight miles back to his rig, sped down the icy mountain road, and crashed his truck. Another rider, emotionally distraught and hypothermic, plunked his butt in the snow, unable to help. The leader of the foursome probed the slope alone. None of them had avalanche beacons for locating each other, and they had no rescue gear on their snowmobiles. Hours after the slide, thirty search-and-rescue members from Chaffee County scoured the slope until their sheriff called off the mission due to high winds, dipping temperatures, and darkness.

On the cliffs twelve hundred feet above me, a jagged fracture line on the convex peak reveals the top of the slab avalanche. Below the cliffs, which are now sheered raw of snow, a half mile of white debris sits packed with lumps, some the size of basketballs, others more like baseballs, in an irregular moonscape. A fresh layer of snow, deposited overnight by swirly winds, spreads across the bumps like frosting. Clumps of trees are scattered throughout the avalanche path. A coating of thick, stucco-like snow plasters the firs—evidence of the tremendous wind that the avalanche had pushed down the slope.

My shoulders drop. I want Tasha to get this find, the mission we've prepared for since I first harnessed her on the snow, her paws the size of quarters. But the immensity of the avalanche reduces the chance for success. Canine successes are rare when the slide is this big and deep. Time also pressures us. We'll have only one pass to find the guy before a horde of family members, friends, and searchers show up and churn up the slope and any potential scent. If the victim had been wearing an avalanche beacon, he would have been found yesterday. Tasha's oblivious to my anxieties. She pounces on Patti and her dog, Sandy, when they walk over to meet me.

"Snow is fifty feet up in the trees," I belt out to Patti. "This is the biggest avalanche I've ever seen."

"One of the largest in my twenty years."

I consider the nuances Patti reads in the scene as we discuss strategy. With the winds blowing across the slope, we plan to walk our two dogs toward the last point seen via the outside, downwind perimeter on the slide's left.

The avalanche technician from the Colorado Avalanche Information Center, Doug, Patti, and I assess the weather and talk about how we can stay safe in the event of hang fire. With a few new arrivals to schlep gear, we leave our skis behind to trudge in our ski boots, uneven snow making us struggle for solid steps. The chill forces me to wear my helmet, three layers of winter clothing, and my heavy pack, filled with survival gear.

The Chaffee County sheriff is counting on us to find the snowmobiler before another set of March storms pummel the mountains. The pressure to perform weighs heavy on me.

"Sit," I pull Tasha to the side. Slapping her black butt onto white, chunked-up, machine-tracked snow, she whines, and then hops up to dance like a nervous horse, too excited to obey. I offer her leniency as I feel pretty much the same way. Tasha squirms in her harness, licking her chops. I command her attention, "Ready girl?" Her eyes fix on the whirling wall of snow that's blowing in our faces. She leans into the make-believe starting gate. Her nose points straight ahead, ears up, eyes wide open, skin stretching slightly across her skull. She stomps the snow like a racehorse ready to run. She licks her chops one last time.

"Go find!"

Tasha hurtles uphill, her bell jingling. Nose to snow, she combs the toe of the avalanche.

Patti, Doug, and I stomp forward while the dogs work in front of us. As we climb the left side of the slope, more snowmobiles enter the staging area below us. People mill about like ants. They are forbidden to enter the avalanche until we are done working the dogs, a promise I'd extracted from the sheriff when he solicited my help.

The dogs move out like runaway vacuum cleaners, scouring the surface of the avalanche debris with occasional grunts and snorts. We lag behind, huffing in the thin air, breaking into a sweat as we hurry to catch up. Whirling winds buffet us. At the far-left side of a tree island on the slope, Tasha's bell stops ringing. She shows interest by jumping up on a tree trunk, then whines and claws at the bark. Jumping away from the tree, Tasha lifts her nose upward, pointing to the top of a tall evergreen. Attacking the tree, she jumps on her hind legs as if wanting to climb it.

Pulling out my probe pole, I shove it down in the snow. It hits rock within three feet.

I contemplate Tasha's behavior. Whining does not equal her double-dig alert.

"Patti, Tasha has something here."

"Hmmm ... my dog is not so interested. We'll keep moving."

Tasha whines again. I probe a ten-foot-radius around the tree, hoping to find an arm, a backpack, something. "It's so shallow, he can't be here, but she's telling me there's scent."

"Just mark it."

Patti and Sandy climb upslope. They traverse across the avalanche. "Sandy's got some scent," she yells. The duo aims for the apex of another clump of trees in the slide's center.

After marking the spot with a flag, I practice patience and hang back to avoid forcing an alert on Tasha, my failure at the Purina Dog Challenge still raw. But Tasha, apparently done checking, notices Sandy's growing interest above a group of trees in the center of the path. Tasha, perhaps in competition with Sandy or just curious, dashes to join in, her bell tinkling as she prances across the avalanche. Patti keeps pace with Sandy. Tasha follows Patti. Both dogs round the uphill side of the tree island and turn into an opening cut by previous avalanches. When the dogs enter the swath of cleared timber, both Patti and I recognize a change in their behavior, from sniffing the snow to lifting their noses skyward.

"Patti, they're on scent."

"Yeah, I agree. He's here somewhere."

The dogs chase scent, noses to the snow, zipping across the path in a zigzag motion, as if bouncing off both sides of the path bound by timber. Tasha's bell tinkles nonstop. Swiping sweat from my face from the rising heat within my body, I shed my pack to strip a layer and analyze the wind. "This wind is pushing the victims scent into the trees?"

"My dog's telling me his scent is blown everywhere." She explains how trees can collect blown scent, acting like chimneys or giant scent pumps. She tells me to imagine a decomposing body as a log burning in a wood stove. In a stove, the smoke rises, and the wind outside takes it away.

"This is so complicated. It's like looking for a morsel of cheese in the forest."

"This is where we need to combine all of our search-training tactics— wilderness, water, avalanche, and cadaver."

All tactics. Patti's words put a new twist on the search, but just as I think I might be figuring something out, both radios erupt with demands from the incident command in the staging area. We can see that the crowd, far down the slope, has tripled in size. Many hold shovels, ready to march up. Trailing behind me, Doug notes thirty minutes has passed.

"Sue, how long are you going to hold these people back?"

I glare at him and address my radio instead. "A few more minutes. The dogs are on to something."

Patti and Sandy peel left into the wind, toward another patch of trees. I stick to the right, determined to not interfere with Tasha. As I secure my parka to the outside of my pack, Tasha disappears into the dense trees.

"Crap. She's gone." Shouldering my pack, I leave Doug behind and follow Tasha's paw prints in the snow, stumbling as I go. Her jingle grows fainter. Diving into the forest, I squeeze in between trees, slipping and sliding, catching my jacket on sharp branches. Every second seems to stretch into an hour, but I stay hot on her tracks, stopping only to gulp thin air and listen for her bell.

The tinkle ends.

My heart bangs like sticks on a tight drum, a mix of exertion and fear of losing Tasha. The sound diminishes my ability to hear, even the wind overhead. I round a cluster of trees to where the tight forest meets the open slope.

With feet planted into deep snow, Tasha's tugging on something, something that's not budging. I peer closer. Tasha has latched her powerful jaws onto a black glove sticking out of the snow. She yanks. Nothing gives.

She tugs on a glove attached to a red sleeve of a jacket that disappears under the snow. Tasha wrenches one last time, and the glove releases from the corpse, exposing a white, stiff hand. Plunging backward, Tasha lands on her bum, the glove clamped in her mouth. She rights, tail wagging, and prances toward me.

I stare at Tasha, my mouth gaping in a muddle of surprise, and fumble for my radio. "Patti. Doug. We found him. Come help."

A change of movement in the staging area below catches my attention. Like a kicked ant nest, searchers pop into high speed, a swarm climbing up the debris field.

"Oh, shit, what have I done?" I cover my mouth looking for Doug to rescue me from my blunder. Instead of broadcasting to everyone on the radio that we found the snowmobiler, I should have cackled our customary, "Wa-whoo," the signal we use to locate each other in the woods. A few minutes to reward the dogs would have been ideal. But no, I blew it. It also would have been nice to conduct a quick investigation of the avalanche burial and a moment of silence in memory of the snowmobiler.

Within minutes, an army of people attacks the site. Friends of the victim look horrified when they glimpse the partially exposed arm poking out from beneath the snow. Searchers wield probes and shovels. What had been a controlled, organized search scene mutates into chaos. Doug takes the lead to dig around the victim's body. My snowmobile driver jumps in to help. Soon a hole big enough to fit a Volkswagen bug and a posse of men surround the man, who is slammed against the tree trunk. Impatient for her reward, Tasha attacks me by nipping at my arm, then pant leg. I stand rigid as a statue, torn between the desire to lavish her with verbal cheers and maintain solemn respect for family of the dead.

As searchers dig through the compacted snow, more of the missing man becomes visible. The force of the avalanche has plastered him to the tree. His head sits upright, but his body doubles unnaturally upward, with his feet above his head. No doubt the impact snapped his spine, pelvis, and femurs. Searchers use a saw to remove tree limbs to get at his body. The grisly scene curdles my stomach, but I surrender in awe at the power of the avalanche.

Watching the diggers, I realize probing would have never found the snowmobiler, given how pancaked into the tree he was. The family would have had to wait four long months for his body to melt out. At least Tasha saved them that misery.

Done with her work, Tasha demands my attention. I remove her harness to reward her by first scratching her back then tossing the schlong. She leaps two feet into the air to catch her toy.

Looking across the avalanche where Tasha alerted, I see the path of the scent. Using my geology skills, I draw a mental map of how the scent had dispersed across the slope. It drifted up this tree, like smoke in a chimney, and blew across to the next place to land, the group of trees where Tasha jumped on the first tree.

As diggers work to extricate the dead man, other snowmobilers sweep the slope with a metal detector to locate the missing machine. A few minutes later, shovelers crawl a hundred feet upslope to extract the snowmobile. Abandoning the schlong, Tasha chases snow chunks that are flinging in the air from the diggers. I trail behind. She devours each chunk with her front paws as they hit the snow. Determined to save the snow-mobile, the victim's friend turns the key, still in the ignition. The beaten machine starts up and he drives it back to the trailhead.

Rescuers slide the lifeless, stiff corpse, covered by one small airplane blanket, into the metal toboggan. Members of the local search team ski him down the slope to a waiting snowmobile and coroner.

In the aftermath, I talk to the group leader who left his friend for dead. His face pinches with guilt when I ask about the accident.

"I couldn't find him. I couldn't sleep at all that night. Every time I closed my eyes, I could see him freezing under the snow." His voice cracks as he says, "There's no worse feeling than leaving your buddy behind."

He describes his buddy as a thirty-three-year-old construction worker, husband, and father of two small children. He rode a borrowed snowmobile for his third ride ever, tagging along for the adventure. Since only two of the four riders owned avalanche beacons, they voted to leave them behind. "We had a plan at lunch. We intended to stay on packed trails rather than high pointing or riding cornices, after hearing snow collapse under our machines, but we couldn't resist when we saw this field of untouched snow. After lunch, when I crested the pass, my snowmobile got stuck. One of my buddies made it to the pass to help me, but another couldn't get up and turned around. When our last rider gunned up toward us, the slope gave way. It was horrible—the wave of snow must have been a hundred feet high when it hit him."

I keep my mouth shut.

"Yeah. Watching it was almost worse than when I got caught in an avalanche last year." He catches his breath and adds, "The exact same spot."

As Doug maneuvers the icy roads home, Tasha curls in the back seat, sleeping with a soft snore, belly full of prime rib leftovers. I vent my pent-up anger for the snowmobile leader. "How could he be so stupid to not read all the warning signs—a collapse of the depth hoar layer in the snowpack at lunch, riding over a convexity, new snow, high winds, avalanche terrain. He violated all of them. How could those snowmobilers not be paying attention?"

"I know. It's just that the adrenaline rush takes over, probably a little testosterone poisoning and competition, the lure of powder ..."

"Easier to ignore the warning signs than to acknowledge it, right?" I tap his leg for a response.

We settle into silence. I rub Tasha's ear, admiring her ability to drop into sleep so fast. Still antsy from the adrenaline of the day, I stare out the window while sorting my thoughts. Sad, confused, elated, lonely. I wish Doug would grab my hand, kiss it, and check in with me emotionally. But he doesn't. *Maybe our relationship is evolving into search-and-rescue partners rather than marriage partners.* I push down my feelings to finish the debrief. "I had an epiphany out there. Knowing where Tasha finds scent is just as important as where she doesn't find it. It's no different than exploring for gold: where we don't find gold says as much as where we find it. This mission was really a giant wilderness problem, and we figured it out.

"And another thing, I'll never blab into the radio again. I swear, I lost control. Not cool. Next time, I need to calm down and compose myself before I speak."

For once, I'm my own judge, and it doesn't feel anything like *being* judged.

My lips spread into a grin, despite the gruesome circumstances of the snowmobiler's death and the haunting memory of the expression on his face. While most avalanche dog teams never get the chance to deploy on missions, Tasha and I did. Our moment arrived. Tasha's nose performed. From the time her toes first touched the avalanche debris to the time she found her gold, ninety minutes clocked by.

I turn to Tasha and rub her ear once more. "Pretty impressive, ol' girl."

CHAPTER 25

Second Time up the Mountain

Spring 2003
Ptarmigan Pass, Colorado

"Are you joking?" I pull the phone from my ear to stare at it. The dispatcher's report sounds like déjà vu. Only three days have passed since our last mission.

"Dead serious, ma'am. One snowmobiler, not wearing a beacon. Just happened on the Continental Divide."

I look at my watch. *Not even eleven o'clock in the morning. Another avalanche has buried another snowmobiler.* The same mountain range, same sheriff, same search-and-rescue team, same set of circumstances, only two miles from the last one. Unseasonably warm, my thermometer in the shade reads above freezing.

Doug interrupts packing for his trip to the Dominican Republic early tomorrow morning to flip open the gazetteer to locate Ptarmigan Pass. On the map, the pass sits a stone's throw from Crested Butte, but getting to the trailhead requires another three-hour drive, around to the east entrances to the Sawatch Range.

A helicopter pickup would make the trip much faster, less than an hour. But the Colorado Avalanche Deployment Program uses a helicopter that is based in Frisco, Colorado, three hours away, and the program normally deploys dog teams from Summit County. Heaving a woe-is-me sigh into the phone, I don't bother asking about a helicopter. After all, this is a wilderness avalanche, for which Tasha and I have the skills. I don't dare risk losing the opportunity.

After requesting the Chaffee sheriff send the Gunnison sheriff a teletype asking for my services, the dispatcher gives me pertinent details of the avalanche. A husband and wife each rode snowmobiles. The husband, who wasn't wearing an avalanche beacon, opted to high-mark a thirty-eight-degree, east-facing slope—in other words, he'd tried to run up the slope till his snowmobile wouldn't go any higher. Halfway up, he disappeared beneath a tumbling wall of snow. Having noted his last seen point, the wife and other nearby snowmobilers tried to find him. A deputy with his police dog responded to the avalanche, but in his rush, he slid off the road and rolled his vehicle, sending him to the hospital. Another local dog handler brought an untrained, uncertified German shepherd to the scene but hadn't found anything yet.

"Are you calling any other *certified* dogs?" I clip off each word to bite back my anger.

"We're working on it."

After hanging up, I slam the phone in the cradle and holler for Doug.

"Aghhh. These people make me crazy with their untrained dogs. That policeman had no business risking his life or his dog's life just to be a hero. And who is this handler with his pet dog?" I shout to Doug as he enters my office. "By the time we drive there, it will be midafternoon, a horrible time to work Tasha. Winds will be swirling around."

"You could decline."

I glare at Doug.

En route to the Sawatch Range trailhead, I call Patti Burnett to join us. While driving up the narrow, icy, two-lane road threading into the range, a tow truck passes. I swivel my eyes to catch a look at the smashed-up deputy's car in tow. I wonder what happened to his dog.

We pick up chatter on the radio channel from the avalanche scene. At the news the pet German shepherd alerted in the snow, I grind my teeth.

They report the depth of the debris at more than twenty feet in some locations. Then we hear a request go out for fifteen-foot-long probe poles—the six-foot personal rescue probes everyone is carrying can only scratch the surface of the debris field.

I turn around to check Tasha, still sleeping. I squeeze her front paw, the one with the middle nail that's bent sideways from all the years of digging. "You ready to go to work? This is going to be a deep one."

When we arrive, familiar sheriff vehicles pack the scene, along with search-and-rescue vans, sleds and trucks, and various snowmobile trailers and crews. Bystanders and friends of the victim huddle in small groups, holding onto one another. I high-five the same snowmobile drivers who transported Tasha and me three days ago.

"How's the avalanche danger in the area?" I ask my driver.

"There's nothing left to come down. The entire mountainside slid. Over three-quarters of a mile of avalanche. It's safe now."

Not waiting around for Patti or a snow-safety technician from the avalanche center, we load up for the eight-mile snowmobile trek to 12,400 feet. During the twenty-five-minute ride, I mull over strategies as I eye Tasha traveling ahead of me on another snowmobile. Doug follows us. The sun cants lower in the midafternoon western sky. As we approach the site, far above tree line, I gape at the mountains. It looks like the entire range has avalanched.

Avalanches are all about releasing tension on a slope. When one avalanche goes, it can trigger an adjacent one in a *sympathetic release.* Fractures within the snowpack propagate along weak layers, causing slope failure elsewhere. Entire mountainsides, several miles long, can avalanche sympathetically with each other—even from somebody's stupidity around the corner. An overwhelming sense of relief comes over me—my driver was right, there's almost no chance of hang fire.

We dismount the snowmobiles on an island of bare rock, not covered by avalanche debris. The wind howls, gusting up to forty miles per hour, through the chaotic upheaval of the debris, a monstrous, serrated jungle of broken slabs. Thick angular cakes of snow sprawl across the slope. It looks like a thirty-story concrete building collapsed here—a disarray of jagged shapes point skyward in a mishmash of angles, creating a horizontal climbing gym.

Like Hancock Pass, Ptarmigan Pass sits on the Continental Divide. In the three days since we worked the Hancock avalanche, twenty-four inches of new snow has dropped here. And it wasn't like nobody knew or understood what was happening; avalanche forecasters had bumped the danger rating from *considerable* to *high*.

In contrast to Hancock, where we arrived in the morning to a fresh scene in a barren bowl in and above the trees, the Ptarmigan scene is bedlam. Eighteen snowmobiles in a rainbow of colors rim the toe of the avalanche. A dog runs across the slope. A counselor attends to the wife. At least thirty people—search-and-rescue teams, plus sheriff deputies—mingle around, some probing the slope haphazardly. Amid the chaos, I locate the incident commander.

"I refuse to work Tasha while that shepherd is on the slope." I deliver my working terms. "I don't know the dog, and I don't want the threat of my dog getting beaten up. It's either Tasha or the shepherd. Your choice."

Within minutes, the owner secures the shepherd to a snowmobile. I thank him for his cooperation.

To gather more detail, I speak with the wife, a woman in her early forties. Five hours had elapsed since her husband went missing. Her haggard face reveals the strain.

"He's a snowmobile racer. He's an expert. He's really, really good," she convulses into sobbing. "And he's outraced two avalanches before."

Rubbing her arm in consolation, I wince internally at the bravado that propels people to take such risks. She soon calms down.

"I sat on the rocky outcrop at the base of the bowl while he high-marked the bowl above," she resumes. "This is our favorite area to snowmobile. We saw an avalanche come down last night, but not in the bowl."

"So, what happened?"

"I got off my sled and called for him. But couldn't see anything. The mounds of snow were so high," she whimpers. "I tried to walk on the debris, yelling and digging with my hands. I didn't have a shovel. A couple people snowmobiling nearby showed up to help with probe poles." Her voice chokes again. "Now, all these people."

I pat her shoulder and ask, "No beacon?"

"Neither of us have beacons. We've been snowmobiling for years and never needed them."

I bite my tongue. The wife grabs my arm.

"Please help me. He still could have an air pocket in there."

I let her cling to hope, despite knowing the grim statistics to the contrary. Staring up at the haphazard probers on the slope, I run the pros and cons of the scene through my head to design my strategy. Tasha, primed from the Hancock avalanche, should be ready, but the scene will be complex because the other searchers will have laid down so many scents, and the huge slabs of snow, hefty winds, sunbaked slopes, and arid high-altitude air all make Tasha's job more difficult. With only two hours to search before dusk, I must get to the point last seen.

Confirming that location with the wife, Doug, Tasha, and I head uphill over the debris to the point last seen. I kneel down and whisper into her warm ear, "Go find!" We pass random probers. Rather than leading, Tasha struggles to keep up, slipping off the blocks. After yanking her up yet another slab by her harness, I check my watch. Twenty minutes have gone by, and she hasn't picked up any scent. Halfway down the avalanche path, thirteen probers are lined up along a twenty-foot-high swell of heaped snow slabs. Tasha aims for the men. She checks out each one, jamming her nose in the probe holes. In the lineup, she targets the sheriff, squaring herself in front of him with a stare. *Why him out of all the men?*

One loud bark comes from her mouth.

"What?" Confusion pinches my face, and I shrug at Doug. Not interest. Not an alert. The last time Tasha gave a walloping one-bark alert was when her tossed schlong caught out of reach in a tree. The sheriff looks at me to explain what Tasha means, but I have no clue. Deflecting a response, I step two feet back.

"Let's get back to work, Tasha."

I let Tasha make the decision about how to proceed: dig, sit, bark, or move out? She reverses to walk toward me. At her direction, we head down the ridge, away from the probers, toward the far edge of the avalanche.

Winds rail against us. Swirling, they race every which way across the slope, swapping direction at a whim. That means we must cover every inch of the monstrous slope on foot to pick up scent.

Five minutes later, as we zigzag downhill, Tasha tenses. Her nose lifts into the air. She snorts like a pig, sucking up scent like a vacuum cleaner, and points her tail upward. She zooms back and forth following the scent. But she can't seem to find the scent cone. I stand back to watch.

The radio clogs with traffic, fast-paced blips of conversation between Patti and the sheriff. The sheriff tells her to stand down as he plans to call off the mission in a few minutes due to the increasing winds, dropping temperatures, and oncoming darkness are making the search more dangerous by the minute.

"Doug, Tasha's on scent. We can't stop now."

"I'll go talk to the sheriff and tell him we need Patti."

I look at my watch. Four p.m. On scene one hour. Doug descends to the side of the avalanche to speak to the sheriff. Tasha bolts after him.

"Tasha!" I scream. "You can't abandon your job!"

As she hits the interface between the avalanche debris and wind-scoured rock, I see her nose pop. She touches the rock and loops just as fast back to my feet. Like a fox on hind legs, she drives her shoulders and front paws into the snow at my feet.

Snow flies. She digs faster.

"Doug, Tasha's got a double-dig! Grab your probe pole." Racing back uphill, Doug stuffs his probe pole into the snow, pushing it deeper and deeper. With his hand at the tip of the six-foot pole, he drives the probe all the way into the snow. Only an inch of metal remains. I stare at the visible inch.

"Don't tell me he's not there?"

"I'm at six feet."

Doug gives one last little shove, pressing the tip of pole beneath the snow. The pole springs back in his hand.

"I just hit something. I think it's him. Sue, you try."

I pull the pole out and poke it back into the snow two inches to the side. Again, when my probe hand reaches the surface of the snow, the pole springs back.

"It's got to be him. Feels kinda squishy, humanlike, rather than rock or snow." But we'd had little practice with the feel of a human as we rarely used probes to locate a hiding victim due to the sharp points that could pierce skin or puncture an eye.

Tasha digs and snow flies. Intent on her prey, her eyes focus in front of her paws. She breathes through her nose. Doug and I move another foot sideways to confirm a soft body beneath. His scent had to have gone straight up through the snow in a perfect vertical line. I glance at my watch for the umpteenth time: ninety minutes from when we started.

To avoid my mistake on the radio from the last avalanche search, I send Doug to ask the sheriff for five shovelers. They dig around the probe pole opening a crater the size of a small room. To avoid getting injured by the shovel blades, Tasha and I play schlong off to the side. After a few fetch games, Tasha chases after scoops of snow flung into the air from the giant pit. A crowd, including the wife, rims the hole. Doug uncovers the snow-mobiler's helmet first, the face shield crammed solid with snow. The wife melts into a quick bout of weeping, but quickly recovers herself with what she most likely already knew to be true. Relief and grief tangle in her face.

I peer down into the hole. Pride swells that Tasha homed in on the man's face.

"Is it okay for Tasha to say 'hello' to your husband?" I ask the wife.

"Yes, of course."

I lead Tasha, who falls into the pit, for her reward and closure. She sniffs him.

"Good girl, Tasha. That's decomp." I whisper privately in her ear. She snaps her head around to stare at me, barks, and dives for my chest for her reward. I pull out the schlong again, tossing it up out of the pit for her to follow. She leaps off the edge and into the air, missing the schlong and landing on chunky debris.

As the diggers uncover the rest of the body, I stand with the wife, my arm around her. Tears flow.

In contrast to the Hancock Pass snowmobiler, this body reveals less trauma. One glove is missing. Boot laces dangle untied. One boot clings halfway off his foot. Flat on his back in the snow, he appears peaceful, almost as if he's making a snow angel.

Tasha returns, schlong clamped in her teeth. She demands more reward. I toss the schlong again. When Tasha begs for more, the wife breaks into a small, awkward smile and throws the schlong.

For the second time in three days, Doug and I prepare to depart the Sawatch Range for home, but this time we're in a hurry. Doug takes off for the Dominican Republic in eight hours. In the chill of descending darkness, the wife embraces me once more. Then she kneels and hugs my chunky dog, who clamps a large tree limb between her teeth.

Empathy is my teacher.

CHAPTER 26

Finding My Voice

Summer 2003
Boulder, Colorado

Spring melt has begun when I retrieve Tasha from my friend Kathy's suburban house in Boulder, Colorado. I have just finished a work stint in the Dominican Republic logging core (looking with a hand lens for itty-bitty specs of gold and other precious metals in rocks, drilled from hundreds of feet underground).

Two weeks ago, when I'd said goodbye, the expression of betrayal and desertion in her dark-brown eyes haunted me. She was belly down on Kathy's porch and didn't even lift her head or thump her tail when I kissed her. She knows my departure routine: the shirt, roller bag, briefcase, fancy shoes, her bed placed in the corner of some friend's house. I've left her twenty times over the years, at times dropping her off at my friend Suzanna's house, complete with a swimming pond and her field-trial Lab, Molly, other times holding her in my lap as we fly to my parents' home in Michigan.

Now reacquainted, I allow her to ride in my shopping cart at Whole Foods, my traditional second stop after returning from the tropics. I pick out a steak for Tasha and organic green salads, sushi rolls, rustic bread, gourmet cheeses, and ice cream for me. A nice change from *arroz con habichuelas*, the traditional dish of rice and beans, served daily in the DR.

Teaching three back-to-back wilderness courses over the next thirty days lies ahead of me, so I load the cart with staples to get me through. When the phone interrupts my shopping, the sheriff's department from a neighboring county asks if we could help with a search. A forty-seven-year-old woman, last seen in her apartment. There was a break-in, now she's been missing for several days. The department suspects foul play and is uncertain of exactly where to start the search. When the sheriff confesses that they've barely begun to search, I decline, but offer to help later when I get home and the parameters narrow down enough to make us more useful.

Four days later, the deputy calls again. "Her disappearance is surrounded by very suspicious behavior. We still can't rule out homicide, but until we have more information, we won't need you."

Homicide. My hackles go up at the creep factor. Many calls for searches never amount to anything, but I phone Doug in the DR to update him on the potential victim search.

"No way. I don't want you being involved with cops and criminals. You have no business helping these guys solve a homicide. It's too risky. You'll end up in court trying to validate Tasha's work."

"You're right," I admit. I've heard all the stories in cadaver class about dog handlers testifying. "But I'm not like that Michigan dog handler who planted cadaver parts at scenes for glory and got arrested by the FBI. I have meticulous logs."

"Just don't get me involved …"

"But what if this happened to your mom or sister?" I imagine him shaking his head at me like a schoolteacher admonishing a student. But I fumble to find the right words to explain to Doug my compulsion to help, to learn all I can about forensics.

On the tail of a demonstration of Tasha's trailing skills to the Gunnison Police Department, several water training sessions, the completion of two medical courses, the return of Doug from Latin America, and preparation for a five-day class, a reporter from the *Wall Street Journal* arrives to write a story on our next course. During dinner, my local search-and-rescue pager goes off. A young man is missing in the mountains near Crested Butte.

"Want to go on a real mission?" I challenge the reporter.

While I outfit her with appropriate mountain-search gear, dispatch calls again, this time to cancel our participation. The missing man is now considered armed, dangerous, and a potential suicide.

"Welcome to my world," I shrug my shoulders in explanation to the reporter, who lives in an apartment building in Manhattan. "We never know what we're getting called to or where we are going. Tasha's had a great career. And this month, we've been called for a possible homicide and now a suicide."

"I thought you just looked for people buried in the snow?"

When she had visited me years ago to write an article for the *Wall Street Journal* about the effects of high-altitude sickness on tourists traveling to Colorado, she knew I was only pursuing avalanche certification.

"A lot has changed since then." I smile. "We do it all."

The next day, students from around the nation cram into our instructional room. They include another Secret Service agent, a paramedic, the journalist, and a dozen others. I settle into a rhythm, lecturing on general principles of wilderness and rescue medicine, the core foundations of our courses.

Scott keeps his radio on, searching for chatter regarding the whereabouts of the potential suicide victim. Several times, he disappears out of the room to concentrate on the ramp-up of that search. As the urgency to find the armed man escalates, so does the call for resources, including us. In our years as business partners teaching wilderness medicine, several missions have transpired during classes.

I try to ignore the radio and focus on teaching. Later, on a break, Scott tells me the twenty-year-old man left a suicide note, stole a handgun from his sister's house, and walked on foot toward the Castle Mountains. A nearby rancher saw the man walking and later heard a single gunshot, which he thought came from a meadow, now the staging area for the mission.

After class, I give in to the lure of the search. I figure if the rancher's story is true, Tasha should be able to find the body. Full of confidence,

I drive Tasha and the journalist thirty minutes south of Crested Butte to Ohio Creek. In the cool evening, we pull into a huge green meadow rimmed with quaking aspens. Vehicles crowd the staging area. Several law enforcement agencies, search-and-rescue teams from the college and Crested Butte, and the family of the missing man mill in clusters that seem to vibrate with something close to panic. Men on horseback and ATV drivers comb the meadow fringes for signs of the man. Cloaked in worry, family and friends of the missing man pace nearby.

"This is a circus," I tell the reporter. "I'd rather wait until morning to search with Tasha, when everyone's gone."

She looks wide-eyed at the chaos. The scarcity of missions has lured everyone out to help—law enforcement and search-and-rescue teams stepping on one another, everyone clamoring to find the young man. Unless you live near a large metropolitan center with adjacent wilderness nearby like the front range of Colorado, the chances of responding to a call are few and far between. "There are just not a lot of wilderness missions going on out there," a colleague once told me. "When they do come, things get competitive because everybody wants to prove they're the best around, to be the first to make the find."

I clamp my mouth shut to avoid saying anything derogatory in front of the reporter, but my shoulders hunch in disapproval. I should peel right back home, but my desire to serve—or, like everybody else, to prove myself again—forces me to stay.

With Tasha on leash, we report to the incident commander, a young climber from the college team. Recounting what I already know, he gives us the background and assigns me a search area.

"But I'm not sure about working Tasha here."

"Why not?"

"Conditions are not ideal for a search dog. Based on the number of people walking around, the time of day, and swirling wind, I'll need to come up with my own search strategy. Do you mind?"

"Do what you need to do." Handing me a map, the incident commander moves to the next team of searchers.

Scrunching my brow at the chaos that will surely make Tasha fail, I stare at her, weighing the pressure to work her after being cooped up all day. The journalist adds another of layer of pressure. As we return to the truck, a Gunnison County deputy pulls up. Over the past couple of years, I helped train his police German shepherd.

"Is it okay if I tag along with you?" he begs. "I really want to see how you work Tasha on a real mission." His big grin makes me think he made a special trip out here just to watch us work. Because of his eagerness, I decide to do a quick pass with Tasha, right through the middle of the chaos, perhaps locating the young man in a place searchers might miss.

As Tasha, the journalist, the observing deputy, and I ready to depart on the search, the incident commander's voice blares over the radio: "The other Crested Butte dog team is en route. They are also on standby for tomorrow."

My blood boils. I know it's Buck. Buck bugs me—immensely. He convinced everyone on my team that he and his dog were trained and deployable, despite the fact that they'd dropped out of SARDOC. For alternate certification, the duo took the National Association of Search and Rescue test. They flunked that, too. Despite all this, Buck and the team seem to think that *saying* that Buck and his dog are trained and qualified is the same as them *being* trained and qualified.

Earlier, I had convinced the sheriff, who dispatches our search-and-rescue team, to adopt SARDOC protocols. He agreed, but I knew that out in the field, pressure to finish the search adds another dimension. Many law enforcement agencies tend to subscribe to a search-dog motto: "Any dog is better than no dog."

Yanking on Tasha's leash, I march to the incident commander and marshal my anger, preparing to speak my mind about Buck. While he does train with ski patrol, he knows better than to deploy in wilderness. No doubt his dog has not even been imprinted on cadavers.

"That kid and his dog cannot work this scene. Absolutely not!" I face off with the incident commander, who gives me a blank stare. "That team is not certified. They have no business being out here, clearing areas in a cadaver search."

My mentors have told me that dogs who are not imprinted on cadavers and human remains can have an aversion to the smell, and they will walk right past bodies, because they are trained to find *live* scent. Buck and his dog will serve no purpose if his dog ignores a body in a bush. Uncertified, invalidated teams destroy all the reputations of other dog teams that work so hard for certification. And they can destroy the effectiveness of a search.

"It's not up to us." The incident commander avoids my eyes. "I'm just passing along the information. The sheriff decides who is called."

"But the sheriff adopted protocols to use only certified dogs!"

The incident commander glares at me to bore in the point that it's not his call.

I throw my hands in the air, feeling like I am the only one in the sandbox playing by the rules. Fighting an implosion and feeling sucker punched, I wrangle Tasha, the journalist, and the deputy in tow and stomp off to search. Fuming, I can barely see straight as we walk ten minutes to a search zone downwind of the greater meadow.

The radio broadcasts that Buck and his dog are on scene. My neck's nape hair rises, but I force my focus onto my task. Swallowing back the rotten taste of conflict, I unclip Tasha, lean over, and give her the cadaver command: "Decomp!"

Tasha's ears perk up. In her new red vest, she trots ahead, her bell tinkling. To catch up with Tasha, we pick up our pace, climbing over downed trees as the setting sunlight filters through the quaking aspen grove.

"Watch her work. Notice her tail is wagging, and her nose is up," I explain Tasha's work to my observers. "Her actions are telling me that she is working but hasn't found cadaver scent."

The deputy glues his eyes to Tasha. She hops and leaps, zigs and zags through the forest. He also eyes me, mentally taking notes. The journalist writes in her notebook.

"See how I allow Tasha to check everything out? We can't micromanage our dogs. When they have something, they'll come back and tell us. That's their job."

"Wow. I need to stop talking so much to my dog. You don't talk much to Tasha."

"Gibber just confuses dogs. It's better to keep your mouth shut and let your dog work."

He nods in understanding. The journalist scrawls more words. Tasha bolts out of sight, her bell cadence slowing.

Climbing over fallen logs and bushwhacking through thick, high vegetation, we see Tasha working a grassy clearing. She darts back and forth to the edges, snorting at the knee-high bushes on the circumference, mapping scent.

"I think she's just sorting out all the search teams' tracks. Scent has collected on the grass and in the bushes. Let's just stand back and watch."

Abandoning the meadow, Tasha moves out. We follow. After an hour, Tasha finds no scent of the young man.

"He's not here," I report to incident command, handing over my map.

The incident commander grunts acknowledgment.

Buck and his dog stand nearby, ready to work, but not yet deployed. The sight of him makes me seethe. To avoid a confrontation, I steer toward my truck.

"He's not going to find the guy cause he doesn't know jack about strategy," I vent to the journalist.

Anger eats at me the entire way home and all night, as I flip and flop, entangling myself in the sheets. Eight years of training to be reputable, reliable, and dependable paved the way for us to work missions. But bad behavior from that disrespectful punk and his untrained dog could destroy the standing of certified dog teams so badly, we might never be called again. I pray incident command doesn't deploy the duo.

The next day, during a midafternoon break from class, Scott corners me. With his pager on one hip, his radio on the other, Scott looks like an action figure search-and-rescue doll.

"Buck worked his dog," he announces.

"What?" *How dare him.* I don't even question if they found the guy. I know they couldn't.

"And you created a big stink at the mission staging area. Everybody is talking about the scene you made. Who are you to say who can or can't work their dog?" Standing only a few inches taller than me, Scott squares his nose at my eyes to speak as a board member, not as my business partner.

"Are you kidding me? All I said was they need to get certified cadaver dogs in here, not someone pretending he's got a qualified dog. Besides, the sheriff's department adopted the protocols."

"Well, you've embarrassed our team. People are disgusted that the two of you are fighting at a mission. There will be repercussions."

"What do you mean?"

"I guess after you left last night, Buck raised a big stink—unprofessional and petty—in front of the missing man's family. The sheriff's search-and-rescue coordinator is upset with the behavior of *both of you* out there."

I think I know who's behind this: Stink Face and the coordinator. They're out to discredit everything I've done. I stare at Scott, trying to convince him with my eyes.

Scott turns to stomp off but swings back. Spittle flies out of his mouth, his temporal artery pulses as his volume escalates. "And one more thing. Why did the sheriff call you and Tasha for that missing hunter and not our SAR team?"

Because we're good. Because one dog can comb an area in the same amount of time it takes twenty-five searchers. Because we save law enforcement agencies time and money. Because a dog's nose can work beyond the eyes and ears of a search-and-rescue team. Because we're cute and nice. Because … I curb the torrent of words running through my head before they explode from my mouth. Instead, I fling a challenge. "What are they going to do—suspend me?"

The following week, I march into the sheriff's office to ask why Buck and his dog were allowed to search on the last mission. But I already know the reason: new staff, overworked deputies. Stuff just falls through the cracks. They just want bodies and resources out there searching. The sheriff agrees with me that certified dogs and handlers are what he wants to put in the field, and he enlists my help in drafting a two-page reminder memo to his department.

"And Sue, I'll have our investigator call you," he says as he ushers me out the door. "We'd like you and Tasha to go back out there to search a wider perimeter with our detective."

Another wilderness-medicine class comes and goes interrupted by another call to find a drowned toddler in an alpine lake in the San Juan Mountains in southwest Colorado. We decline the search, and I send a colleague from Silverton. He calls me from the scene to go over his search strategy on the phone. Later in the day, his German shepherd, Kai, alerts on the toddler's body in the water.

A couple weeks after the incident with Buck, I receive a letter in the mail from Crested Butte Search and Rescue. I tear open the envelope.

One word leaps off the page.

Suspended.

CHAPTER 27

Barking Back

2003–2004
Crested Butte, Colorado, and Beyond

"How come I never have these problems when I work elsewhere?" Flopping in a chair, I unload on Doug. The letter from the Crested Butte Search and Rescue board demands that I write apologies to all the agencies involved, plus the family. Buck has to apologize, too.

"They have it in for you. You're competition for them."

"When did search and rescue become so competitive?" I don't like this. I'm made out to be arrogant just because we have standards.

Too bad Patti hadn't yet written her book, *Avalanche! Hasty Search*, eight years ago. If I had been able to read it, I would have learned early on to be cautious of the petty politics and growing pains of any SAR team, and that many highly skilled dog handlers have abandoned SAR because they were unable to develop the thick skin necessary for dealing with political quagmires. In this blossoming small town, I find Patti's words to be true of not only the SAR team but also of the local clinics and ski patrol, everybody fighting and competing to be top dog or a big fish in a small pond.

"Think about it," Doug says. "There are four search-and-rescue teams in Gunnison County, all vying for the action, all wanting to be heroes. You're getting called for missions all over the state, and your SAR team isn't. You work above and beyond. People get jealous when you're the best."

"I never thought it'd be like this. I think I want to quit."

"Why not use an apology as a chance to educate the greater search-and-rescue and law enforcement agencies on the benefits of having a trained, certified search dog on scene?"

How many times am I going to have to educate people? To be heard?

Doug's words sink in, and my anger shifts to assertiveness. I can use my apologies as an educational opportunity, a way to explain the value of certified versus untrained dogs.

A few days later, I reflect on my conversation with Doug. Maybe I am just like the men I complain so much about. I love the adrenaline rush, being the hero. It gives me self-worth. I'm known as the "lady with the avalanche dog." My thoughts are interrupted when the deputy who had shadowed me on the search for the suicidal man calls. Thinking he was going to reprimand me for my outburst on the last mission, I take a tentative stance.

"Guess what?" his voice beams through the phone.

"What?"

"My boy just had his first apprehension. My shepherd tracked a fugitive who fled from his car. He ran through the mountains. I did everything you said, and my boy tracked him and got him!"

"No way!"

He rambles on. I listen. Feeling like a proud parent, I congratulate him. But I'm too embarrassed to confess my suspension.

Two days later, the neighboring sheriff dispatch phones once again about the missing forty-seven-year-old woman, six weeks after the initial call.

"Her remains have been located," dispatch updates me.

Eeeeek. But human remains intrigue me.

Tasha and I are requested to assist the department and the Colorado Bureau of Investigation with searching the property for more human remains. Despite the eeriness, I commit our services once permission and paperwork to deploy us is complete. I neglect to disclose my suspension. I tell Doug about the mission.

"Sue, what the hell?" he lobs his concern. "You're dabbling in turf where you don't belong."

"But we spent a week at cadaver dog boot camp."

"You need to spell out to them that you're not certified! You just told stoner boy he couldn't work his dog because he's not certified. Now you're doing the same thing."

"But look at our track record. We find cadavers and human remains. Tasha found the guy in the lake and the three avalanche victims. Our record speaks for our skills. Besides, SARDOC doesn't have a certification for human remains detection."

When I call my sheriff's department to obtain their blessing for the homicide mission, my deputy buddy answers. Wanting to burst into tears from shame, I confess. "My team suspended me."

The deputy laughs. "Sue, we don't give a shit if they suspended you. We deploy you, not your search-and-rescue team. We value your skills and Tasha's nose."

The deputy's words lift a weight from my conscience.

Tasha and I drive two-and-a-half hours, out of the mountains, to the edge of the high, dry desert. Despite Doug's objections to our deploying, he joins us, too.

In the heat and blasting midday wind, we meet the coroner. Yellow crime-scene tape surrounds the entrance to the 360-acre compound with a residence and stone quarry. A large white van serves as a mobile laboratory. Investigators buzz around in white moon suits, blue gloves, and face masks. Dressed in blue jeans and cowboy boots, the coroner looks more like a wrangler.

"Glad you made it, Sue. Good to see you again." Over the years, Tasha and I had earned his respect. As a fellow member of the search-and-rescue community, he'd been following our progress.

Tasha walks to him and sniffs every inch of his boot and lower leg, her nose a millimeter away from the denim and leather. Her little snorts tell me he's been walking around in the stinky stuff. She smells it.

"You've been around human remains, yes?"

"Sure have."

I pull out my clicker. "Good girl, Tasha. That's decomp, isn't it?"

Her big brown eyes meet mine. Tail wagging, she lets out her signature, one-time, loud alert. "Wooof." Then she rams my pocket for a reward. But I tote neither kibble nor schlong. I pet her head instead, cooing her with praises.

"I never miss a moment to train. So, what's the scoop?"

"Well, we think she's been shot, chopped up, burned, and buried."

My eyes swell to the size of saucers. Doug lobs me his I-told-you-so look.

"We believe she was shot in her town-house apartment and transported in a vehicle's trunk. At some point, she was brought out here, to her property, and cut up in the stone crusher." He points to an orange, eight-foot-tall rock-crushing machine. "We believe after she was crushed, they dug a hole, burned her, then buried her. CBI is sifting through her remains right now."

"What, then, are we doing here if you've found her?"

"Can Tasha tell if that machine has crushed human remains?"

"Well, she just told me there's human remains on your pants. We're here. Might as well try it."

I laugh. Doug's head swivels back and forth across the scene. He locks his eyes on mine, conveying his unease. I avert my eyes back to the coroner.

As the coroner turns to attend to the radio, Doug elbows me. "How do we know the killer isn't watching all of this and writing down our license plate number? This is bad. We don't even know if they have a suspect yet. The killer could be watching us."

I concur about the creepiness—but we're here. When the coroner gets off the radio, he supplies more details. "This property is owned by the woman and her estranged husband. They are in the midst of getting divorced. Apparently, it's been quite bitter, with lots of fighting over custody of the daughters and division of the property. We believe that after her body was chopped in the rock crusher and burned, they buried what was left, and then covered the grave site with two tons of stone pallets."

"Workers put stone pallets right over her? So, how'd you find her?"

"Some pipe fitters installing a water hydrant had to move the pallets and found some recognizable bits and pieces."

I wipe sweat from my forehead, blaming the blazing evening sun. Doug's head pivots, eyeing hiding spots around the property.

"So, what exactly do you want us to do?"

"First, we want your dog to determine if the crusher was used to chop her up. If so, we'll haul that baby out of here for analysis. Next, we want you to check some spots in vehicles and trailers where they might have stashed her body before they tore it apart. Then, we'd like you to search the entire property to see if there are any other human remains anywhere."

I nearly choke on the list.

"And one more thing. They had a few pigs fenced on the property ..."

Pigs eat humans. Andy had told our cadaver class that some criminals used pigs to eat human remains to hide the evidence. "We could look in the pig scat for bones," I tell him.

I spell out my terms for the coroner. Because the air is too hot, too windy, and too contaminated with lab people, I defer working Tasha until daybreak and a fresh scene. I add we'll need a law enforcement escort for our safety and to assist us with the scene.

After a sleepless night in the motel, thrashing about, wracked with visions of fingers clawing out of the ground to grab my ankle, I get up at 4:00 a.m. to prep. Before going to bed, I'd left messages for all my cadaver-boot-camp instructors, asking for advice. I hadn't heard back from any of them.

When we arrive at the compound, a gentle breeze sways sagebrush, and a few cicadas chirp. My plan entails starting far away from the scent-pool chaos. We aim for the southern, upwind side of the property. I keep Tasha on lead because of potential crime-scene hazards.

Dry vegetation crunches under our feet. We dodge prickly pear cactus and rattlesnake hidey-holes. When the deputy shows us the trunk of an abandoned car, I unleash Tasha. After I give her the decomp command, she hangs her front paws onto the rim of the trunk. Shoving her nose inside, she sniffs and jumps away.

"Nothing there."

We check a gutted mobile home with a dangling door. Doug lifts Tasha inside. She tiptoes through broken glass, but she shows no interest.

The deputy directs us to the pigsty. I glance into the pen, looking for human bones sticking out of feces. But the pen seems clean, so I suggest we move on.

Then, with Tasha on leash, we move into the crime-scene area we had scouted the day before from the road. The one-ton stone crusher sits on the desert floor a hundred feet from the pit where the human remains were burned. I keep a wide berth between the giant metal contraption and us. About twenty feet upwind of the crusher, I whisper the decomp command to Tasha and unclip her leash. She runs to the crusher and sniffs. She loops around it once then stands on her hind legs with her front paws up on the crusher. She hops on her hind legs trying to reach upward. Doug and I look at each other, knowing what's about to happen. She lets out a slow, high-pitched whine. We stand still. She lets out her one monotone, loud bark.

"That's her alert."

I examine the crusher, noticing a brown leather glove two feet above Tasha's nose. But whether she alerted on the glove with cadaver scent on it, the machine, or the lab techs walking back and forth, I didn't know. Nevertheless, I mark the spot on my map.

We circle the crusher to verify the findings. Tasha cues in on the same spot, jumps up, and gives the same alert. Now I know the crusher holds human remains—she hadn't alerted on the glove or techs. Whipping out a piece of cheese from a plastic bag, I reward her.

With a shift in focus, Tasha darts to the nearby pit. As I watch, she disappears into a three-foot-deep hole. Seconds later, she prances back to me with her tail wagging, head up, and ears perked. Her head bobs in pride, and her mouth is clamped onto something. As she comes closer, I see a three-inch-long human bone fragment.

Shit, she's not supposed to pick up evidence. I pull out my clicker. "Good girl, Tasha. Drop it."

She stares at me without dropping the bone. I try to encourage her to drop it by growling and stomping toward her, without letting the law enforcement officer understand what just happened.

Succumbing to my visual threat, she opens her mouth. The bone plunks to the ground. I click the clicker to reward her, while smirking to myself that she found a bone that the lab techs missed.

As with avalanche work, I need to redirect her in case more human remains hide on the grounds. I nudge her away with my knee. Walking past the hole, I scowl at the ash, imagining the murderer burning the chopped corpse.

After an hour of searching we find nothing else. I report that human-remains scent is on the stone crusher. I give the deputy my map. Doug, Tasha, and I depart for home, pleading with them to avoid calling me into court.

Two days later, a Congressional Record appears in my mail. Unlike my last piece of mail, with a suspension from my search-and-rescue team, this surprise honors Tasha and me. A Colorado congressman I'd never met has paid tribute, in front of the United States of America House of Representatives, to Tasha and me for our finds on the two avalanche missions. My fingers fondle the thick, elegant, cream-colored stationary. I read the last paragraph that praises how Tasha and I go into the Colorado backcountry to help families find closure. "That unselfish spirit of neighbor-helping-neighbor is what helped make this country great." I read it again. And again.

Later, family members of the Ptarmigan Pass avalanche victim write me thank-you letters. The Chaffee County sheriff applauds Tasha, Doug, and me in a newspaper editorial.

My team ignores us. They never ask for details of what happened on our other missions, never congratulate us on Tasha's finds or even mention our appearance in the Congressional Record. I tell myself I no longer care what that rinky-dink group thinks. But, I do. I'm human.

❧ ❧ ❧

Closure for some missions takes months, even years—if ever at all. I resume my schedule of teaching classes, working at the clinic, and flying to Latin America on short-term work stints to earn money. As my human-canine relationship with Tasha strengthens, my human-human marriage weakens.

One day, a few years back, when Doug and I were drilling for potable water in Tobago, West Indies, he broke down. Uncharacteristically, he asked me to go for a walk. At first, I blamed it on the monthlong project in the hot equatorial sun and our living conditions.

"A walk? Sure, I'll go." What an odd request, I thought as we marched out into the heat of the day from our air-conditioned office.

"I can't do this anymore."

"Do what?" I asked, thinking his distress was about the job.

"Take care of you."

"What do you mean? Where is this coming from?"

"I promised your mom and dad I'd take care of you." Between bouts of sniveling he confessed, "I can't ..."

I hugged him and whispered in his ear, like I had done a dozen times with Tasha, "Shhhh ... It's going to be okay. You're just stressed out." Looking back, I think it was his way of trying to tell me something. Something too painful for me to hear or want to feel. I recalled another outburst Doug had while visiting my parents' house after we got back together after our minidivorce.

"I can't sit here anymore," he shouted and got up from the table occupied by my parents and their friends. We were all in a community center, sitting at the table, watching our hometown college hockey team in the playoff game. My mother was bragging about me to her friends, and Doug snapped. "You think your daughter is so great, and you go on and on as if she's a saint." If flames could have spewed out of his mouth, they would have. "Did she ever tell you what she did to me?"

I swallowed and waited for a war to break out between my protective mama bear and the son-in-law.

"Yes, of course," my mother replied in a matter-of-fact, loving way.

"She met that writer guy. So, what?" As if to say, *get over it.* "That happened years ago."

He sat back down, drank four more beers, and never brought up the subject again. He just buried his pain and shame a little deeper. In the back of my mind, I wondered if the two out-of-character events were connected. But instead of asking him, I pressed on, avoiding the underlying issue— my denial as strong as any lost boy's.

Months after the mission to find the young suicidal man has been called off, I join a Gunnison sheriff's investigator at the location, to clear the broader search area one more time, in hopes of finding any clue to his whereabouts. Tasha locates blood drops from a wounded animal, but nothing else within a mile surrounding the meadow. Based on our work, the investigator concludes that the young man left the area. If I had the time, money, and resources, I would expand the search area, to bring closure for the family. But I don't. I just have to let go.

In autumn, hunters finally find the remains of the young man. Dead from a gunshot wound, he had walked miles from the point last seen before finally killing himself.

Later, I follow up about the homicide case, and to find out the lab results of remains on the crusher. The initial CBI lab report had detected no human remains. I recoil at the discrepancy between Tasha's response and the lab report. But final reports show that the woman was indeed crushed before she was burned and buried. The authorities had jailed a Mexican man working for the family's business in connection to the crime.

The homicide scene haunts me in nightmares long enough that I decide to decline further criminal human-remains detection.

"Disarticulated body parts and urban disasters are for other teams." Doug applauds my decision.

In November, Tasha and I travel four hours to take our official SARDOC water-certification test. From a boat, Tasha pinpoints a scent article, a sock, submerged twelve feet underwater. We add another badge to our credits.

When Scott asks me to apologize to my search-and-rescue team in person, I agree. Just to mend relationships. By the end of the year, my suspension from the team ends. They officially admit Tasha and me once again to the organization. But the readmission is just a formality. Our reputation has ballooned far beyond our tiny town, and it brings us calls for searches from five different sheriff's departments in Colorado, from neighboring states, and even another country.

During a break in class, after my lecture on acute mountain sickness, one of my students pulls me aside. In his late forties, with a slight South African accent and a leathery face, Frankie shows the wear from more than twenty years of pioneering expeditions across the African continent. "Man, I love your class. This information is brilliant." Standing eye level with me, he lobs me a question. "Should my African guides with no medical training be carrying medications like Diamox and Dex?" He refers to two drugs used to ward off acute mountain sickness and brain swelling, also known as high-altitude cerebral edema (HACE).

"We've gotten into some serious trouble over the years leading clients up Mount Kilimanjaro, even lost a few. Well, recently, we had a client at Crater Camp with high-altitude cerebral edema. He got really goofy on us, acting like he was drunk. He started to vomit and couldn't walk. We were stuck at eighteen thousand feet with no help, no helicopters, nothing. Luckily, a neurosurgeon on our trip gave the guy some Dexamethasone. It literally saved his life."

At the end of class, Frankie corners me again and asks me if I would come to climb Kili and teach a high-altitude medical course for his guides.

With Doug in the Dominican Republic, I arrange to squeeze in the trip to Africa. I wait until details are confirmed before informing Doug about the volunteer trip. He doesn't like it, especially my traveling with Frankie, but it's the kind of challenge I've been waiting for. Amy and the boys agree to care for Tasha. But before the plane tickets are even purchased, I dive into designing a custom course to teach African guides—some who speak little English and have had minimal schooling—how to monitor their clients' vital signs, medical conditions, handle altitude emergencies, treat medical situations, and execute rescues.

But before I fly to Africa, Scott, my partner for the last seven years, and I agree to split. After years of working together to build a highly-visible wilderness-medicine teaching company that attracted worldwide clientele, I blame our separation on the fact that two alpha cooks can no longer work in the same kitchen. But it was more than that. Maybe it was jealousy or envy or losing control of what we were. I am sure the inability to communicate clearly about the past and future was a contributing factor to our separation.

Seven years was a long time together. We had always joked, "Scott's my second husband," and, "Sue's my second wife." I felt like I had just lost a best friend. However, instead of talking about my loss with Doug, I pushed those feelings of loss deep inside. Doug got what he wanted, 100 percent of my future earnings and a wife he didn't have to share. After I buy out Scott's interest in Crested Butte Outdoors, he starts a new company. And with that, the little town of Crested Butte falls farther and farther into my rearview mirror.

As I continue to build Crested Butte Outdoors, International, on my own, I stretch like a kid on a Twister mat, each extremity reaching as far as it can to opposing corners. My work with Tasha has served as the base to get me this far, but it's my overseas work, clinical experience, and in-the-field SAR successes that have put our names on the map. And that changes everything.

Colorado avalanche season comes crashing down on us again in March of 2004. One year after Tasha found the two snowmobilers in three days, the same sheriff wants Tasha and me to search for a young man who was swept off the 14,360-foot La Plata Peak. Wearing hiking boots, he stepped in shallow snow, triggering an avalanche. He slid two thousand feet down a narrow chute. It was clear that he was dead, but his two friends lost visual track of him halfway down the mountain. The survivors scoured the debris until dark then postholed through, thigh-deep snow to their vehicle, only to remember that the victim had the keys. They hiked to a highway, hitched a ride, and called 911 after midnight.

At daybreak, at the trailhead near Aspen, I greet the same crew that transported us last year to the Hancock and Ptarmigan Pass avalanches. Tasha and I lift off in a helicopter and land at the base of the cement-like avalanche debris. With the sun rising over the mountain, Tasha pinpoints cadaver scent within ten minutes, but when I test the spot, the concrete-dense snow snaps my probe pole. Search crews probe and dig for more than thirty minutes to finally uncover the crushed body, buried under four feet of snow.

A few weeks later, while teaching a wilderness medical course in Wyoming to members of the Teton County Search and Rescue Team and Teton National Park employees, my Chaffee County search family calls again with news of an April avalanche claiming another life. A few mountains away from La Plata Peak, a visiting hiker traversing across a steep slope triggered an avalanche. Unable to respond to the mission, I recommend Patti and another dog team from Breckenridge. My friend's dog finds the victim just before the sheriff calls off the mission due to hang fire.

In June, as snow melts off the high country, I head to Virginia to speak at the National Association for Search and Rescue (NASAR) Conference. Standing in front of the giant lecture hall filled with my peers from around the nation, I address the audience to speak about avalanche, wilderness, and rescue medicine.

While at the conference, the Gunnison County coroner asks me to assist in finding a suicidal person and a sheriff's deputy requests my help in locating a fisherman who fell overboard in a reservoir. When I return home, Poodle Lady and I take our dogs to the murky reservoir to check for the fisherman's scent. Tasha alerts on one spot, but with conditions too dangerous to dive, the sheriff aborts the mission. Weeks later, the body is discovered floating on the water surface close to Tasha's alert.

By the time the aspens turn gold, my travel goes global and I find myself volunteering abroad. Where I once longed to cut the airtime to Latin America in favor of settling down in Colorado, flight miles pile up. I return to the jungles of Tanzania with an improved high-altitude medical course for Frankie's twenty African guides on Kilimanjaro. I wind up lecturing again at the 2005 NASAR conference in California, and I head to Utah for the Wasatch Backcountry Rescue Avalanche Dog School—the one I attended as a student when Tasha was eighteen months old. This time, I serve as the first out-of-town female instructor at the prestigious school, sharing lessons learned from my avalanche missions. When asked to educate Mount Everest Sherpa guides on wilderness and rescue medicine, I fly to Lukla, Nepal, and trek four days on foot to reach the village of Kunde and teach my class.

My one-time fear of stumbling in a foreign language back in Santo Domingo goes global, too. But I learn to swap between English, Spanish, Dog, Swahili, Sherpa, and Nepali.

As the calendar fills, my purpose spreads. Each step puts Tasha and me in position to help more people, but I always know that our clock is ticking.

CHAPTER 28

Go Find

Summer 2005
Lake Tahoe, California, and Colorado

A year later, my arm hanging over the back of a patio chair for support, I sink with fatigue under the midmorning June sun at a Starbucks in Lake Tahoe. Tasha flops on the shaded, cool concrete slab at my feet, with her head between her front paws, eyes shut.

"You're famous, you know that?" I nudge her shoulder with my clog. "Hey, I'm talking to you."

Tasha acknowledges me by lifting her head and rolling to her side, moaning a slow sigh. She looks weary from hustling from one activity to the next.

On the tail of a trip to Africa, where I left Tasha behind, my three-week California road trip kept us busy, schlepping through airports to speak at the NASAR conference and teaching an eight-day wilderness-medicine course in Lake Tahoe. My clothes are rumpled, and my hair is wadded up in a clip, errant strands hanging down my neck.

I prod Tasha again with my foot, trying to rouse her. "Your vacation starts in five days. You'll be at Kathy's house for a month while I go to the DR to work."

Tasha's head stays stuck to the concrete, eyes closed. She thumps her tail once.

Wrung out from interaction with too many people in the past three weeks, the idea of being in the Dominican Republic with its torrid heat and tumult of people makes acid bubble up in my stomach. As I slosh down a sip of strong, milky latte to settle it, my cell phone rings.

"We need your help." Jeff Skoloda, a technical climber from Ouray Mountain Rescue, introduces himself. "Your colleague told me you had the best avalanche dog in the state."

"Really? That's nice to hear." The flattery helps me punch a little personality into my voice. Jeff starts to relate his story, but I interrupt him. Balancing the phone on my shoulder, I rustle through my hot-pink computer bag, readying to take notes.

Jeff delivers snippets of images: a small airplane ripping apart, a steep mountainside, avalanches, victims, Richard (the missing family member), and the distraught uncle, Ed Jones. As I kink my neck to hold the cell phone, I scrawl notes with one hand. A bead of sweat drops from my forehead onto the table. Was it the hot coffee, the sun, or the adrenaline pumping through me? Sweat soaks through my one remaining clean travel shirt.

Jeff recounts his Ouray team's several-week search for the remains of Ed Jones' family. Ed's brother, Patrick, the owner and pilot of a single-engine Cessna 210, had been flying from California to Colorado with his wife, son, and grandson. Radar had shown the aircraft lifting from seven thousand to twenty thousand feet, over the San Juan Mountains, in a matter of seconds, probably by wind shear. Investigators believed a mountain updraft ripped the plane apart, the wings dropping to one side of the cone-shaped peak of Whitehouse Mountain and the fuselage on the other.

"It's been a pretty intense mission. One by one, we take a helicopter thirteen thousand feet up the side of Whitehouse Mountain to search."

"Sounds really dangerous."

"Ed is not leaving Ouray until all his family members' bodies are recovered. We're still missing his nephew, Richard. He's still somewhere up there."

"Have any other dog teams been called?"

"No. You're our first choice. We need a team that can get in and out on snow at high elevation."

When I lift my eyes from my notes, I see a young couple kissing at the table in front of me. Their affection reminds me I haven't seen my husband in a month—and I can't remember the last time we touched lips. I am sitting a long way from our condo in Colorado and from him, currently in the Dominican Republic. I turn my eyes toward Tasha, looking for any little clue. Should I accept this mission? Just a head lift, a tail twitch, an ear perk, a small stretch—something to tell me she would like to find this guy.

I send Tasha a telepathic message: *Tash, this could be your last major mission. You're almost eleven, and I'm over forty. Pretty soon, both of us won't be strong enough to take on the tough missions.*

A mission like this only comes around once in a team's career, if that. Even Jeff's bare-bones description tells me that this mission will tax all our skills: wilderness air-scent, human remains, and avalanche techniques, plus our mountaineering abilities. It doesn't help that the mission demands working with an unfamiliar search-and-rescue team, albeit one with a strong reputation for hauling people out of ravines, plucking stranded climbers off mountains, and rescuing those inside vehicles that plunge off the deadly Red Mountain Pass Highway.

"How are we going to get on the mountain?" I ask.

"A private pilot from down valley. He's a crop duster in the Colorado corn capital." Jeff laughs.

"What, no National Guard or Flight for Life helicopter that has enough power at altitude?"

"Nope."

Our lives will be in the hands of Jeff's team and a pilot who sprays chemicals on corn. *Should I risk our lives to find a dead guy—all for no pay, for nothing?* Tasha fails to sense my agonizing over the decision, or she ignores me.

"How long ago did the crash happen?

"Thirty-two days ago."

Jeff explains the intervening events. Two days after the aircraft crashed, the Civil Air Patrol homed in on the emergency transponder and performed a flyby, discovering the fuselage on a couloir, a steep narrow chute, on the side of Whitehouse Mountain. They could see bodies on the slope. Since the crash, one spring storm after another has piled several feet of new snow on the mountain. As the days warmed up and more snow piled up, wet slab avalanches sent thousands of tons of snow roaring down the mountain. The wreckage had disappeared under the snow and reappeared multiple times as the movement of the snow scattered the pieces across three quarters of a mile.

"Recovery has been difficult and dangerous. The sheriff has only let a select few climbers go up to search. Twisted metal, toys, clothing, and the bodies were all over the place, which means Ed's nephew could be anywhere. At this point, we're giving it one more shot. You're our last-ditch effort."

That's why they're calling me. Straightening my neck, I swap the phone to my other hand.

If only a national database of certified search-dog teams existed, law enforcement could easily call on trained volunteers like Tasha and me *first* instead of last. I want to scream about how many cases like this come down to a "last-ditch effort." I think about the Elizabeth Smart case or the fact that Chandra Levy's body lay in a Washington, DC, park for a year because nobody called qualified human-remains dog teams to search for her.

This moment, this phone call, provides me an opportunity to help the Jones family through the worst tragedy of their lives. This time, a dog team can make a difference. Without hesitation, I agree to the mission.

Tossing the phone on the table, I lean back in my chair and rub my temples. Reality slaps me in the face. *Sue, you dumbass. Why did you say yes?* It's only five days until my departure for the Dominican Republic, with a monthlong work stint to convince my husband that I'm contributing, to make him happy, even though I have no desire to spend weeks logging gold core samples.

The short time frame between California, Colorado, and the Dominican Republic means that I will have very little time for this mission. Once home, I'll have to gather up all my mountaineering and avalanche rescue gear to drive three hours west to Ouray to execute a treacherous body recovery. Then, after what will undoubtedly be a physically and emotionally exhausting mission, I'll have to drive ten hours to Boulder to drop Tasha off before racing to Denver to board the flight to Santo Domingo.

Five days. When will I breathe? I hit the redial button on the phone to inform Jeff I need to be on a plane for the Dominican Republic on Sunday. Red tape could put snags in the mission. Either Jeff's sheriff or mine could deny our participation. Permission must come from both.

At home in Crested Butte, I wait for my phone to ring. Anxiety mounts as Tuesday passes. In my bare feet, I pace in my living room, chewing on my dry nails. Tasha eyes my nervous energy from her bed.

I unpack boxes of teaching supplies and wash fake blood off my gear. I check on my international flights and throw travel essentials into my open suitcase: business shirt and slacks to avoid being hassled at customs and immigration, Bose noise-canceling headphones (so I don't have to hear or talk to anyone), a blow-up neck-support pillow for sleeping, and a travel purse with passport, credit cards, and a two-inch wad of US one dollar bills for tips.

On Wednesday, I respond with my local search-and-rescue team to a horse-riding accident up the road from my house. An inexperienced rider fell off his rental horse, landing on his back. Fearing a pelvic or spinal injury, our ten-person team, along with the ambulance crew, carries the oversize man off Snodgrass Mountain in a litter. I offer to determine if he has a spine injury by using our wilderness-medicine protocol, but the paramedic refuses my help. Another slap down for my confidence.

I want to share the details about my pending Whitehouse Mountain mission with my teammates, but bite back my desire in fear of another suspension. When I return home from the horse accident an hour later, Tasha perks her head up. I sink back into obsessing about Richard's body, high on the mountainside.

"We are running out of time," I snap at Tasha.

With a big yawn, she watches me pace. I plan in detail how to work the couloir with Tasha. I imagine the crash site—the towering cliffs, fields of broken snow, the hot June sun, twisted metal—and a cadaver. My pacing speeds up. I postpone apprising Doug of the mission. I already know his response: *"No! Hell, no. You're not risking your life to find a dead body."* So, I don't call him.

Wednesday night and Thursday morning pass.

"I need to know what is going on!" I throw my hands up in the air and yank the telephone so hard that I pull its stand off the counter. Dialing Jeff's number, I muscle my voice into calm tones, but it frays at the edges, ragged with aggression.

"What is going on? Why haven't you guys called? I'm running out of time."

"Sorry, Sue. The sheriff doesn't know what he wants to do."

My search-dog self-esteem deflates. I flop onto the couch with exasperation.

"It's the danger that's making him hesitate," Jeff tells me. He tells me all the things that have the sheriff second-guessing himself: having multiple flights starting at first light, helicopter insertion with blades spinning on a forty-five-degree slope, wind shifts, rocks pelting down, extraction of everyone by 9:00 a.m.—and, always, the hang fire risk.

"I have the same concerns. This one's really dangerous. But I can assure you that if Richard is still on that mountain, Tasha will find him."

"I'm sure she can. While we wait for a decision, we're working on a plan. We have to negotiate around the pilot's schedule. Ed Jones has been paying a hundred dollars per hour for helicopter time, and he wants to fly you into the site. Saturday would be the last possible opportunity to deploy."

Thursday night passes with no word. No calls come on Friday.

On Saturday morning, I submit to defeat. I hang up my rescue pack in exchange for my airport roller bag and flip-flops.

CHAPTER 29

Water Mission

Summer 2005
Crested Butte, Colorado

"Why aren't you and Tasha at the lake looking for the drowned kid?" A phone call from the coroner interrupts my Saturday mountain-bike ride during the few remaining free hours before I have to take Tasha to Boulder and catch my plane to the Dominican Republic.

"What kid? What lake?"

"A twenty-year-old who got dumped out of a canoe last night in Nicholson Lake. I'm on standby to retrieve the body, but they haven't found him yet. The Crested Butte police, the fire department, and a dive team have been looking since midnight."

"Nobody called us."

"What? You just live a few minutes from the lake, and you're the only certified water dog in the county."

Blood races to my face. I look at my watch. Eleven hours ago. Stink Face excluded me. If we had been called when it happened, it's possible that Tasha could have saved the young man's life. But now too much time has elapsed for a live find.

Pacing in small circles on the side of the dirt road, I absorb the accident details from the coroner. At midnight, several young adults grabbed some canoes and went paddling without life jackets. Within fifty feet of shore, on the opposite side of the lake from the house, the boat capsized, dumping everyone into the water. The victim couldn't swim. He cried out for help. One friend tried to get him back to shore, but desperate for his own safety, the friend let go. The victim sank.

"Tasha could have pinpointed that kid within the first hour of submersion if given the chance. Why didn't they call?"

Silence reverberates across the phone. The coroner's radio squawks in the background.

"They're calling in a new set of divers."

"That's good. I would love to work with them. If the police want me to respond with Tasha, have them call me."

The local emergency service crews on the scene—the police, divers, and the fire department, several of whom are members of my search-and-rescue team—know that Tasha and I found the college kid who jumped off the bridge at night into Blue Mesa Reservoir. The crews have my telephone number, know I live fifteen minutes from the lake, and know our qualifications as the only local certified water team. But I suspect Stink Face dissuaded the others from calling me.

For the past decade, he's used his power—as leader of my search-and-rescue team and as a member of the board of directors—to keep me out of the field. Even though his crew participated by providing lights for the divers, he should have told the cops to call me the minute they responded. But he didn't. I twist my foot into the dirt, longing to extinguish a few burning egos, including my own, like I would a smoldering cigarette.

There it is, front and center in my face. Politics getting in the way of saving lives. Tears cloud my vision as I bike toward home.

While I climb the steep mountain road on my bicycle before turning the corner to my condo, a police officer calls to ask for our help on the water mission.

Really? Are you calling us this late to cover your ass? The parochialism and egos of these exclusive boys' clubs dictate death over change, death over education, death over their own egos—the death of an innocent who might have been saved by a dog team. Screw politics and egos! I agree to show up with Tasha. I'll stand tall, pull my shoulders back, keep my chin up, and chew out Stink Face with a glare instead of making a verbal scene. I know damn well he had a say in my suspension.

I race up the stairs, ripping off my sweat-soaked biking apparel, tripping over my bike shorts. "Tasha, are you ready to go to work?"

She digs her claws into the wood floors, scrabbling with her short, stiff hind legs to move out of the way of my runaway freight train. Her head snaps back and forth as she watches me chuck clothes out of the closet in search of light polypropylene water-mission clothes for warmth on the lake. Tasha charges me, her wet nose nuzzling deep into the flesh above my waist. She nips at me gently with her upper and lower teeth.

"Ouch! That hurt. You little stinker." Shoving her away, I lift my shirt. "You left a welt."

On the way out the door with Tasha's marker buoys and our life jackets, I grab a banana, shoving it in my mouth. Tasha slurps up half-chewed banana bits that drop to the ground. I boost Tasha's rear end as she jumps up into my pickup. At age ten, she can't make the leap by herself anymore.

As I swing around curves to the lake, my phone chimes for the third time in twenty minutes. I pull over to the shoulder to take the call from a SARDOC number I recognize.

"You're not calling me about this water mission, are you?"

"No, I don't know anything about a water mission. We just got a call from this guy named Ed Jones. I think you know him. He's asked specifically for you. He's asking you to respond to Ouray for that missing person in the plane crash? You'll need to be there tonight."

"Tonight? You have to be kidding." Four anxiety-ridden days of waiting and *now* they call while I'm en route to another mission.

With the time crunch, I defer discussion of the plane crash until we finish the water mission. Two missions, back-to-back. Dog missions occur few and far between, sometimes months or years apart, yet today two mission requests compete for our time. I wonder how to juggle them both and still fly to the Dominican Republic tomorrow morning. *I must be nuts.*

When my truck crests the small hill above the kidney-bean-shaped lake, I slow to size up the scene. I'm expecting to see men in black suits with yellow tanks bobbing in the water alongside a small fleet of red-and-white rescue boats and anxious family members pacing the shore. Instead, towering, snow-covered peaks reflect in a peaceful, glassy mountain lake like a postcard. For a split second, I forget about the mission until I spot a dozen rescue vehicles parked bumper to bumper along the shore, spanning half the length of the lake. Rescue boats sit empty near the shore.

Nearby, a group of people hovers on the porch of a home overlooking the lake—family members and friends of the victim. Some pace while others cling to each other. The sadness of the situation spreads over me. Once again, Tasha and I are the clean-up crew rather than the save-a-life crew. The young man's life may have been sacrificed on the altar of Stink Face's ego.

Before I let Tasha out of the truck, I switch into search-dog-handler mode, my only protection. I release my fragile emotions, bury my ego, and don my invisible search-handler mask, the one that keeps me focused and calm. I gather my gear.

"Tasha, help," I command, stretching my arms for her to plop into them. Securing a leash around her neck, I aim for the policeman who seems to be in charge amid the loitering firefighters, scuba divers, and ambulance crews.

I want to sneak by the emergency personnel unnoticed, come up with a plan, give Tasha the search command, and be home in an hour. But all eyes focus on the black furry Lab wearing her red search vest and a decade of confidence. Stink Face's eyes lob angry bombs at me. I avert my attention toward the adjacent policeman, who extends his hand to shake mine.

I don't even ask why they hadn't called me eleven hours earlier. It doesn't matter anymore. The idea of shaking hands with Stink Face makes me queasy. Instead, I fold my arms across my body and ask about the point last seen. As he moves away, but within earshot, the policeman recaps the details of the accident and rescue efforts for me.

"The point last seen is there, where the lake narrows."

"How long before the National Park Service dive team arrives?"

"An hour."

Tasha and I must act fast before the divers arrive and launch boats back onto the water, clogging the air with human scent and making Tasha's job more difficult. Grabbing my waterproof notebook and pen from my radio harness, I draw a quick map of the lake, scratching an *X* where the victim was seen last and an arrow to note the wind direction, which I test with a strip of pink tape. I sketch another *X* with a circle, indicating "no people" for the policeman.

"See this search area downwind? I need it clean. Scents from other people will reduce our chances for success."

"I'll do what I can." He looks everywhere but at my map.

"Please. Keep everyone out of the area until we're done." Nodding my head, as if to prompt his agreement, I look into his eyes for confirmation. He offers none. From appearances, our search efforts might be discarded. I wonder if I am only a pawn in this rescue chess game, a ploy to placate the family.

"After Tasha scans the shoreline for scent, I'll need a boat with a driver."

"We'll send a river raft your way when you need it. That's all we got."

I agree. On foot, Tasha and I set out to circumnavigate the lake. I release her leash.

Nose hovering two inches above the shoreline, Tasha tracks three-inch-deep footprints in the mud where frantic friends, family members, and rescuers had run back and forth on shore in the dark. I haven't given her the search command, but she knows what to do. Tasha runs through the muck, flinging muddy water from her paws as she sorts out the different scents. As we walk around the lake's north rim, I wallow, sinking ankle deep in mud. I mark wind direction and her route on my map.

After seeking higher ground, Tasha wriggles onto her back, bucking the air with her mud-thickened paws. I let her romp to release pent-up energy. From her behavior, I can tell we are still upwind of the victim's scent. Dreading the reaction of the EMS onlookers, I dare not turn my head back toward the staging area. No doubt they're thinking, *Heck, my dog does that. What's so special about her dog?*

Minutes later, Tasha and I arrive at the spot where witnesses said the victim drowned thirty feet offshore. I peer into the cloudy, dark lake. No bubbles rise to the surface. At midnight, when the accident occurred, eyewitnesses may have erred in pinpointing the victim's last location due to the pitch-black lake, lack of clear vision at night, possible alcohol, and dubious memories. Depending on Tasha to tell me the truth of the victim's location, I give the decomp command.

She snaps her head, acknowledging me, and launches her body in a full belly flop into the water.

While Tasha paddles in circles, I stand with my hands clasped behind my hips, my body erect, to prevent steering Tasha with any physical suggestions. She must find the scent from the gases escaping from a dead man's body, not signals from me. Tasha swims twenty feet from shore, whipping her tail back and forth like a rudder, steering her body in a zigzag pattern.

The wind direction thwarts her. Instead of the wind blowing at our faces, making it possible for her to smell his body, the wind blows parallel to shore. I command Tasha to swim further away from me. Instead, she swims toward me.

"Tasha, you're not cooperating."

She hauls herself out of the water to shake at my feet. I radio the policeman to send the boat. Pointing with my arms, I indicate where to pick us up, downwind of the point last seen. A city policeman in full uniform rows a clumsy fourteen-foot raft designed for whitewater rapids. I bite my lip, knowing the tip of Tasha's nose will have to be several feet above the water, less than ideal for finding percolating scent.

While the oarsman rows ever so slowly across the lake, Tasha and I walk downwind to meet him where the lake hooks right on the flat, marshy shoreline, which is dotted with spruce trees and low brush. At the bend in the lake, Tasha's nose lifts, and her nostrils dilate. Tiny water droplets spew from her nasal passages on her exhales. The tip of her tail points skyward, and her ears perk forward. Sprinting, she hunts an invisible scent like a cat chases a mouse.

Low-lying plants, moist and shaded from the sun, have molecules of the drowning victim's scent clinging to them. I recognize a scent pool, a collection spot where decomposition gases bubbling up from the lake bottom blew to be trapped by the brush.

"Atta girl. You found his scent. Decomp."

Like a shot, the black dog bounces from bush to bush, running down the lake, bounding back and forth, in and out of the scent cone. She runs to the water's edge, lifting her nose as the wind blows her ears back, and stares straight into the wind. She lets out a high-pitched, guttural whine, as her lips remain closed. Her body quivers.

When the boat arrives, she bounces on her paws, gaining momentum to launch herself into the raft. Unable to brake once she hits the rubber tubes, she falls face-first onto the floor. I pick her up, positioning her in the front. The oarsman struggles to maneuver the awkward raft as midday winds blow us away from the scent.

"We need to grid back and forth, perpendicular to the wind," I direct him. "When the victim's scent reaches the surface, the wind pushes it away, like a fan blowing smoke from a campfire. Our job is to get Tasha to show me the boundaries of that scent cone. When you hear her whining, you'll know we're in it."

He grunts, struggling with the sluggish boat. On the beach, a new set of divers are gearing up. Grappling with the oars, the oarsman fights against the now-steady wind. He backstrokes to gain momentum.

Tasha's eyes sparkle as we enter the saturated scent cone. She stretches from the rim of the raft with her front paws, and whines, trying to reach out with her nose to touch the invisible gas. She snaps her head forward into the wind, her eyes fixed straight ahead. The rest of her body freezes as her nostrils flare in and out. Like a small lawn mower rumbling to life, Tasha grumbles from deep within, bellowing up into a monstrous, prolonged, "Wooooooofffff!"

"Crap, Tash, you scared the bejesus out of me with that noise."

The oarsman's eyes swell as big as plums.

I drop an orange buoy for the divers and mark the spot on my GPS unit. The mark is sixty feet offshore and ninety feet downwind from the point last seen. Under the buoy, seventy-five feet of white line uncoils, pulled downward into the murky water by a two-pound anchor.

"Keep rowing," I urge. "I need to get Tasha closer to pinpoint the scent source."

Fumbling, the oarsman attempts to row the bulky craft into the wind. The buoy, twirling in the water, captures Tasha's attention. But her nose still twitches, picking up scent.

A motorboat sputters. In unison, Tasha and I jerk our heads in the direction of the motor, our concentration shattering like dropped crystal goblets. An older man in plainclothes pilots the small boat, which contains a barking golden retriever.

"What the hell are this old man and his barking dog doing out here? I asked the cop to keep everyone off the water!" I grit my teeth. Stink Face must have sent him. He wants us to fail. Tasha rivets on the golden.

"He's hoping to find the victim using his depth finder." The oarsman tries to placate me.

"While we're searching? He had all day to use his depth finder. This is ridiculous! His pet dog is a huge distraction to Tasha." I glare at the man across fifteen feet of water.

Tasha leans over the edge of the raft, sniffing for the barking golden. As the boat motors portside to us, Tasha pounces across the raft for closer proximity.

The old man waves his hand like a rider in a slow-motion parade. As he passes, waves rock us off course and mix up the scent cone in a tornado of spiraling air.

Rage wells up. But I force my shoulders down and shift my attention back to Tasha.

Dangling her paws, Tasha's elbows rest on the raft tube. Her back legs shake in an effort to balance herself. As the boat motors off, she fixes her eyes, mesmerized again by the orange buoy.

I slap my hands on the taut tube attempting to distract her stare. "Leave it."

Her ears perk forward as she shuffles her behind in preparation to jump.

"Don't you dare …"

She catapults off the tube, belly-flopping in a splash of water. Like a greyhound hot after a rabbit, she beelines for the buoy which doesn't even resembles her favorite toy, the schlong.

"Tasha, leave it! Leave it!" I throw my hands in the air. "That's it. The search is over."

Tasha seizes the buoy in locked jaws and heads for shore. But, to her surprise, her athletic dog paddle gives her no forward propulsion. Her stubby legs tangle in the buoy line, with the two-pound weight dragging her snout underwater. With a few web-footed underwater punches, she pops to the surface, inching forward, struggling against the buoy line. She takes three more strokes forward. The snarled mess pulls her snout underwater again. Coughing, she surfaces and grips her jaw tighter to tug her prize to shore.

"Quick," I beg my oarsman. "We have to get her before she drowns."

Last summer Tasha nearly drowned at our favorite camping spot in the Black Canyon of the Gunnison, a narrow river gorge cut several thousand feet through some of North America's oldest rocks. As she retrieved a giant stick from the river, the fast-moving current swept her under a monstrous boulder. She popped up a quarter-mile downstream, coughing and gagging, but with the stick still in her mouth.

The oarsman swings the boat around to paddle toward Tasha.

"Tasha! Drop, leave it."

Tasha gives me an over-the-shoulder, eyeballs-as-big-as-tennis-balls look. She clamps her jaw harder on the buoy.

"NO!"

Against the weighted buoy's resistance, she powers her hind legs through the tangled line to swim. Her head strains sideways with the buoy's weight, but she moves forward. When she reaches the beach, she crawls onto the mud, struggling to all fours. She drops her prize, shakes, and turns to me, beaming pride, her tail wagging.

"Bad dog! Really bad dog!"

Jumping out of the boat, I grab her by the scruff of the neck. With my feet sinking ankle deep into the muck, I shove her into the boat. As she squirms, I unwind a cobweb of string from her legs.

Back in the boat, Tasha leans toward me with ears drooped in contrition.

"Good dog, Tasha. You found his scent. But we weren't done."

Despite Tasha ripping out the buoy, the location is saved in my GPS.

At the staging area, Stink Face stands in front with arms crossed. I spout off about Tasha's alert.

"Don't tell me," he scowls. "I'm not in charge."

I huff toward Jon, the lead diver with the National Park Service. Regaining my composure, I smile as I approach him.

"Would you like to know where Tasha alerted?"

"Absolutely. Tasha's a rock star."

Handing him my map, I circle where Tasha alerted and tell him to dive thirty feet upwind. He turns to brief his teammates.

On the drive home, I call SARDOC first to say that I am free of the water mission, then I call Ed Jones. Ed's voice sounds so desperate. "You're it. You have to find my nephew, or I'll never be able to bring him home." His plea for help dissolves the anger that's been percolating in me since Tasha and I arrived at the lake. I tell Ed the protocol, how I need the Ouray sheriff to request permission from my sheriff.

At home, I help Tasha out of the truck and tie her outside in the sun to dry. As I shoulder my gear upstairs, my telephone chimes once again. I expect the sheriff confirming permission protocols, but instead a friend from the lake calls with news that the divers found the young man's body.

Running downstairs, I untie Tasha, shove her in the truck, and zoom back to the lake. I speed-dial Doug in the Dominican Republic.

"After they spent twelve hours dinking around, Tasha shows up, alerts, and the divers find the body within five minutes," I brag and slightly exaggerate to Doug. "Can you believe it?"

"Make sure you reward her with a big steak tonight. I can't wait to see you tomorrow."

My elation drops, realizing I can no longer avoid the inevitable: I must break the news to him that I won't be flying in to the Dominican Republic tomorrow.

"Ed Jones just called," I hesitate, anticipating a negative response. "They want us to work a plane crash tomorrow. So, I'm not sure when I can get to the DR. I'll call you as soon as I am done with it." I wince, feeling guilty, and snap the phone shut before Doug can respond.

Tasha and I rush back to the lake, where Jon greets me with a big smile and the news that the dive team found the young man within minutes in about thirty feet of water with no visibility. While the local fire and emergency crews keep their distance, I snag a passing deputy.

"Can Tasha see the body?"

"Sure, I guess it's okay."

The more times I expose Tasha to a corpse, the more successful she will be when searching for bodies.

Out of respect for the body and the victim's family, Tasha and I tiptoe behind the deputy to the black bag near the shore. Tasha's hackles rise, and her shoulders drop as she crouches near the bag, stopping within nose distance. She takes quick, shallow snorts.

Leaning over, the deputy unzips the bag partway, revealing the young man's wet, black hair rather than his face. Startled at his body lying face down, I jump back.

Tasha nudges the bag with her nose. She moves in closer, smelling his head. Her hackles relax. She sniffs a few more seconds and wrenches her neck to make eye contact with me.

"Woooooooffff."

"Yes, decomp. That's him."

She lunges at my waist, begging for her reward. I yank out the bright-orange, floating schlong, tucked in the back of my pants. Stepping away from the bag, I fling her toy into the water. Like a platform diver ready to execute the leap, Tasha takes ten running steps and, with outstretched legs, lands smack on her belly. She swims to the reward, latching onto the toy to parade it through the crowd, brushing her wet, sandy body against legs as she goes.

CHAPTER 30

A Promise

Summer 2005
Ouray, Colorado

I put off calling Doug again until the very last minute. Making myself sound as pert as possible, I spell out my change in plans—to helicopter onto Whitehouse Mountain to look for the body of Ed's nephew and delay my flight to the Dominican Republic by a few days.

"No, you aren't going on that mission. You have to be here at work tomorrow, and that's your responsibility. You can't pay thousands of dollars to change an international flight to go on a volunteer rescue mission."

"But—"

"You haven't worked in a month. You're just goofing off. What about me?"

"A couple days wouldn't make a difference. I could extend my stay on the other end to finish the work."

"No."

"What if I ask Ed to pay my flight-change fee?"

That mollifies Doug. Another phone call to Ed secures his agreement to pay for delaying my flight to the Dominican Republic. But when I call Doug back, letting him know that Ed will pay the flight fees, he says, "No, you can't go. You won't go. It's not right. I don't want you risking your life or Tasha's life for someone who is dead."

At least that makes sense: he doesn't want me risking our lives.

"But I have to do this mission. We are the only ones with all the skills—water, wilderness, and avalanche. We're the only ones who can pull this off. Ed needs us. This is what our last decade of training and work has been for."

"You belong here. I need for you to be here tomorrow."

I read between the lines: he is suffering, sweltering in the tropical heat, in a cloud of mosquitoes. He wants me there—to be miserable *with him*.

"I can't. I have to do this mission." I clap the phone shut and throw it on the passenger seat. *What just happened? He no doubt thinks my partnership with Tasha takes priority. Is he right? Are we two people going in two different directions?* I gun the gas pedal toward Ouray in answer.

During the three-hour drive from Crested Butte to Ouray, I fight back fatigue by inhaling a Subway steak-and-cheese sandwich, and then I crack open shelled sunflower seeds between my teeth, one at a time, and spit the hulls out the window. Air rushes inside the cab, tossing my hair across my face.

At the ugly memory of my phone conversation with Doug, I reach around to stroke Tasha's soft coat with my fingers. Tasha stretches out across the back seat, sleeping on a full belly of canned tuna, brown rice, salmon oil, and two raw eggs. She snores.

I long to be curled up in Doug's arms, but my stomach tightens, knowing I hung up on his objections and defied his desires. During Tasha's training, Doug had been there, volunteering to hide buried in snow, listening to my gripes about macho search-and-rescue egos, and assisting on missions. He should understand better than anyone how much this mission means to me. But instead of sharing my passion, he's become a control freak over the years. Perhaps I agreed to this mission because it was easier for me to risk my life searching for a dead man than talk to my husband about our deteriorating relationship. I spit self-doubt out the window with my sunflower-seed shells.

As the sun sets behind the Colorado Plateau, I find myself falling asleep at the wheel. I force my eyes wide-open and turn south at Montrose, toward the heart of the San Juan Mountains. Tasha and I arrive at the quaint resort after dark. We're the only occupants of the hotel, and I drive to the unlit backside, looking for our room in complete darkness. Adjacent to the hotel, the Uncompahgre River thunders vibrations through the pavement. Between the river's deafening roar, the inky night, and the creepy solitude, I grip the steering wheel hard enough to whiten my knuckles.

"Tash, stay. You're not going anywhere until I get your collar and leash out of my suitcase. If I don't, you'll end up in the river, never to be seen again, or I'll find you in town with the bears, looking for garbage. That's the last thing I need tonight."

I shut her in the air-conditioned truck. Her nose presses to the window, fogging the glass. Her eyes droop.

From the back of the truck, I lug one overstuffed suitcase toward the dark room, looking over my shoulder several times. Tasha's glow-in-the-dark collar with her leash are snuggled deep in the suitcase, somewhere beneath the heap of ski boots, fleece, down, and Gore-Tex outerwear.

When I enter the room, a wave of musty hot air rushes me, knocking me backward with its sickly-sweet smell. The heat reminds me of the roaster-oven nights I endured in the Caribbean with biting insects. Dropping my suitcase on the floor, I throw open the window, hoping the cool mountain air will penetrate the mesh screen and flow into the room.

I groan, dreading my 4:30 a.m. wake-up call. Tasha and I need sleep, but the sauna atmosphere in the room make her pant to cool down, and that's enough to keep me awake. Alternatives mean sleeping with the door open, risking toothy gorge rats crawling into our room, or sleeping in the back of my truck without my sleeping pad or bag. Neither sounds appealing.

I open my suitcase and rummage for Tasha's collar and leash, locating them below a large Ziploc containing a three-day supply of dog kibble. At the truck, I secure the bright green luminescent collar on her neck. She pulls me to the edge of the parking lot for a quick pee and poop. I stand in mindless exhaustion, rubbing my dry, itchy eyes, anticipating the moment of collapsing on the bed to fall into a coma.

"Okay, girl, let's go."

I tug her toward the sizzling room. Closing her inside, I point my finger at her shiny black nose, prompting her to be good.

Crawling into the back of my truck on my knees, I ruffle through the rest of my bags: the Boulder bag, the shoe bag, the search bag, the avalanche pack, the food bag, the Dominican bag—searching for everything I might need for the mission. In the avalanche pack, I stuff my beacon, personal radio, shovel, probe, snacks, two liters of water, first-aid kit, wands for marking alerts, and Tasha's vest.

Four minutes later, I barge into the hotel room with my arms full of gear. I scan the room for Tasha's whereabouts. I expect to see her sprawled on the concrete slab panting, queasy from the oven-like temperatures. Instead, she stands on all fours, tail wagging, head and snout buried deep in my suitcase.

"Tasha. What are you doing?"

Her head dives deeper, as if pouncing on a field mouse. Then, I hear that all too familiar sound—the snorting grunt of an underfed piglet suckling a teat. Tasha inhales dog kibble without chewing.

"No!"

I yank at her collar only to feel the snaps explode open. I fall backward, my avalanche rescue pack full of electronics and expensive gadgets hitting the concrete floor with a thud. A Tasha trademark, she gobbles up the bits of food like an emaciated street dog that hasn't eaten in days. Only short bursts of stomach contractions interrupt her snorts.

As I scramble upright, dry heaves ensue. She gags. She coughs, trying to expel bits of kibble piling up in her esophagus. While she dry heaves the undigested food, she inhales more, with no breaths in between. I hear movement from her stomach, through her esophagus, and into her mouth. Her tail wags freely behind her.

"Noooooooooooooo!"

Half the kibble seems to go into her lungs or down her nose. Her chest muscles pulse in and out, making her wretch again. Worried she might suffocate from kibble asphyxiation, I grab her neck like a mother dog picks up her pup. Resisting me, she lunges forward into the heap of winter jackets and pants to suck up the last remaining kibble, including shreds of plastic from the Ziploc baggie.

I want to strangle her.

I clench the scruff of her neck until she lets out a yelp.

"Shit, Tasha. I can't believe you did that." I slide her overstuffed body across the concrete floor. A clear plastic tendril clings to her nose.

I feel like Steve Irwin, the crocodile hunter from Australia, wrestling a wild croc. With my legs nearly doing the splits, I use my right foot to slam the door shut, to prevent her from sneaking out into the dark streets of Ouray, while my other foot holds her barreled muscular chest back from the suitcase. When I turn to lock the door, she makes one last dash to gulp at the upchucked mess.

I stop the action, slamming the empty suitcase lid on her head. She backs out. I want to laugh and cry. I want to kill her and sob on her shoulder. In six hours, we will be boarding a helicopter for the most dangerous mission of our life. Now she's overheated and has a bloated belly. In the morning, she may be too sick to search or even move.

Swallowing the last of the kibble, she leans forward to dry heave three more times, but nothing comes out.

I sit on the bed, shaking my head, fingers rubbing my temples. I try to succumb to tears. But nothing comes out.

"What am I going to do with you? It's eleven o'clock at night and we have to be up and ready at four forty. You're a mess."

From the center of the room, Tasha stares at me, licking crumbs from her chops, then tilts her head to the side. She has slurped up all remaining crumbs from the floor. Only shreds of plastic remain, strewn around my suitcase. I fall on my back on the bed, covering my face with a pillow, longing to escape into sleep.

A wet nose nudges me from my stupor. Thinking I slept through the alarm clock, I spring to my feet. The clock says only ten minutes lapsed. I splash water on my face to wake up.

Tasha's long, pasty dry tongue hangs halfway down to the floor. She paces. She pants, her head drooping low.

I fill the ice-cube container with water. Tasha slurps up half the contents in seconds.

Ten minutes later, after I finish organizing my pack, I watch her stomach expand. Her hide feels like an overstretched elk skin on a Native American drum frame. I collapse into bed.

"Good night. Don't bug me."

Tasha splays her kibble-packed belly on the cool concrete floor and pants, then paces. Tasha's belly slowly swells as dry nuggets expand, tripling her gut size. Every forty minutes, she paces, toenails clacking across the concrete. Desperately looking for relief, she jumps on and off my bed a half-dozen times.

I flop around like beached fish. Tangled in sweaty sheets, I reach for my phone to check the time every half hour for fear of sleeping through the alarm. As Tasha labors in her panting, she taps tight circles, nose chasing tail, until she finds the perfect place to plop down on the concrete for a few minutes—until she rises to repeat the pattern again.

Sleeping thirty minutes at a time, I throw my sheet to the side, hop up, and take Tasha outside. Standing in the pitch-dark night, half-naked, I scream alongside the torrent of the raging Uncompahgre River. The Milky Way glitters above. I look for any sign that Tasha's girdle size will shrink in half before sunup.

Just before daybreak on mission day, we drive to the designated meeting place with three members of Ouray Mountain Rescue. In an open meadow, rescue vehicles gather around the makeshift helicopter landing zone. Dimmed headlights glow off aspen trees and illuminate the grass.

With my assistance, Tasha rolls out of the truck to plop on the damp ground. A sharp high-pitched sound of gas escapes her, resonating through the silence. My dry cheeks crack a big smile despite myself, and despite a nearly sleepless night. I grip Tasha's leash that's attached to her bright-red search harness. She pants heavily. The back half of her body waddles with every movement, and she resembles a sixty-pound barrel with four squat legs and a head.

I can't imagine heaving this puffed-up, semicomatose black Lab onto a helicopter and flying one mile straight up, to a mountainside where no one else dares venture. What if her gut explodes at altitude?

Tasha pants, crouching with her tail tucked between her hindquarters. I drag her to greet Ed Jones and Sheriff Mattivi, her head hanging low. I dread disappointment when they see Tasha.

"I'm so happy you're here, Susan." A tear streaks down Ed's face. He sniffs back his embarrassment by pulling me into his big frame to give me a you-just-saved-my-life bear hug. I return his hug with one even tighter. His sorrow flows into me, forming an unspoken bond between us. I gulp, and neither of us speaks for a few moments.

As we settle into exchanging information, two headlights approach from the north sky, looking like cat eyes glowing in the dark. The whack of twirling blades echoes against the canyon walls. Three Ouray search-and-rescue climbers—Bill Whitt, Jeff Skoloda, and his wife, Nicole—stand behind us. Ferried one at a time in the small chopper, the three of us will meet on the mountain a mile above where we now stand.

"Don't worry, Mr. Jones," I reach for his hand. Shouting over the helicopter noise, I holler, "Tasha and I will find your nephew. I promise."

I have never said those words to a grieving family member before. Ever.

The pilot waves the first member of the Ouray team to approach him. Bill Whitt slides into the helicopter and waves goodbye. As morning light creeps into the mountain community of Ouray, the pilot lifts the helicopter above our heads toward Whitehouse Mountain. All too soon, Tasha and I will join him in another world, one painted with rock, ice, and snow.

Tasha bucks against my grip when the pilot returns to settle his helicopter skids onto the grassy meadow. With blades spinning, the pilot cues me to hot-load the helicopter. I crouch low.

I muster all my strength to hoist Tasha by her vest strap. "You can't hop in because your guts are stuffed." My one-hand bicep curl fails to lift her heavy body into the vibrating machine. I trip. Her chest and legs slam against the metal frame. Scrabbling her front paws, she catches the ledge. One final shove under her butt, and she's in.

She scoots across the bench seat toward the pilot. I yank her leash as she's just short of his lap.

"Sit."

Her butt obediently taps the seat.

Slinging off my avalanche pack, I toss it at her and haul myself into the bird. Tasha lunges toward my lap. I press my shoulder into hers, shoving her back into the seat gap between the pilot and me, while keeping a secure grip on her leash.

"Move it, Tasha. You can't sit in my lap yet."

As the pilot revs up the spinning blades, thrumming vibrates inside the bird. Tasha's body shakes as she hunches her head forward, digging her claws into the seat to brace herself. From training and working in helicopter flights, she knows the routine. Her eyes gaze at a distant spot out the window. Her pink tongue hangs to the side of her mouth, coated in white foam. Her tail tucks under her hindquarters. She waits for me to pat my hands on my lap, giving her permission to sit on me.

"You're okay, girl." Those words help me focus, too, as my hands fumble for the seat belt then the helmet.

The pilot taps my helmet and points to the intercom device.

"If you want to talk to me, push this button."

I test the intercom.

"You ready, Sue?"

"Ready."

He gives me a simple nod and smiles. The helicopter lifts, shifting me sideways. Tasha falls into my lap.

CHAPTER 31

My Everest

Summer 2005
Whitehouse Mountain, Colorado

Tasha's weight pins my legs. I glom on to her, bear-hugging her neck. Her leash, circled multiple times around one palm, nearly cuts off the circulation in my hand. I slide my other hand into the grab handle above the door.

As the helicopter rises, the ring of rescue vehicles shrinks below us on the lush valley bottom. The chopper climbs fast, departing the dark morning shadows on the valley floor to burst into the sunlight, mirrored intensely off the snow-covered peaks.

The chopper ascends toward a snow-covered mountain that plunges down into a tangled chasm, choked with trees, snow, and gushing water. Even expert mountaineers don't climb through these crumbling cliff walls to summit Whitehouse Mountain. I wheeze for breath as the oxygen depletes with the gain of altitude.

The helicopter, a mosquito in comparison to the hulking mountain, seems so frail—a loose collection of mechanical parts that could quit cooperating with each other at any moment. The pilot aims straight for the vertical wall of rock that's cut with white couloirs, the largest one plummeting one-and-a-half vertical miles. Somewhere on that face lies the body of Richard Mills. Panic threatens to overcome me. Squeezing Tasha's torso, I feel her fast heartbeat in my hands.

I scan the narrow, steep couloir for anything that looks like plane wreckage. But we're too far away. The couloir slices a white tongue through massive upright rock slabs, golden in the morning sunlight. Like teeth ready to crunch prey, walls tower on both sides of the couloir, pinching the snow chute. We're about to land near its toe.

The pilot reduces power and inches closer to the vertical rock wall bounding the couloir.

"We're about to land." The pilot's voice blares through the headset.

"You've got to be joking. What? Where? Where is Bill? I don't see him."

"He's below us. See that little speck in the middle of the slope. That's him."

"Way down there?"

"Yep."

While the pilot descends, I scan a search area that's the size of eight football fields standing vertically on end. Bill appears, wielding an ice ax, chipping a tiny flat strip in the snow on the steep slope adjacent to a small rock fin. As we inch toward him, he runs behind that little fin for protection against the rotor wash.

I brace for impact. The helicopter teeters. Its blades seem ready to shave the icy slope, then we lurch toward the rock fin where Bill is hunkered down. I dig my fingers deeper into Tasha, who's panting like a steam engine, reminding me I'm not the only nervous soul on board.

The pilot drops this tin-can-whirligig into a small slot that's bounded on both sides by rock walls.

"Ready?"

The chopper bobbles. Deep in concentration, the pilot balances his side skid on a flattened sliver of the slope strip and signals Bill to approach.

"Hand me Tasha." He finds stable footing, his arms reaching overhead.

Blinded by the early morning sun, I squint at Bill. His fingers barely reach above the skid. I shout Tasha's command, "Help!" the cue for her to fall into someone's arms, but she can't hear me, so I give her a flick of my wrist. Tasha's pads claw at the air. I release her leash and harness handle.

Whipping off the helicopter helmet, I swap it for my search-and-rescue helmet. The noise of the motor deafens me, and the vibration rattles my teeth. My side skid hangs several feet above the ground, a reasonable jump, but with an angled landing.

Slipping off my seat, I search for a purchase for my plastic ski boots on the skid, one at a time until my lug-soles cling to the icy metal. Grabbing my pack, I leap off the bird, arms extended. The short free fall plops me feetfirst on solid snow. Anticipating a slip, I chip my boots into the snow to avoid sliding ass-first onto the slope and off the cliff. My boots anchor, the top layer of snow softer than expected. Momentary relief floods over me, knowing Tasha and I will be able to hike on soft snow instead of crawling across something like a giant ice rink. But my relief is short-lived when I remember the warming sun and the threat it brings.

Blades revolve above me and I duck, scrambling on hands and feet. Turbulence pushes me into the safety of the rock fin. Reaching the duo, I drop to my knees to play, Tasha's reward.

She flips on her back, sliding on her avalanche vest, her feet pumping the air. With the tension of the flight over, I laugh at both of us. Tasha with her lips fluttering and me with my curly blond hair escaping from my goggle-covered helmet, my tight, stretchy mountaineering clothes, and my heavy pack. *A mountain-woman action figure, ready to conquer the world.*

The bird lifts, sending a blast of turbulent air toward us. I look at the vast treeless slope, bounded by rock walls. Below us, the couloir plunges into air, thousands of feet down toward the little mountain community of Ouray. As the helicopter's faint *thud-thud-thud* echoes far below in the canyon, silence settles around us.

Above, the June sun is warming the east-facing slopes, releasing pea-sized rocks off the cliffs. Pebbles ping down on us. I shed a midlayer of clothing in the heat but keep the helmet on. Tasha rolls, jostling her guts packed full of kibble.

I glance at my watch: one hour to find Richard Mills.

Setting my pack down, I unload unnecessary equipment in order to be light and fast. Tasha continues to roll around, squatting to pee, trying to poop. I squeeze out water for her to drink from the hose connected to the bladder inside my pack. She sniffs the tube, jerking her head away in refusal.

"What do you want me to do, Sue?" Bill interrupts.

"Tell me—where did you find the three bodies?"

He points at an isolated boulder perched in the middle of the slope, a football field's length away. "We found the little boy on the upside of that big rock. Due to the sun and warm temperatures melting away the snow, part of his body was exposed on the surface of the snow. The last time we were here, there must have been twenty more feet of snow up here."

I gulp, a grim image of what we might find popping out of the ice comes into my head. Snow conditions had really changed, and so could a decomposing body.

"And the grandpa? Where was he?"

"About a hundred feet upslope from the boy."

"And granny?"

"She was found around the corner." With his finger, he draws a map in the snow. "She got hung up on a different boulder. You just can't see it from here. Part of her body was exposed by the snow melt."

I pull a notebook out of my radio harness and sketch a map just like at the water mission eighteen hours earlier. From Bill's description, I draw a couloir branching to the right, unseen from my current location.

"So, here's the deal," I tell him. "If Tasha shows interest, I'll place a wand in the snow. When Jeff and Nicole arrive on scene, tell them to look for my flags to poke around with probe poles. With any luck, they'll find something squishy underneath."

I pull a red-flagged wand out of my pack and stuff another eight wands inside my shirt for quick access.

He hands me a team radio. "Just remember, you need to be back here in an hour."

"Yep. I have one pass to get this right. Let's hope Tasha will work her magic."

Dropping to my knees, I lean over to unclip Tasha. I whisper the familiar command in Tasha's ear.

"Are you ready to go to work?"

Her ears perk forward, she licks her chops, and her snout rams mine. I flinch, taking the hit.

"Go find!"

On command, she dashes sixty feet up the undulating snow slope and hooks toward the rock wall bounding the north side of the couloir, her snout guiding every move. I watch her scour the area where two of the victims were found.

Her nose rises to twelve o'clock, and her nostrils pulse in the air, two inches from the rock wall. She produces a high pitch whine, an indication she's found scent. The position of her nose tells me she smells decomp drifting somewhere from higher up the slope.

My chest heaving in the thin air, I lope to her location to search for flesh or a piece of clothing.

Nothing.

With my aluminum six-foot probe pole ready, I lean over a huge gap where snow melted away from the rock wall. A void of darkness yawns. I peek into the dark hole. The sound of water rages below. My body tenses at the complication: We could be standing on a thin, fragile snow bridge that could collapse without warning, sweeping Tasha and me into caverns of water to drown beneath the snow. The abyss also complicates the scent picture: Richard's scent could be flowing in water from a mile away. The scent of one of the other bodies found weeks ago could drift through the cavern, too, causing Tasha to react.

With the scent's origin unknown, I whip a wand from my jacket, drive it into the snow, and get ready to follow Tasha's next move. Yanking her nose from the rock wall, Tasha sprints toward an SUV-sized boulder in the center of the slope. Her nimble short legs and wide paws sidestep rocky rubble with ease. She shoves her head into the dark void ringing the boulder. I hustle toward her, dodging calf-high rocks that have been flung catawampus onto the snow from above. Tasha circles the boulder twice, and then stops. She tosses her nose up to the sky and whines.

"Is that him? Did you find him?"

Inching up to probe around the rock, I see a five-foot-wide gap between stone and snow. My probe shoots through snow, hits surging water, and then rock. I repeat several spots, with the same results.

I flip open my cell phone. Bold red numbers flash across the screen. 6:32 a.m.

Standing, dwarfed by the lone SUV-rock perched in the middle of the couloir, I radio to Bill for more information. Below me at the makeshift helipad, he looks like a miniature G.I. Joe doll.

"Can you see me? Did you guys find a body here?"

"Yep. The four-year-old boy."

"That's what I thought. Tasha's right on. When did you find him?"

"About nineteen days ago."

"Yeah, and that large boulder was buried under snow. That's how fast this place is changing."

Tasha inches toward the boulder again to get a better whiff. But I order her back for fear she might fall in.

Sweat drips down my face. The couloir we're in is like a convection oven. The intense solar radiation is melting the ice that normally keeps countless tiny rocks cemented to the frozen walls. Like buckshot exploding from a gun barrel, a steady stream of pebbles ricochets off the side of the mountain. I scrunch my shoulders to my ears and spin my back to the wall to protect my face, hoping to prevent the rocks from tearing into my flesh.

Tasha turns away from the SUV-boulder and bounds upslope toward a flash of silver twisted metal the size of a coffee table, glinting in the morning sun. She investigates, sniffing with caution, her moist nose wafting close to the sharp edge. She races further up the slope, wheezing heavily in the thin air.

I scan the slope, peppered with small black rocks and airplane debris. The melted snow holds remnants of the fatal disaster. A new toothbrush. Pages of a children's book, wet and tattered. The mild downdraft breeze isn't strong enough to flutter the sodden pages, but water under the snow flows with the smell of decomposed human scent. I scratch my forehead, walking in circles, wondering where Richard Mills might be entombed.

Curiosity draws me to pick up the book. But I drop it before gleaning the title. If I miss one of Tasha's behaviors, one subtle nose twitch, I might miss an important piece of the puzzle.

I trail Tasha, glancing again at my phone.

Thirty minutes left.

Scurrying to keep up, I gasp as the dry mountain air pierces my lungs. I shove a palm-full of snow in my mouth. Ice melts to water instantly, offering me some cooling relief.

"Where is he?" I cheer her on. Tasha directs the mission. I surrender control to her and follow. Our partnership shares an understanding with just a few simple words and hand signals.

With renewed energy, I stomp my feet, sidestepping fist-sized rocks, and march behind her, gripping my probe pole. By Tasha's behavior, I read that she hasn't pinpointed the scent source. She returns to the rock wall, pounces on the volcanic rocks with her front paws. Looking upward, she emits a series of long high-pitched whimpers.

"Tash, he can't be up there. The pilot would have spotted him lying on the bare rock. What are you trying to tell me?"

We ram against our communication barrier. For all our training—voice commands, hand signals, whines, and alerts—I can't decipher what she is trying to tell me. Her behavior says she smells something. Hoping to catch a whiff of something, I inhale air percolating from the snow. But I can't smell anything.

"Tash, the scent has got to be flowing in the water. We've got to keep following it."

Tasha pushes her paws off the wall, flips around, and runs for the center of the couloir again. I follow, glancing at the time.

Twenty-two minutes remain.

We pick our way across the white moonscape, which reminds me of what a meteorite explosion might look like. Black rocks and twisted silver metal plane debris hamper our path. Pieces of metal jut from the snow's surface, hinting at the force of the plane's impact.

Tasha's pace picks up. She zigs then zags, working a couple hundred feet in front of me. My pace lags. Feeling like I had just sprinted to the top of the Empire State Building, I buckle over and try to catch my breath.

Tasha reaches another isolated rock the size of a small house, perched at the intersection of the main couloir and a right-branching chute. Her audible panting fades as she pulls further away from me.

I hustle again to catch her, heaving in frantic rapid breaths from urgency and thin oxygen. Tasha disappears behind the house-sized rock for what seems like eternity: no doubt the location where they found grandma. I wonder if Tasha will come around the corner with something in her mouth: a brush tangled with human hair or a child's soggy teddy bear missing an ear. I grimace at the thought, waiting for her to bark or reappear.

"Tash, where are you?"

As I stare at the boulder, Tasha barrels around its corner, head bobbing up and down, nostrils flaring, tail wagging. Her eyes meet mine, briefly. She continues her clockwise rotation around the boulder seeming to chase scent in a circle. As she presses forward, running to the opposite side of the slope, I probe around the boulder with no results, but leave another wand and verify the site with Bill.

Tasha speeds back to me. She squats on her hind legs, pushes her bum down one inch from the snow, and squirts out a massive pile of poo—the mound of kibble from last night. Enough to fill a large cake pan. While relieving herself, she taps her feet forward and keeps her nose in the air, sucking in information only detectable to a working canine. Pooping doesn't even break her forward momentum with her nose. When finished, she flies by me, sniffing the snow at my feet, no doubt feeling ten pounds lighter.

The thud of the helicopter bringing the third and fourth searchers echoes against the mountain.

I face upslope and, for the first time, focus on the smaller couloir on my right, which funnels toward me into the main slope. A trail of plane debris shambles down the slope. The flotsam-strewn couloir helps me formulate a plan: to let Tasha follow the scent cone. The immense rock walls bounding the steep slopes throw my usual plan off-kilter, but the couloir unkinks my mind. The couloir stretches up about half the height of a New York skyscraper. At its apex, it butts up against a thirty-story vertical cliff. I imagine how the wingless metal shell, with four family members strapped into their seat belts, slid a half mile down upper Whitehouse Mountain, tumbling and bouncing, before launching like a chunk of snow over the cliff to explode into bits on impact.

Richard Mills' body could be broken into bits and pieces anywhere.

I look at my phone.

Sixteen minutes remain.

My stomach clenches into a burning bundle.

When the thuds of the helicopter blades resound against the gray rock-and-ice amphitheater one more time, I know the last two searchers, Nicole and Jeff, have arrived. After the helicopter departs again, with its diminishing echo, more pea-sized rocks shower down on me. Snow crunches underfoot.

Tasha stays on task, circling, trying to sort out the rivers of scent pouring at her from the main and right-hand couloir. She stands at the intersection of the two slopes. Time only permits choosing one of the couloirs. Her nose flares as short bursts of scent siphon in.

I plant my feet in the snow, clasp my hands behind my back, and watch Tasha. She doesn't look to me for advice. She veers off the main slope and climbs right.

The sun rising higher in the sky causes me to squint. In comparison to the main couloir, this smaller one pitches on an angle steeper than stadium stairs, along a quarter-mile-long incline. There are mangled pieces of the plane here, too. An inflated tire attaches to the landing gear. A seat flips upside down. The control panel is ripped in several pieces. Across the disarray, the cliffs above disgorge rocks of all sizes—pebbles, fist-sized stones, basketballs, pumpkins, and boulders. Each element in the scene screams for attention. Each element competes with the others in a miasma of confusion.

In the rising heat, beads of sweat pour from my head. I wipe my brow with my bare hand and push back my helmet to cool myself in the gentle breeze blowing downslope.

I step over a red cotton shirt, a seat cushion, and dismembered cables to keep pace with Tasha. Attacking her search area like a guided missile zooming in on its preprogrammed target, she zigzags across the pockmarked slope.

Bill's voice interrupts over the radio, "Sue, where should I send Nicole?"

"Have her meet me up here. Tasha's onto something. I have to follow." I wave my arms, so he can see me before I round a corner out of his sight.

I glance at my phone.

Thirteen minutes left.

Tasha sprints uphill with her tail erect. She makes quick cuts across the potholed snow, dodging metal, avoiding rocks, almost ping-ponging off the sheer rock walls. Half football player and half ballerina, she dances over torn metal and sharp rocks that could at any moment slice her pads off. Her nose scours the landscape.

"It's the scent cone—and you're in it!" I can't smell the scent cone, see it, or feel it, but I sense its invisible outline from Tasha's behavior. I mentally map its dimensions—shaped like an upside-down funnel—with Tasha heading right for the spout.

I scurry uphill, darting around a broken suitcase to catch up to Tasha. The effort in the thin air makes me wheeze. During my rush toward Tasha, my phone jangles. Its intrusion cuts into my concentration. Tasha charges ahead to crest the slope out of my sight. Irritated at the interruption, I grab the phone from my pocket in case the sheriff demands our return.

"Sue?"

"Doug?"

"Where are you?"

"I'm in the middle of the frickin' search!" I yowl into the phone. Of all the people, Doug should know better than barging in at a critical moment in a mission. "Tasha's in the scent cone. She's got him. She just took off. Gotta go."

I slam the phone shut. Anger at the intrusion pumps adrenaline through me, allowing me to tramp up the slope with renewed vigor. After dashing a few feet, I stop to breathe before the reduced oxygen drops me to my knees. With Tasha out of sight, my fear for her safety threatens to smother me.

"This is it, girl. You found him," I yell to her. "You need to bark or come back to me!"

Below my feet sprawl a pink sweater with white buttons, a ripped gray sweatshirt, a container of deodorant, a half-used toothpaste tube tightly rolled, a broken toy, a decomposing box of crayons, a torn coloring book, one white tennis shoe, and a slipper. I ignore them to look for Tasha, who peeks over the lip at me. Her hooded brown eyes pierce me with a resolute stare, and she sits down. She's done working.

"He better be there." I bolt full speed ahead, pumping my arms to charge up the last pitch around a knee-high boulder-covered mound as Tasha sits her ground.

I glance once more at my phone.

Ten minutes remain.

"Tasha, where is he?"

She stares at me, not budging from her perch. Her tongue hangs from her mouth to cool off.

"Now what? You're the expert, the trained search dog. Why can't you behave like all the other search dogs and lead me right to where he is?"

Her behavior says she is finished searching, but I don't see anything that looks like a body. I want to wring her neck.

Vexed, I look back downslope as Nicole and Jeff round the corner into view. My eyes cloud with failure. But Tasha sits in a perfect pose, showing me she's proud of her work.

"But Tasha, I don't see him. Show me!"

Her return stare into my eyes gives zero insight to the location of Richard Mills.

"What are you trying to tell me? I know you're not sitting on him; otherwise, you'd be digging through the snow." I walk a tight circle around her.

Nicole and Jeff edge closer. Their voices echo off the rock walls.

Gray rocks, dirty snow, plane parts, and clothing clutter my vision. Tasha's posture suggests Richard isn't under the snow. If he were buried, she'd dig. If he's on the surface, I should see him. I stick my probe pole into the snow where she sits. The metal tip hits rock. I pick up my pace, kicking my boots around Tasha in wider and wider concentric circles.

I pass a white sock, a shoe, and the leg of blue jeans buried in the dirty snow. With each larger concentric circle, I poke my probe pole into the rutted snow in between pebbles and rocks, kicking wreckage aside with my toe.

"He's got to be here somewhere."

Jeff and Nicole close in. Tasha fixes her unblinking eyes on me from fifty feet away, her bum still glued to the slope. Dripping sweat tickles the back of my neck.

In my circling, I walk between rocks, lumps of snow, and rubble. Heading downslope, I stop at a car-sized boulder near a vertical rock wall that's blocking the morning sun. An oxygen cylinder from inside the plane lies nearby, and I hear water rushing under my boots. Downdraft winds cool my perspiring face. I peek into the dark hole between the snow and the wall, like I had already done twice at other locations. Shoving my head deeper into the opening, I hope to find something.

I do.

Clutching my throat, I shoot backward coughing. The gagging stench of human decay wafts from the hole—the reek of a decomposing thirty-seven-day-old corpse. I back away, retching.

I'd been following Tasha for five thousand plus steps now, sticking my face into scary dark holes expecting open eyeballs to stare back. Smell is here, but no eyes, face, or body.

"Where is the body?!" I raise my hands in the air to demand an answer from the mountain.

Tasha darts toward me, tail wagging, ears pressing back. She loops around my feet and doubles-back upslope, leading me to her exact same spot, snapping her butt down in her perfect pose.

Stumbling on rocks back uphill, my eyes dart between Tasha, the uneven snow, and over my left shoulder. Nicole and Jeff stomp up the steep slope, probing at a snail's pace.

Five minutes remain.

I circle a wide berth toward Tasha, covering new ground, just in case new clues have surfaced. But there are too many thrashed plane parts and the annihilated contents of luggage, spewed across the ice in a sprawling jumble of color. The mishmash prevents me from homing in on a clue. My eyes scan across the slope, struggling to decipher what might look like pieces of a body or pertinent clothing versus metal airplane parts—there are a million little pieces of stuff scattered on the pitted, rock-strewn snow. I spear my probe into a blue shirt in hopes that an arm lies beneath.

Nothing.

"Tash. You've been to this spot twice. You're telling me he is right here. But, I don't see him."

I flash back on my avalanche lectures and field simulations for help, calling up the advice I told hundreds of students over the years.

"Of course. Lift up the glove, a hand might be attached. Pull on the ski pole, the strap could be wrapped to a wrist. Probe your pole beneath the backpack: a body could be connected. That's avalanche rescue 101."

I shift my eyes from Tasha to the snow, fixing on white fabric resembling a sock, two feet to her side. Like stalking prey, I take a half step closer to stand between Tasha and the sock. All of the other clothing I'd seen lay pancaked against the ice, but the rounded sock sprouts bulbous from the snow, different from the surrounding, undulating, pebble-covered bumps. I peer closer: a swatch of blue jeans meeting the sock arches with substance, too.

I do what I should have done ten minutes earlier. Grazing the metal tip of my probe on its fibers did not collapse it. The sock holds something more than air. I wield my probe like a fisherman's harpoon. Lightly denting the end of the probe deeper into the white fabric, I feel a bounce. I push with more resistance. The probe springs back. There it is, that familiar feeling. That sensation of metal pushing on human flesh, of touching skin stretched tight over a bloated extremity. Prodding a little harder, I feel the resistance of a heel bone. The white sock and the lower leg of the blue jeans protrude from the snow, but no more of the body.

"Tash, it's him!"

Tasha springs to her feet, startling me. Planting at my side, she brushes against my pant leg, inching her nose toward the end of my wand. She sniffs the blue jean leg.

I inch closer, turning my nose up in the air just like Tasha. I move my probe from the sock, up the pant leg, touching the denim jeans. I probe a soft spot on the back of a knee. Because the jean leg disappears beneath the snow, my next probe dips into the snow, but hit ice and rock, preventing me from locating the rest of Richard's body.

If Richard is intact, his body is cemented in the ice. Like most avalanche victims, tossed and tumbled around, his foot and lower leg skim closest to the surface while his body probably curls below, frozen in the tomb of ice and snow. I reach for my radio.

"It's him. We found him!"

I do little to contain my euphoria. Dropping my probe pole, I bend down on one knee to kiss Tasha's forehead.

"My good girl, you found him. You sat next to him like a good little soldier. You did what I asked of you."

I place my hand over my heart, preparing for what I might say to Mr. Jones: *"Thanks for believing in search-and-rescue dog teams. Thanks for never giving up on your family. Thanks for finding my name on the internet and calling me."* But that would have to wait until seeing Ed face-to-face.

Even though Tasha's and my work has ended, Bill, Nicole, and Jeff's work has just started. They have less than thirty minutes to chip out Richard Mills' body, zip it into the black body bag, and attach it to a hundred-foot line below the helicopter, which will deliver it to the meadow where Ed waits.

Quite over being the patient little soldier, Tasha demands her due. After all, she just completed a job that only a handful of skilled dogs in the nation could have performed. She flings her nose, jabbing me with her snout. Attacking me with too much exuberance, she bonks me in my nose.

"What is it, girl?"

She stands back, cocks her head, and freezes. Two brown eyes stare unwavering. At twelve thousand feet, in the San Juan Mountains, on an early summer morning, and with no words exchanged, I try for the umpteenth time in less than one hour to understand the unspoken language that only Tasha and I share.

"I know what you want. You want your reward for a hard day's work, just like the rest of us."

Whipping the glove from my sweaty hand, I throw it into the mountain air for her to chase.

CHAPTER 32

Buried Alive

2005–2008
Colorado & Montana

Shortly after Tasha found Richard Mills' body, cracks that had been hidden in my marriage for years started to surface. Somehow, balancing past and future commitments felt like I was carrying two tons of snow on my shoulders. I prayed I wouldn't crumble under its weight. I finally made it to the DR, but almost as soon as we got back I took a medical-consulting job on an icebreaker traveling to Antarctica.

"Doug, it's only for two weeks. It's a trip of a lifetime." I justified my decisions by telling him, "Think of the doors that will open for me. I'm getting paid to practice medicine in Antarctica."

"I don't want you to go."

"They called me. They're paying me well. You should be happy," I argued back as I headed out the door to teach twenty-seven students.

"Do not go."

That's all he said before he slammed the door behind me.

I recognized Tasha was old enough that her career was nearly over, which meant it was time for me to change mine. I didn't have the time or the heart to train another dog partner—Tasha was my one and only. But I did have more to offer. Two weeks later, I flew to the tip of South America in the dead of winter and boarded the SS *Gould* for a trip across the Drake Passage to the Antarctic Peninsula. In hindsight, maybe I shouldn't have gone, but I felt like I had to leave. I didn't recognize at the time that Doug's wounds from the first time I went to Antarctica were still hurting despite being two decades deep. And he expressed his hurt through anger and attempts at controlling me. My second trip to Antarctica was the equivalent of one of those skiers moving across an unstable slope—a huge avalanche was coming.

When I got home, Doug gave me the silent treatment for a few days. Then he insisted it was time of us to "get the hell out of Crested Butte" and move to Montana, the place where our love story first began. I blamed his unhappiness on exhaustion, the commute, and bad neighbors at the condo. I agreed to leave, though I suspected that he was hoping I'd stay. I told myself over and over that I'd give up everything to keep Doug's love, even if it meant losing the things I'd worked so hard for—my business, Poodle Lady, and Amy, Big, and their two sons. These things, these people were what held me together, and I knew I had their support and love.

We rented a house in Boulder, Colorado, for a while to make Doug's commute bearable. He'd transitioned his work from the Dominican Republic to southern Mexico. After twenty years of searching for gold, he finally found the thing he was looking for—a minable ore deposit in Chiapas, Mexico. That was the good news. The bad news was that it was a place riddled with unrest and violence, a place where he feared for our lives. Worse news: we were contract employees and wouldn't reap any monetary benefits from the discovery beyond our consulting wages.

When we packed up in Crested Butte, I believed in my heart that once we got to Montana, all our problems would just go away. Tasha was eleven now, and her muzzle was more gray than black. Her arthritic joints made climbing into the truck and skiing alongside me more difficult. Her search career was nearing its end, and it was a reality we could both handle.

In her semiretirement, my original dream for Tasha came true when we were hired as the first Colorado Rapid Avalanche Deployment (C-RAD) dog team at Eldora Ski Resort near Boulder. Each morning she'd sit alongside me, and we'd ride the chairlift together. Her webbed feet, splayed wide from years of digging, dangled over the edge, and her ears flapped in the wind.

Doug fumed when I told him I was making thirteen fifty an hour, but I supplemented my meager salary by offering medical and rescue courses. Tasha quickly found her lounging spot on the top-shack couch, overlooking the Continental Divide and South Arapaho Peak, the location of our first avalanche mission. It was a great spot to contemplate the sixty-five missions my partner and I had been called to in our tenure. Out of all of them, the one that was still haunting me during those days was the last mission of Tasha's career.

❖ ❖ ❖

Five days had passed since a Denver homemaker vanished near the summit of the Mount of the Holy Cross. My ole buddy Tim Cochrane had called us as the last-ditch effort after a multiagency, high-profile search-and-rescue operation failed to find her.

Cochrane had me on speed dial because a month earlier he had dispatched a Civil Air Patrol plane to drag us into a search for a missing park ranger while we were on vacation in Montana. At the Colorado-Wyoming border, as Tasha and I dozed in the back seat of the tiny plane, our pilot was told to take us back to Montana. On the sixth day of the search, friends had found the missing park ranger at the base of a cliff.

Now, Cochrane's plea for help summoned me back to the site of my first search-dog mission. It had been eight years since I partnered with legendary handler Ann Wichmann and her dog, Jenner, on that mountain. This time all eyes were on Tasha and me. If we failed to find the missing mother of four young children, Cochrane would suspend all other search efforts. We were filling some big shoes.

Cochrane had confided in me before we loaded the Huey, "You're it, our last shot. If you don't find her, the search is over."

"Give us until tomorrow afternoon," I told him. He knew Tasha needed to catch the downdrafts at night and early the next morning and to work the slope long after all other searchers and contamination were gone. If the missing woman were up high on the mountain, her scent would pool down into the meadow where we were about to land.

Tasha and I lifted off, just hours before sunset, with our camping gear and a support person I had just met. Looking out at the massive peak, I wondered if we'd find her alive like Cochrane's team had found the red-jacket lady hidden under a rock years before.

But by noon the next day, Tasha hadn't picked up one molecule of the victim's scent. The helicopter touched down in the dried alpine meadow at ten thousand feet to bring us back to base. We flew above treetops, looking down on hundreds of volunteers as they exited the forest. Cochrane instructed the pilot to land in a football field that was ringed by family and friends, clinging to the chain-link fence, waiting for a miracle.

Tasha jumped from the Huey into my waiting arms. Grabbing my pack, we scrambled across the grass toward the family. The incident commander addressed the crowd. "Sue and Tasha did everything they could. I'm sorry to announce, the search is over."

What? We hadn't done everything *we* could. We simply ran out of time. But it wasn't my call to make or the place to do it. I didn't say anything to the family. I kept my shoulders back, my warrior face on, and beelined it to my truck with Tasha in tow.

The next day, I collapsed. I was sitting on the couch, staring out the window and eating a pint of ice cream out of the carton, when Doug swooped in and said, "Don't eat that ice cream for breakfast. You'll get fat."

The container and spoon fell out of my hands onto the wood floor. I ran down the stairs and out of the condo with Tasha trailing behind. She didn't even stop and gobble up the mess. I dropped to my knees on the pavement outside and sobbed uncontrollably. Tasha licked salty tears as they dripped off my face.

"I wasn't able to keep my promise," I told her. I cried for a long time that morning thinking about the promise I had made a decade ago when I whispered into Tasha's vulnerable eight-week-old ears, *"How'd you like to be a dog that saves lives?"* (It was also the same year I said to Doug, *"Till death do us part."*) I promised Tasha we'd never leave anyone behind—and we had just left a mother behind. Had we been called on the first day of the search and not the sixth, maybe she would have been found. I don't know. That's just how it happened. Tasha must have felt my pain because she didn't leave my side the rest of the day.

My position at Eldora Ski Resort lasted only one winter because we moved to Montana. Once we were settled in, my secret plan was to find a way to reconnect with Doug and then segue into retirement, just like Tasha had done. Despite all the red flags dangling off our home life, I believed that if we stopped and smelled the roses, you know, built a fire—like a lost person is supposed to do when they get disoriented in the woods—we could still live happily ever after until we figured out our next career move.

I soon realized my dream wasn't working when Doug refused to hang up his rock hammer and left for yet another business trip. So, I pressed on like I always did. My phone continued to ring even though I was long gone from Colorado. The search-and-rescue teams and law enforcement agencies I'd created relationships with would call asking my opinion about where to look or who to use for their missing-persons cases. I zigzagged across the country, teaching courses and speaking at national conferences. My role as a wilderness medic landed me jobs as a medical consultant in the television and film industry. There were a lot of things I didn't know about our marriage, but I did know that Doug and I were moving in different directions.

Five months after we arrived in Montana, I traveled to the Danakil Depression, considered the hottest place on earth and located in the northern part of the Afar Triangle in Ethiopia, to work on a science documentary that eventually aired on the BBC and Discovery Channel. Even though Doug resented that I was going, he agreed to stay home and take care of Tasha. Twenty pounds lighter and a month later, I returned from Africa. Only then did Doug agree to travel with me to the Everest region of Nepal. With more demand to train Sherpa guides, I had set up collaboration with multiple international organizations, including the Khumbu Climbing Center.

Again, I believed time together, this time in Nepal, would fix everything.

We dropped off Tasha to stay with our new Montana friend, Kim. While we were away, Kim left a message. "Does Tasha come with operating instructions? Three men were caught in an out-of-bounds avalanche near the ski resort here. Search and rescue can't find one of them. Should I bring her to the scene?"

When I finally got her message in Nepal, I emailed her, saying, "Just tell Tasha to 'Go find!' and she'll know what to do." But by then, it was too late for Tasha to deploy. Human searchers using probes, not the local avalanche dogs, had found the last of the victims buried under tons of snow. He left behind a wife and two small children.

In Nepal, where I'd hoped for happiness, Doug and I fought nonstop. On the first day of class, I stood inside a stone-cold teahouse at thirteen thousand feet to address thirty Sherpa guides-in-training, a handful of wilderness-medicine colleagues, and Doug, who sat alone in the corner, his face hidden beneath his oversized down-parka hood. "Thanks for coming, everyone." I took a deep breath and said with a smile, "I want to thank Doug for all his love and support over the years and making this trip possible." As the Sherpas jumped to their feet to honor him by clapping, Doug didn't crack a smile or even acknowledge their accolades. My watery eyes met his. He had emotionally left the room a long time ago, and in that moment, I felt more alone than I ever had before.

On that trip I realized that I couldn't solve my marriage problems as long as I was still denying their existence. As soon as I stopped denying the problems, I realized that he'd already checked out. I was as much on my own and unable to go forward in this as Tasha trying to run a search mission without me while I was in Nepal.

Upon our return, I made one last effort to make my mental map fit my world.

One day, when Doug returned to the house after walking Tasha, I handed him a schedule I'd just sketched out.

"Look," I said, "I'm going to write a book about our adventures with Tasha and here's how I'm going to do it." I'd worked up a timetable with slots for writing, exercise, 'Doug and Sue Time,' and Tasha walks.

"Huh?"

"I need to write this story. I've been looking at office space, so I can buckle down."

His face went flat.

I wasn't done with my denial, evidently. I thought he'd welcome my dream with open arms.

Instead, the handwritten note dropped from his hand as his blue eyes met mine.

"Not on my watch."

My world changed.

On the surface our marriage was like those perfect snowflakes accumulating on a mountain snowpack. Beautiful, but concealing cracks, much like a snow-packed slope hides layers as it grows through the winter. Afraid of what I might find, I didn't dig too deeply into the snow. I didn't go looking for where the instabilities lay, knowing that the whole thing could give way and bury everything in its path. Instead, I sidestepped the slope, hoping I wouldn't get caught.

For a decade, I had avoided marital confrontation by following my real passion—training Tasha and helping people find their way. I believed my marriage was supposed to last forever, even as I wandered ever further away from my husband.

On April Fools' morning, a few days after Doug had returned from a ski trip in Japan and a month since we had seen each other, he rolled over in bed. I tried to kiss him, but he pushed me away. "We need to talk."

Doug had never said those four words. I immediately went into victim mode: *What have I done now? Go ahead, punish me. I can take it.*

Then without hesitation, he spurted out unforgettable words: "I have never loved you."

"What?"

"And I have never been in love with you. Our life together is over."

My world collapsed. This time, I was the one caught in the belly of the avalanche, the one needing help—I screamed, spinning upside down, slamming into rocks, unable to find reason. Choking on mouthfuls of snow, I could no longer mutter the excuses, "It's Antarctica, isn't it? Or … the book? Or … just as soon as …"

Wham … I triggered the sweet spot. All those years traveling in avalanche country with Tasha, I'd avoided burial beneath the snow, but denial about my most important relationship finally came crashing down on me. Lost is lost, whether you're turned around in the forest, suffocating in an avalanche, misguided in business, or, in my case, adrift in a marriage that doesn't actually have all the pieces it needs.

People go through five stages of loss: denial, panic, bargaining, depression, and acceptance. I didn't get this from Kübler-Ross. I first learned about it from studying the psychology of lost-person behavior. I know how far mushroom pickers wander in the woods before admitting they are lost. I understand why a disoriented three-year-old quickly finds a hidey-hole and avoids discovery. I had employed my own expertise at finding lost people. I read about it, trained a dog to do it, and mastered it. Yet, I had failed to recognize the *lostness* of my entire marriage.

Those who are lost face *denial* at their disorientation. I remember this first phase happening several years into my marriage. My gut instincts warned me, yet my ability to say something failed me. I felt the lack of intimacy, the absence of kissing and physical closeness, but when anger inflamed our words I blamed myself or our hectic work schedules.

Emotionally, I strayed off course. I lost track of my footing, my intuition, the man who had my back, my rock in life, my lover.

By the time I responded to his decision to leave me, my voice could no longer be heard over the roar of violent words. I felt crushed. I sank further into the white abyss. Nothing I said or did mattered anymore. He had made up his mind. His decision squashed my heart. My breath left me as I clawed my nails deep into the weight of the snow.

He left.

I gasped.

My body ached.

I couldn't move.

If I wanted to survive, I had to lie quietly in a cold, snowy tomb, motionless, until I could assess my emotions, feel their pain, and dig into my core, exploring every decision to see how I got here in the first place.

With any luck, I'd be found.

Maybe I would be found with the help of Tasha.

Those lost, me included, soon settle into *panic,* the second phase. For me, the frenzy hit when Doug moved out. He left for a monthlong bike trip to Spain, and when he came home, he asked me if I wanted the house, the dog, the truck, the raft, the couch, the tent, half of his retirement, the sleeping bag he'd just borrowed, and the spatula.

How the hell did I know? My grief-stricken mind couldn't focus long enough to make a decision. What would I do? How would I carry on? I thought I was going to die. I called our mutual friends to ask for advice. When I gathered my family members around to tell them, I believed they'd tell me I had let him make terrible mistake. Instead, they told me, "Thank god he's gone. He wasn't very nice to you."

And still, I hoped he'd come back. I wanted to tell him that out of our marriage, I only wanted him and not the stuff.

He never returned to me.

While sobbing on the porch one day, I called my mother and asked, "Mom, why couldn't I just have a 'normal' dog? Why did I have to go train her to be a search-and-rescue dog?"

She paused and cleared her throat. Then she asked, "Why is it that a mother can raise three children, and they all come out so differently?"

She eventually replied to my question. "Sue, you got Tasha to go on adventures with. You were lonely. Doug wasn't available. He was busy working. That's why."

Exhausted, I tried to rationalize the situation. I entered the third stage, *bargaining.* Those who are lost often drift into negotiation to escape their predicament. The mind deteriorates, playing tricks on the psyche. I used all the tools in my search-and-rescue pack to bargain my way out from under the debris. I pleaded with Doug in person to reconsider the deal. I tried to tell him, without being explicit (something I was never good at), that he was making the biggest mistake of his life. When that didn't work, I asked him if he could love me again.

But Doug held firm.

He quit on me and moved out. Tasha never did.

We agreed on joint custody of her. That was about the only thing we did agree on.

My blood turned to sludge. My *bargaining* then subsided into *depression*.

The realization that, "Oh, shit! I'm really lost," left me emotionally paralyzed at age forty-six, unable to do anything except cry about my future. I believed I'd be broke, broken, unloved, and unwanted personally and professionally. I slept through an entire summer, like a hiker so lost that she sits down in the snow, unable to go another step. Warm, clear August days are the only reasons a sane person lives in Montana, and I missed it all. Instead of hiking with Tasha in the mountains on glorious sunny days followed by gold-and-red sunsets, I stayed under my white down comforter, believing I would never survive. Pillows pressed against my ears and sealed me into a white tomb. I couldn't hear, see, or think. I only saw daylight when I opened the door to let Tasha in or out.

She knew I had nothing to give and expected nothing. She just curled up alongside me, cherishing the infrequent belly scratches and quiet cooing in her ears.

My depression soon gave way to one last fight.

❖ ❖ ❖

After six months, Tasha nudges me out from under my feather tomb with her wet snout. I claw the covers aside to see what she needs. That's when I notice something is terribly wrong.

There, all alone and nearly lifeless in my white room, I see my partner and best friend. She stumbles toward me, dragging her hindquarters, and crumples at my feet.

As I cuddle her, she seizes violently. Her head slaps the floor and white froth flows from her mouth, oozing onto the carpet. I watch, helpless, as her eyes roll upward, disappearing into her skull. Her body stiffens like the frozen bodies we'd dug out from under the snow. Her expression reminds me of the horror-stricken faces of victims we had found.

"Please don't leave me." I stroke her soft black fur. I blame her seizures on my lack of attention, a reflection of my sad inner state.

But it's more than that. "Tasha has an inoperable brain tumor," Doug tells me over the phone. He's driven her four hours to the nearest animal teaching hospital that had an MRI machine. I didn't have the courage to go with him. I knew the outcome wasn't going to be good.

Days later, when her pain seems too much to bear, I confront Doug about her end-of-life care.

He argues for pumping her full of medications. "We can prolong her life. She can still have a good life for a while longer."

"No. We need to end her suffering now." *My suffering.*

"Nope. No way. We can make her feel better with meds."

Suppressed once again, I struggle in futility to make my voice heard, but he wins.

We stuff her full of phenobarbital and prednisone. The drugs reduce the inflammation and smooth out the uncoordinated electrical activity in her brain. The little white pills I feed her twice a day turn her once-bright eyes into dull, listless, brown pools. Her energy fades. She sleeps a lot. She drags her hindquarters, her tail tucked underneath her.

In the end, I surrender to *acceptance,* the fifth and final stage of *lostness.* Nothing I can do or say can change my situation. I have to let go of a life that no longer exists, surrender to the fact that the two beings I love most in my life are leaving, have already left. I need death for my rebirth. I am now on a journey alone.

Tasha has one last rescue to perform—saving me from being buried in my own avalanche, one that might permanently damage me. Caring for her forces me to emerge from my depression.

Once Tasha has been seizure-free for five months, I start to wean her off the medications to bring back her liveliness. Over two days in March, I cut back her doses.

But that day, she convulses with a grand mal seizure. Her head whacks the wooden floorboards, and her limbs spasm with erratic jerks.

Shit. I berate myself for inducing these spasms. But rather than depending on someone else to assist with her seizures, I resort to my years at the clinic—using medication to sedate the patient. Rifling through the kitchen, I pull out a Ziploc bag containing a brown vial of liquid Valium. Drawing two milligrams into a syringe, I inject the drug into Tasha.

Time stands still. One minute later, her seizure activity stops. She lies on her side as if dead, but I see her heart beat through her chest wall. She gasps as more drool froths from the side of her mouth.

For another thirty seconds, her body quivers intermittently. Then she quiets. I caress her matted, lusterless black coat. Her limp body does little more than breathe. I stroke her.

"You're going to be okay, Black Dog."

With the sleeve of my red sweatshirt, I wipe the wet watery goop oozing from her eyes and then my own.

A few minutes later, Tasha struggles to right herself. Panting, she wobbles, shaking from exhaustion. She drags her hindquarters across the floor, her toenails scraping on the wood floor. She bumps into a chair, a table, and a wall. She winds her way to the sliding-glass door to go outside.

"This is it. You're on your journey."

I open the sliding-glass door and watch her look for her final resting place in my backyard, outside under the pine tree, in the snow. What could be more appropriate for an avalanche dog that spent her entire career in snow?

The morning is crisp and clear, the first one in months. There's a sunny feel to it. Tasha's behavior makes sense to me, finding a safe spot with a view to die for.

I have to let her go.

I suck back my tears to follow her, just like I had a hundred times before across avalanche slopes, in the wilderness, and on mountainsides.

She stumbles, making her way along the snowy trail behind my house. She uses her snout to right herself, determined to make this walk on her own. Fresh snow clings to her nose.

Swaying back and forth, Tasha spots an opening under a tall, lone pine tree with views of Big Mountain. She plants all four paws in the snow to steady herself.

Holding my breath, I prepare for her death. I envision her exhaling her last breath and slowly collapsing into the cold snow.

Rocking like a boat tied to a buoy, Tasha squats, then pees.

"That's it? You struggled all this way just to pee?"

Tasha ambles back inside the house to sleep the rest of the day.

The reprieve lasted one good month.

During that month, I endured lessons that I didn't understand at the time but would later. My personal avalanche was the best thing that could have happened. The forces of destruction are great at pushing things to die away in our lives, so we can become more alive. Eventually I came to recognize the contrast between my partnership with Tasha and my marriage to Doug. One partnership worked, the other didn't. Why?

Getting married didn't solve our problems. Doug and I weren't vulnerable to each other. We never looked at each other closely or honestly. But the biggest problem we had was our inability to communicate. We never created an intimate language between us that forged a strong bond, not like the bond Tasha and I shared. Even without words, Tasha and I truly communicated. We understood each other's needs, wants, and desires. Doug and I never managed to do that, not for a single day. It was easier to be in denial than to feel the real, raw pain of our situation.

And we lacked forgiveness. I could forgive Tasha for her many escapes or for gobbling a week's ration of food the night before a critical rescue. She could forgive my fumbling and mistakes or pushing her too hard while trying to train her to save lives. Looking back, Doug and I never even tried to build a bridge out of words of understanding, compassion, love, and forgiveness. We didn't really understand *how* to forgive each other. What Tasha and the Poodle Lady and my mentors and the other rescuers gave me was my real gold: the tools, the capacity, and the wisdom to keep reinventing myself for a life worth living—one full of purpose and meaning, one I found by carving out a career saving lives and teaching others to do the same.

❧   ❧   ❧

Six months after Tasha had her first seizure and a year after Doug left, I have to face the inevitable. Between bouts of rain and sunshine, I arrange for the magic potion—the lethal injection—from the animal clinic. Two women in purple scrubs make a house call in my backyard.

Doug throws the ball for Tasha one last time while the technicians prepare the syringe. Exhausted, Tasha lies on her belly on the wet grass. Her chin rests on her paws, and she holds a rawhide chew stick in her mouth. She no longer has the energy to chomp down, so like an old lady without teeth, she gums it. She barely moves. She cannot summon the energy to interact with me anymore.

When the needle enters Tasha's thigh, she doesn't react. Not even a flinch at the needle prick. Within a few seconds, she flops to her side on the green grass. The rawhide chew drops from her mouth. She sleeps with a familiar snore.

I get close on my hands and knees, bury my face into her warm, sweet neck, close to her ear, and hum. Caressing her delicate ears, I cry for her, then for all my losses. "You did everything I asked of you." I hear a low buzz and feel it vibrating against her ribs. My beautiful Tasha is purring. My nose nestles deep into her ear. "You saved many lives ... and mine too. You never left anyone behind." I give her one last command.

"Go find!"

Acknowledgments

Most people search their entire lives to find passion, purpose, and eventually philanthropy.

I found all three in my devotion to train Tasha and myself. This journey has been one of my greatest achievements.

I could have never trained Tasha and crafted this book without all the support I received from search-dog teams and my writing tribe. Both required friendship, honesty, and dedication. It did take a small village to train Tasha and a small city to write *our* memoir. I say *our* because if Tasha could speak (oh yeah, she can) she'd say, "I've hounded you every single day to get that book done. Write what you think you can't. Have fun, enjoy the process, be a finisher, finish it. Just know I've looked after you all these years, while you sat on your bouncy ball in your office, staring out the window, sacrificing powder days and river trips, trying to recollect our story."

I know Tasha hears me each day when I greet her in my sing-song voice, "Hi, Black Dog. Do tee dooo," when I walk through the front door and throw my keys on the granite countertop. The tinkle bell she once wore around her neck now hangs on the door knob. Tasha watches me look around the room, hoping I'll see her tail wagging, nails ticking across the hardwood. But I don't.

The fun part of writing this book was revisiting and appreciating all the people and dogs that touched my life. I consider them teachers and mentors. They all helped me launch this journey—pushing me and making me dig deep to find my truth. Because of that, I am a more compassionate and understanding human.

My thank-you list is huge.

Since most readers might not read beyond this next paragraph, I'll mention the biggest influencers first.

Carla Wheeler, Dottie and Harry Purvis, and my family, Amy B. and the boys, editors extraordinaires: Debbie Burke (superwoman), Becky Lomax (ass cracker), Peggy Hageman, Ember Hood, Bob Mecoy—who said when I signed him on as my literary agent, "We've got to make this dog hunt." Anthony Whittome's encouraging words kept me up late in the tugboat studio, writing for my life. Marnie Jackson and the five writers at the Banff Mountain and Wilderness Writers Program made me dig deeper into the snowpack to find clarity. Keith Liggett, I will always be grateful for the connection, connection. The Montana Women's Writers critique group (Phyllis Quatman, Dawn Peterson, Dr. Betty Kuffel, and Christine) are the beautiful women who encouraged me and patiently waited for me to tell my story one painful word at a time, week after week, month after month, for several years. They never gave up on me and always had my back!

Hanging out with dog handlers is a lot of fun. We all shared the joy of romping around the woods and over snow with our canine companions, discovering their full potential. Avalanche/search-dog teams I'd like to thank that are not included in my narrative are: Carla and her dogs KC Jones and CC, Mark Fisher and Emma, Dennis McLaughlin and Duke, Cheryl Kennedy, Julie and Darren Weibler, Karen Risch and Lira, James Burwick and Kai, Ann Marie Boness and Teal, Elaine Flowers and Sizzle, Deb Tirmenstein and Ruby, Stacie Burkhardt and Sage, Jim Vail and Pepper, Janet Panebaker, Dan Burnett, Ryan Root, Shannon Young, Sara Fuld and Thor. My neighbors Suzanna Linam and Molly, Steve Farley, and the never-replaceable Kathy and Paul Hooge all kept careful watch over Tasha.

Big thanks go out to the awesome 2007 professional ski patrollers at Eldora, some of whom have moved on to fabulous careers as avalanche forecasters and heli-ski guides. I'm proud to have worked in such a supportive team. Sincere appreciation goes out to members of the Crested Butte Search and Rescue and Crested Butte Ski Patrol. Thanks for the opportunity to learn and grow. Later in our tenure, and with the changing of ski-area management, the resort allowed Tasha and me to train alongside their avalanche ski patrol dogs. I even hosted a SARDOC avalanche weekend at the resort.

Thank you to all of the ski resorts who supported our avalanche dog training. In Colorado, the list includes Crested Butte, Copper, Monarch, Vail, Aspen, Beaver Creek, Breckenridge, Loveland, Eldora. Utah Resorts include Snowbird, Alta, the Canyons. Washington state resorts include Snoqualmie and Crystal Mountain.

Outdoor retailers and companies who generously donated essential gear for keeping us safe and looking professional: Marmot, Tom Fritz of Fritz Insight Group and ex-VP of Marketing at Marmot, Patagonia, Backcountry Access, Maui Jim, Nature's Variety dog food, GU Energy Gel, Ruffwear, Lärabar, Cloudveil, Nielsen-Kellerman Kestrel meters, Greatland Laser, Garmin, and Exped.

I'd like to thank the organizations who participated in our search-and-rescue career and kept us safe: Colorado Flight for Life, Colorado Avalanche Information Center (CAIC), American Institute for Avalanche Rescue and Education (AIARE), Colorado Rapid Avalanche Deployment (C-RAD), Wasatch Backcountry Rescue (WBR), Canadian Avalanche Rescue Dog Association (CARDA), National Association for Search and Rescue (NASAR), Montrose, Ouray, Chaffee, and the Gunnison County sheriff's departments, SARDOC, Mountain Rescue Association (MRA), Colorado Search and Rescue Board, Colorado Civil Air Patrol (CAP), Colorado Public Television, Crested Butte Public Television, and the Colorado National Guard.

To the SAR and ski-patrol teams we worked with, thanks for your dedication to saving lives. And to the individuals who lost their lives in the line of duty, I honor you.

Medical mentors and lifesavers not mentioned in this book include the crew at Wilderness Medical Associates, my colleagues at Doc Tom's clinic (Nicole, Amy, Lynn, Sara, Doc Zevan), Kristin Peterson and Mike Tayloe with Katabatic Consulting, Dr. Luanne Freer, Clint Kay, DVM, and Steve Conlin, DVM, who helped navigate Tasha's end-of-life care.

Whitefish, Montana, was my creative haven, and to be honest, writing this book was no different than training Tasha to find the lost. I landed in a new town, had to go find a tribe, and learn the fundamentals of writing. I'll never forget asking my dear friend, Kim Launer, a few months after I arrived in Montana, "Think I can write a book in three months?" She replied, "I don't see why not." Her words kept my wonderful naïveté alive, the same naïveté I had while training Tasha.

My story would have never found its worldwide audience without the help of Authors of the Flathead, Flathead Rivers Writers Conference, Banff Mountain and Writing Workshop, Banff Filmmakers Workshop, Whitefish Review, and the amazing team at Blackstone Publishing for creating this beautiful book.

The list of writers who showed me the way is too long to list. Teacher Dennis Foley and Larry Brooks of Story Fix taught me the basics of story structure.

Professional writing nudges have had lasting impressions on my early drafts. Thanks Scott McMillion with Montana Quarterly, Katherine Fausset of Curtis Brown Agency, and lawyer Scott Wurster for sound advice.

My personal therapists, BFFs and spiritual teachers include Cathy Greer Cole and Sara McClellan Fisher, two women that have been in my life since childhood. Thanks Ms. Peggy Miller, Susie Raffatto, Lauren Walker, Carolyn and Jeff Remmel, Deb Huntington, Thea L., Teresa Hunt, Kathy Tureck, Gigi and Paul Rapport, Rita Braun, and Chuck Stern for holding my hand when things got difficult. Gratitude goes out to my ski partner, David Wagner, for dragging me out into the backcountry even when I said no. To technical advisor Martin Vidak, Osteopath Sara Bonds for keeping my energy flowing, and to Dusty Hosek, who held me together like glue.

And finally, to David, wherever you are.

Author's Note

This memoir tells the true story of searching for life in the high country of Colorado with my avalanche dog, Tasha. From 1995 to 2007, I trained and deployed Tasha. I kept training logs, news articles, magazine publications, and mission reports. Opinions about the details of some of the accidents recollected may vary due to eyewitness accounts being faulty, especially during times of stress.

Mentors, close friends, colleagues, teammates, and incident commanders mentioned in this book are real. For some, I changed their names and looks to protect their identity; others I left in. Victims of this story didn't sign up to be characters in this book, so I changed most of their names. I did my best to tell the story based on my experience. Some statistics mentioned may not be current or exact. For the sake of storytelling, time lines may have been condensed or modified and dialogue approximated in a way that elicits the meaning and feeling of what was said. Forgive me if there are errors. No one is perfect, not even a search dog.